LENNON
THE ALBUMS

By The Same Author

Timeless Flight: The Definitive Biography Of The Byrds
Neil Young: Here We Are In The Years
Roxy Music: Style With Substance
Van Morrison: A Portrait Of The Artist
The Kinks: The Sound And The Fury
Wham ! (Confidential) The Death Of A Supergroup
Starmakers & Svengalis: The History Of British Pop Management
The Football Managers
The Guinness Encyclopaedia Of Popular Music (co-ed.)
Morrissey & Marr: The Severed Alliance
The Smiths: The Visual Documentary
The Complete Guide To The Music Of The Smiths & Morrissey/Marr
The Complete Guide To The Music Of Neil Young
Crosby, Stills, Nash & Young: The Visual Documentary
The Complete Guide To The Music Of John Lennon
The Byrds: Timeless Flight Revisited – The Sequel
The Complete Guide To The Music Of The Kinks
Neil Young: Zero To Sixty: A Critical Biography
Van Morrison: No Surrender
Morrissey: The Albums

Anthology Contributions

The Bowie Companion
The Encyclopedia Of Popular Music
The Mojo Collection
*Oxford Originals: An Anthology Of Writing From Lady Margaret Hall,
  1879–2001*

JOHNNY ROGAN

LENNON
THE ALBUMS

CALIDORE

ISBN 0-95295-406-0
[New ISBN from January 2007 ISBN 13: 978-0-95295-406-4]

Exclusive distributors:
Music Sales Ltd
14–15 Berners Street
London
W1T 3LJ

A catalogue record for this book is available from the British Library.

Cover photo: Andrew Maclear/Redferns.

Published by Calidore.

Typeset by Galleon Typesetting, Ipswich.
Printed in the UK by MPG Books Ltd, Bodmin, Cornwall

NOTES TO THE READER

Lennon: The Albums is a detailed study of the solo recordings of John Lennon. It includes a track by track analysis of every album recorded by the singer in the UK/US territories. Collectors please note that the work concentrates solely upon officially released albums and does not include promotional releases, items exclusively produced for DJs/radio stations, special issues, samplers, cassette releases, various artistes collections, interview discs, videos, DVDs, radio/television appearances, bootlegs or unreleased recordings. Singles are listed separately and also covered in detail throughout the text. The Index at the rear of the book can be used to cross-reference songs.

Within the main text, albums are printed in italics, along with books, poems, radio and television programmes, plays, magazines and newspapers. Individual songs are in single inverted commas along with single word quotes, newspaper headlines, review titles, aphorisms and phrases of less than 10 words; interview quotes and citations from books are in double inverted commas. Numerical units are written out up to nine and numbered thereafter, except in the use of musical time, money, measurements and specific usages such as 8-track recordings. Acronyms have full points omitted, but names of people do not. Group/band names are preceded by a lower case 'the' and only painters are 'artists'. End spellings of verbs are 'ize' in accordance with *The Oxford English Dictionary* rather than computer spell checkers, with the obvious exceptions of words such as advertise, analyse, comprise, demise, improvise, supervise, surprise, televise *et al*. Song and album titles are generally displayed as they appear on the record, even if inaccurately spelt or lacking the necessary commas, hyphens and apostrophes. Nouns and noun compounds are usually not hyphenated except when attributive.

Other rulings are mainly in accordance with those suggested in *The New Oxford Dictionary For Writers And Editors*, an invaluable asset in producing a consistent style guide.

CONTENTS

ACKNOWLEDGEMENTS

This book attempts to rescue Lennon's work from the proprietorial clutches of Beatles' mythology. Beginning with his first collaboration with Yoko Ono, it continues through his solo years, carefully analysing each of his albums. Listening again to Lennon's complete works was both a challenge and a joy. The aural journey was made more comfortable by a handful of written works that dare to see him as more than a Beatle. I would like to thank fellow Omnibus Press author John Robertson whose *The Art And Music Of John Lennon* and *Lennon* were extremely valuable as both reference works and silent sounding boards for further discussion and argument. Robertson, who also wrote *Neil Young: The Visual Documentary*, was described in his blurb as "the pseudonym of a well-known writer" whose *non de plume* was borrowed from the classic Byrds song 'Old John Robertson'. Given the Byrds and Neil Young connections, plus my own writings about Lennon, it was hardly surprising that some people assumed that Robertson must be me. The fact that I also wrote *Crosby, Stills, Nash & Young: The Visual Documentary* in the same series as Robertson's Young book and that I shared the same initials as John Robertson made the comparison even more striking. Thankfully, we can now safely confirm that Robertson was actually the pseudonym used by Peter Doggett, whose superb reference work on Lennon's paintings, drawings, art and music from his childhood through the Beatles' period and beyond has recently been updated and republished. Doggett has always been a fellow enthusiast on all matters relating to CSN&Y and, of course, John Lennon. Although we haven't spoken about Lennon much in recent years, we shared many discussions about the minutiae of his life and work during the mid-Nineties. Peter's knowledge and insightful critical comments were always greatly appreciated.

Over the years, I have interviewed a number of Lennon associates whose contributions are evident in the text. Particular thanks to the late Derek Taylor, the late Clive Epstein and the late George Harrison. In fact, there are far too many dead to mention, from Dick Rowe to Jesse Ed Davis. For some enlightening comments on Lennon's lost weekend and period in Los Angeles, thanks to Tom Slocum. Former IRA leading light Gerry O'Hare provided vital information on the Irish Republican Army's interest in recruiting Lennon for their own propagandist purposes, an account that has never been mentioned or alluded to in any of the extant biographies. Éamonn McCann also offered some fascinating memories of the birth of Free Derry. Mark Lewisohn recalled his involvement in the original *Anthology* project. As you would expect, researching the Byrds' story for over 30 years has also brought me into contact with a number of American rock icons who crossed paths with Lennon during and after the Beatles. I thank them too.

Colleagues, old friends, writers and fans who also helped along the way, directly or in passing, include (in chronological order): Alan Russell, John Regan, Gill Chester, Philip Norman, Anthony Scaduto, Chris Charlesworth, John Tobler and Adrien Van Clute. More recently Jackie Cuddihy, Sarah Bacon, Sharon Kelly, Cian Ó Maidín and Dave 'The Rave' Hill were on hand to help in various ways. On the production front, thanks to designer Lisa Pettibone, Susan Currie at Music Sales, plus Ken Shiplee and reader Pam Balaam at Galleon. Finally, special thanks to Andy Neill for some enlightening last-minute observations, amendments and general discussion on all things Lennon.

John Lennon was probably the best interviewee in rock history and his incisive comments on music and life are captured in several key books, notably Jann Wenner's *Lennon Remembers*, David Sheff's *The Playboy Interviews*, and *The Lennon Tapes*, a transcript of the BBC interview conducted by Andy Peebles. Other books that proved enlightening were Jon Wiener's groundbreaking *Come Together: John Lennon In His Time*, Anthony Fawcett's *One Day At A Time*, *The Lennon Companion* (edited by Elizabeth Thomson & David Gutman), The *Rolling Stone* Editors' *The Ballad Of John And Yoko* and Keith Badman's *The Beatles After The Break-Up 1970–2000*. The weekly British music press covered Lennon's solo career in great detail, sometimes prompting humorous replies from the man himself. Lennon also discussed his music, politics and personal philosophy in countless interviews and pronouncements given to the world's media during his famous bed-ins with Yoko Ono. Later, he conducted many syndicated radio interviews, sometimes speaking to dozens of disc jockeys down the phone line. All these were invaluable sources.

Finally, a word on Beatles-related literature. While the major biographies touch on the work, readers seeking a detailed account of the actual recordings should consult Mark Lewisohn's magnificent *The Complete Beatles Recording Sessions*. Students of the lyrics and music are directed to Tim Riley's *Tell Me Why: A Beatles Commentary*, Ian MacDonald's *Revolution In The Head* and Peter Doggett's *The Art And Music Of John Lennon*. The Beatles' book industry will no doubt continue, buoyed by anniversaries and the cyclic retrospectives that have boosted the circulation figures of monthly music magazines since the mid-Eighties.

Any reader, critic or Lennon associate wishing to clarify any detail or provide updates and corrections, please contact the author via the publisher's e-mail address:

calidore_@hotmail.co.uk

JOHNNY ROGAN

INTRODUCTION

With the probable exception of Bob Dylan, no recording act of the last century has been afforded as many articles and books on their life and work as the Beatles. As their former publicist Derek Taylor once remarked to me: "They deserve endless scrutiny – the work will never age." Lennon's collaboration with Paul McCartney produced some of the finest songs of the last hundred years and attempting to disentangle each one's contribution has often proved contentious. In interviews with Jann Wenner in 1970 and with David Sheff in 1980, Lennon attempted this exercise in miniature, but many of his answers were instinctive, and perhaps impulsive. Paul McCartney put his own case, with full checks and balances, in Barry Miles' *Many Years From Now*. Sometimes, neither ex-Beatle was clear about precisely who did what in the intense fire of composition. But, without ignoring McCartney's input into several of these songs, there is no doubt that certain Beatles' compositions spoke with Lennon's voice. He wrote from several different viewpoints, composing pure pop hits ('Please Please Me', 'Ticket To Ride', 'Day Tripper'), quirky love songs ('I Feel Fine', 'Girl', 'You've Got To Hide Your Love Away'), sang raucous, larynx-lacerating cover versions ('Twist And Shout', 'Money', 'Dizzy Miss Lizzy'), rock numbers ('Revolution', 'Don't Let Me Down'), utopian diktats ('The Word', 'All You Need Is Love') and sound collages ('Revolution 9'). Many compositions were like aural diaries and provided a fascinating biography of his state of mind at various stages of the Beatles' career: 'A Hard Day's Night', 'I'm A Loser', 'Help!', 'In My Life', 'Norwegian Wood', 'Nowhere Man', 'She Said, She Said', 'I'm So Tired', 'The Ballad Of John And Yoko'. There were surreal songs in which Lennon seemed to combine childhood memories of reading Lewis Carroll with a love of drug consumption and the assistance of advanced technical production in order to create such strange visionary works as 'Rain', 'Tomorrow Never Knows', 'Strawberry Fields Forever', 'Lucy In

The Sky With Diamonds', 'A Day In The Life' and 'I Am The Walrus'.

The problem with discussing Lennon's Beatles years is that it is never easy to isolate him totally from the group identity. The Beatles' image as 'four young lads against the world' was not just a PR line but a concise definition of their gang mentality and musical unity. At their best, Lennon and McCartney were interdependent songwriters and personalities: Paul's sentimental side was balanced by a tough, ruthless pragmatism, manifested musically in songs as bizarrely contrasting as 'Till There Was You' and 'Helter Skelter'; John's brusque humour disguised a softer core, the macho man of 'You Can't Do That' quieted by the calm of 'Cry Baby Cry'. They complemented each other's songs with insight, craft and artistry, encouraged healthy competition, and rotated vocal duties which ensured the spotlight was shared.

The Beatles recordings spanned the golden age of the single – an era they almost single-handedly created. Looking back at their early years is like witnessing an uninterrupted trajectory to greatness. 'Love Me Do', 'Please Please Me', 'From Me To You', 'She Loves You', 'I Want To Hold Your Hand', 'Can't Buy Me Love', 'A Hard Day's Night', 'I Feel Fine' – each record subtly improves upon the last, adding new lyrical flourishes and musical innovations. The 1965 trilogy – 'Ticket To Ride', 'Help!', 'We Can Work It Out'/'Day Tripper' – reveals the process even more profoundly: the incandescent, reverberating guitar part, the confessional lyric and the double A-side, the last of which incorporated less as a concession to ego or misplaced democracy than as an admission that the traditionally 'inferior' B-side had no place in their exemplary canon.

If the Beatles had never released a long-playing record, they would still be considered avatars of their age. Their early albums were completed under phenomenal pressure requiring, by modern standards, back-breaking productivity against the studio clock. The début, *Please Please Me*, recorded in under 10 hours, should have been a dog's dinner, but instead helped transform the notion of the pop album. At a time when LPs were usually filled with mediocre tunes and considered as mere postscripts to best-selling singles and a sop to fans, the Beatles effortlessly created a work that was genuinely worth-while. The new cover versions supplemented the material they'd honed during long sessions in Hamburg or at Liverpool's Cavern, while the Lennon/McCartney originals served notice of a potentially powerful songwriting duo. *With The Beatles*, released later in 1963, was even better, a deft mix of Motown covers and stronger originals, including the raucous 'It Won't Be Long', the thoughtful 'All I've Got To Do' and McCartney's early standard, 'All My Loving'.

The Beatles' work rate continued relentlessly during 1964. They not only completed their first film, *A Hard Day's Night*, but filled the album of the same name with 100 per cent self-penned material, another first. They concluded the year with *Beatles For Sale*, which some later critics unfairly saw as a retrograde step on the specious grounds that it again featured a few covers. What they failed to acknowledge was its brave exclusion of singles material, even though 'I Feel Fine' b/w 'She's A Woman' was readily available. Ever resourceful, the Beatles still managed to write three potential number 1 hits on the record – 'No Reply', 'I'm A Loser' and 'Eight Days A Week' (the latter proved the point when it was released as a single in America and topped the charts). Having already furnished the Rolling Stones with 'I Wanna Be Your Man' and provided number 1 hits for Billy J. Kramer & The Dakotas, Lennon/McCartney still found time to offer exclusive new songs to a select few in a busy 1964. Among the major covers, unreleased by the Beatles, were Peter And Gordon's chart-topping 'A World Without Love', Cilla Black's 'It's For You' and Billy J. Kramer's 'From A Window'.

1965 was another watershed year. Amid the frantic composing of new songs and hit singles, Lennon completed his second book, *A Spaniard In The Works*, the follow-up to the critically acclaimed *In His Own Write*. The Beatles' second film *Help!* was released, complete with a hastily recorded soundtrack which nevertheless featured several highlights, not least 'Yesterday', one of the most recorded songs in the history of popular music and 'You've Got To Hide Your Love Away', Lennon's foray into folk rock. The short-lived folk rock boom of 1965 signalled the possibility of a new literary awareness in pop music and, as usual, the Beatles had the final word, issuing *Rubber*

Soul just before Christmas. Its contents captured the group at a pivotal moment in their careers, attempting that uneasy transition from uncomplicated teen idols to rock gurus. The sleeve was a perfect emblem of that tension between the familiar and the new: distinctive mop top hairstyles, viewed through a fish eye lens to create a distorted effect, reinforced by psychedelic lettering. Lyrically and musically, there was that same conflict between two worlds. They looked back to the era of Carl Perkins with the rockabilly influenced 'What Goes On', strove for modernity while simultaneously lampooning rampant American consumerism in 'Drive My Car', revelled in the word play of Bob Dylan while observing the mental vacuity of 'Nowhere Man', and celebrated Ravi Shankar in the raga-influenced adulterer's tale, 'Norwegian Wood'. Even the love songs betrayed different traditions: the neanderthal emotional brutishness of 'Run For Your Life', giving way to the antagonistic self-questioning of 'I'm Looking Through You' and reaching a new sophistication in 'Girl', which disguised emotional exasperation as detached analysis of dolly bird feminism. The album reflected an age of pop democracy in which McCartney's evergreen 'Michelle' nestled alongside the pseudo philosophical 'The Word' without any sense of incongruity. From satires to sitars and safe singalongs, the Beatles oscillated between pop and progressive, while Lennon's 'In My Life' was a crafted elegy documenting all that had been achieved and lost.

It was not until 1966 that the Beatles learned to slow down. This was the year when *NME* felt their crown might be slipping because 'Paperback Writer' took a full *two* weeks to dislodge Frank Sinatra's 'Strangers In The Night' from the number 1 spot. Although the group played at the music paper's annual poll winners' concert, this would be their final stage show in the UK, bar a roof-top appearance at Apple's Savile Row headquarters, three years later. Following a troubled world tour, they retired from live performance to concentrate on studio work. Their decision was vindicated by the positive reaction to *Revolver*. Now routinely regarded as one of the greatest albums of all time, it was originally seen as a novel progression that, according to *NME*'s reviewer, had "broken the bounds of what we used to call pop music". It also represented the flowering of the four Beatles as distinct creative entities. George Harrison was offered the unique opportunity to open a Beatles album. 'Taxman', his lugubrious complaint about Britain's highest tax bands, was executed with a wry wit worthy of Lennon. Ringo Starr also received special treatment and soon found himself singing lead on a number 1 Beatles' single, 'Yellow Submarine'. McCartney revealed the full range of his songwriting skill: 'Eleanor Rigby', a bleak but poignant narrative of old age and loneliness, featuring a stirring string arrangement, became another chart topper and instant standard; 'Good Day Sunshine' and 'Got To Get You Into My Life' celebrated the more optimistic, ebullient side of his character; the stately 'Here, There And Everywhere' was probably the best song he ever wrote. Lennon's major contributions were more downbeat, cerebral and experimental. 'She Said, She Said', a chilling acid-inspired meditation, was set against an engagingly chaotic rhythm which articulated musically its fractured narrative. Finally, there was the awesome 'Tomorrow Never Knows', the Beatles' and pop music's most ambitious work to date. Inspired by the *Tibetan Book Of Dead*, it set out to capture, in sound and lyric, the chaotic temporal and spatial disturbance of a full-blown acid trip, a journey to transcendence leading to the void. Lennon informed producer George Martin that he envisaged the sound of 4,000 monks chanting on a mountain top. He may as well have demanded that Martin capture the music of the spheres. Remarkably, Lennon's vision was partly translated into audibility by filtering his voice through the Leslie speaker of a Hammond organ, then applying tape loops of different sounds to create an other-worldly ambience. It was a stunning achievement that heralded a new phase.

Seemingly determined to surpass *Revolver* and 'Tomorrow Never Knows', the Beatles spent more time in the studio than ever before, even ignoring the seemingly obligatory demands of a Christmas single. It was not until February 1967 that the world experienced the first fruits of their labour and, fittingly, the Beatles chose the singles market to reveal their progress. 'Penny Lane'/'Strawberry Fields Forever', the greatest double-sided single of all time, was the ultimate testament to the complementary talents of Lennon/McCartney and a giant step forward for popular music. It was actually more important than the long player that followed in its wake and paved the way for a generation of musicians. It also ensured that *Sgt Pepper's Lonely Hearts Club Band* was the most eagerly awaited album of its time. Its impact was volcanic. *Newsweek* compared the lyrics to T.S. Eliot's *The Waste Land*, *The New York Times* heralded the arrival of "a new and golden Renaissance of song" and acid king Timothy Leary claimed its creators were "evolutionary agents sent by God with a mysterious power to create a new species". Even by the Beatles' innovative standards, this was a momentous work that revolutionized the production and presentation of the LP record. With its gatefold sleeve, printed lyrics, run-on tracks and cardboard cut-outs, the package was Pop Art *in excelsis*. The lyrical themes embraced Indian philosophy ('Within You, Without You'), social commentary ('She's Leaving Home'), psychedelic fancy ('Lucy In The Sky With Diamonds'), and music hall whimsy ('When I'm 64'). George Martin's groundbreaking production employed an array of sound effects, including animal noises, cut-up Sousa marches, multi-layered tapes, a 40-piece orchestra and, most famously, what John Lennon called "a sound building up from nothing to the end of the world". The climactic 'A Day In The Life' was the ultimate victory of imagination over obsolete technology, establishing the Beatles as experimental leaders and songsmiths whose overreaching imaginations seemingly knew no bounds.

The psychedelic party that *Sgt Pepper's* inspired went cold by Christmas, but not before they closed the flower power era with 'All You Need Is Love' and a British equivalent of the Merry Pranksters' magic bus trip. Always ready to extend traditional formats, the Beatles pioneered the 'double EP' with *Magical Mystery Tour*, the soundtrack to the television film that was broadcast on 26 December 1967. Greeted coolly by the popular press, the travelogue mini-movie was lapped up by fans, who responded positively to the superb six-song set which proved a festive favourite, kept off the top of the charts only by the Beatles' own single 'Hello Goodbye'.

1968 was the year of politics. In America, the assassinations of Martin Luther King and Robert Kennedy symbolized the trauma of a nation already at war with itself. With the escalation of conflict in

Vietnam, peaceful demonstrations had given way to street rioting and hippies were usurped by yippies and political pranksters whose watchword was organized chaos. Musically, Dylan, along with the Byrds and the Band, saw salvation in old wisdom as a panacea to the political hectoring. Irrespective of sales, *John Wesley Harding*, *Sweetheart Of The Rodeo* and *Music From Big Pink*, signalled the need to look back, advice that the Beatles themselves would take a year later. It's usually forgotten, though, that this back–to–roots movement had already been anticipated by the foursome in the understated 'Lady Madonna', a wish–fulfilling attempt to record a genuine rock 'n' roll record which climbed to number 1, months before the release of the aforementioned albums. While McCartney urged the need to 'get back', Lennon was still grappling with the political ambiguities of the present. Those tensions helped produce the last undisputedly great Beatles' single. 'Hey Jude' b/w 'Revolution' should have been a double A-side for it was, in its way, as brilliantly complementary and oppositional as the unsurpassable 'Penny Lane'/'Strawberry Fields Forever'. Lennon was galvanized into action to re-record a blistering take of 'Revolution', bristling with guitar distortion and a passionate vocal. It remains his greatest rock performance as a Beatle.

Having already made history with the first double EP, the Beatles took the next step by issuing a double album, a radical idea at the time, although Dylan had pioneered the trend in 1966 with *Blonde On Blonde*. *The Beatles*, released in November 1968, was a determined attempt to mix the natural with the experimental while removing the obvious artifice of *Sgt Pepper's*. With its plain white cover, the work denoted modesty rather than extravagance, but the music spoke louder. Everything came out on *The Beatles* – a vast, sprawling canvas of musical ideas and genres, embracing rock, pop, folk, blues, country, avant-garde experimental, cartoon comedy, ragtime, vaudeville, and much else. There was seemingly no attempt by the individual composers to fashion their work as 'Beatle songs', although many listeners still felt that they created an illusion of aural cohesion. The album's lack of formal structure was at once frustrating and liberating. In many ways, *The Beatles* served as a template for much of their later solo work. Producer George Martin famously said

it would have made a great 'single album'. Many critics agreed – but
there is no consensus as to what such a précised work might contain.
It seems everyone has a different track listing – which surely explains
why it was a double album in the first place.

After *The Beatles*, the group continued on the road away from *Sgt
Pepper's*. Following the example of 'Lady Madonna', their final run
of singles – 'Get Back', 'The Ballad Of John And Yoko' and 'Come
Together' – owed their loyalty to early rock 'n' roll. Purely from
Lennon's partisan perspective, the final two Beatles albums, *Abbey
Road* and *Let It Be* (which was actually recorded first), were deemed
anti-climactic after the grand run from *Rubber Soul* through to
The Beatles. In their closing years, the Beatles were propelled by
McCartney's singular vision, belief and determination to navigate the
group through a period of disunity and crisis. Understandably, *Abbey
Road*, a more cohesive effort than *The Beatles* and the group's last
hurrah, still appears high in 'All Time Great Albums' lists, but
Lennon always reacted negatively to the work, partly because it saw
McCartney clearly in the ascendant. "John objected very much to
what we did on the second side of *Abbey Road*," George Martin said,
"which was almost entirely Paul and I working together, with contributions from the others." Lennon produced some decent material,
but there was evidence of isolation and creative parsimony, as if he
was in weary retreat from the Beatles. His distrust of craftsmanship at
the expense of inspiration was more evident than ever. By this point,
of course, he had already released his first album with Yoko Ono and
effectively started the second stage of his career.

Contrary to expectations, the recording history of the Beatles did
not end with their break-up in 1970 but continued with the release
of various live albums, the later mammoth *Anthology* series and, of
course, the 1995–96 'resurrection' singles 'Free As A Bird' and 'Real
Love'. These home demos from Lennon's Seventies' archives were
magically transformed into new 'Beatles' projects, with the full
co-operation and involvement of the three surviving members. It
was characteristic of the group that they should defy and transcend
both time and death.

While it was impossible for Lennon to escape the shadow cast by possibly the greatest cultural popular music phenomenon of the twentieth century, his attempted reinvention during the Seventies was a wondrous example of living theatre, punctuated by music that still resonates. This book, which begins at the dawn of his solo career, when he first collaborated with Yoko Ono, attempts to do justice to a decade of his life that has all too often been submerged by the more vivid memories of Beatle John.

LENNON ALBUMS

UNFINISHED MUSIC NO. 1:
TWO VIRGINS

Released: November 1968

Original UK issue: Apple (S)APCOR 2. US issue: Apple T5001. CD reissue with
bonus track: Rykodisc RCD 10411 (UK/US)

John Lennon had already been experimenting with home taping
long before Yoko Ono came into his life, but there is no doubt that
she was the catalyst in pushing him towards avant-garde experimentation. They had first met in November 1966 at John Dunbar's
Indica Gallery, a full 18 months before this album was recorded.
Lennon was heavily into LSD at the time and, in the wake of the
Beatles' groundbreaking *Revolver*, seemed intent on immersing
himself in every mind-expanding experience that the counter-
culture had to offer. Yoko Ono's *Unfinished Paintings And Objects*
exhibition at the Indica appealed to Lennon's sense of the absurd
with its overpriced artefacts such as the Sky Machine that "produces
nothing when a coin is deposited" and the all-white chess set. Later,
Lennon vividly recalled the strong impression left by the show and
that strange first encounter with Yoko Ono. "I got word that this
amazing woman was putting on a show, and there was something
about people in bags, and it was going to be a bit of a happening. So
I went down to a preview. There was an apple on sale there for
£200. I thought it was fantastic. I got the humour in her work
immediately. There was another piece which really decided me for
or against the artist – a ladder which led to a painting which was
hung on the ceiling. I climbed the ladder, looked through a spy glass
and in tiny letters it said, 'Yes'. I felt relieved. John Dunbar insisted
she say hello to the millionaire. She came up and handed me a card
which said 'Breathe' on it, so I just went [pants]. This was our first
meeting!"

When he browsed through the exhibition catalogue, Lennon
learned that there was more to Ono's art than expensive whimsy. Her

13

writing betrayed a philosophic air, guaranteed to appeal to the Beatle who had written such songs as 'The Word' and 'Tomorrow Never Knows'. Two weeks before recording 'Strawberry Fields Forever' (with its key line 'Nothing is real'), Lennon had been reading the following extract from her catalogue:

> "Man is born, educates himself, builds a house and a life and then all that vanishes when he dies. *What is real? Is anything real?* A thing becomes real to us when it is functional and necessary to us. As long as we strive for truth we live in self-induced misery, expecting in life something that is not an illusion. If we recognize that *nothing is true* or illusory . . . then we can proceed from there on to be optimistic and swallow life as it comes."

As Lennon and Ono were both married, their contact over the next year was necessarily sporadic. She sent him a copy of her book *Grapefruit*, which he found both fascinating and infuriating, depending upon his mood and patience level. Before long, he was bombarded with postcards bearing cryptic messages such as 'Watch all the lights until dawn', 'Go to the horizon – measure it' and 'Boil water and watch until it evaporates'. Although she had already infiltrated his mind and would soon invade his household, he still insisted to his wife Cynthia: "She's just another nutter wanting money for all that avant-garde bullshit."

As Lennon's marriage frosted over, so his interest in 'avant-garde bullshit' increased. While Cynthia was persuaded to holiday abroad, he made the bold decision to invite Yoko to his Weybridge house. They retired to a room where Lennon stored his Beatles tapes and works in progress. There, in the early hours of 20 May 1968, they consummated their artistic, musical and sexual union with this abstract collage of electronic sounds.

"I was always shy with Yoko," Lennon insisted, when recalling that evening for the readers of *Playboy* magazine. "My ex-wife was away somewhere and Yoko and I did acid. We had never made love. Because I was shy, instead of making love, we went upstairs and made tapes . . . She was doing her funny voices and I was pushing all different buttons on my tape recorder and getting sound effects.

14

Then, as the sun rose, we made love. That was it. That was *Two Virgins*."

The audio-vérité album consisted of 30 minutes of voices, distorted instruments and various sound effects, including bird calls, falling buildings and snatches of music hall songs. The famous Ono wail opened the work, with Lennon providing growling feedback on his guitar and screaming back at her. At one point, John says, "Who's there?" as Yoko's ghoulish whine segues into a tolling bell. There are also elements of humour, with Lennon adopting a Wilfred Pickles persona and announcing, "It's just me, Hilda, I'm home for tea." Ono responds with the instant aphorism, "Tea's never ready." On side 2, Yoko's eerie wailing becomes more intense and there is a moment of melodrama when Lennon urges, "Go on then." Towards the end, he appears to imitate the solemnity of a sung Mass for a few seconds, but the idea is undeveloped. "I've had enough now, thank you," he announces wearily. "Let's get this over with, if you don't mind," at which point the record concludes.

For most contemporaneous listeners, the album must have sounded like a discordant indulgence. The low volume recording virtually invited surface noise after a handful of plays, although it seems reasonable to assume that few fans regarded the work as a turntable favourite. Of course, for Lennon and Ono it was a stimulating voyage of discovery. Overall, the intention of the work, as underlined in its title, was to create a soundscape that suggested a return to lost innocence.

The Edenic concept still gripped Lennon's imagination when he was considering the album's artwork. With Adam and Eve in mind, he decided upon a provocative sleeve whose notoriety would far outlast any comments on the album's aesthetic or musical appeal. "Originally, I was going to record Yoko, and I thought the best picture of her for an album would be her naked," he reasoned. "I was just going to record her as an artist. We were only on those kind of terms then. So, after that, when we got together, it just seemed natural, if we made an album together, for both of us to be naked. Of course, I've never seen me prick on an album or photo before . . . The album also says: 'Look, lay off, will you? It's two people – what have we done?' "

Yoko Ono confirmed that the nude shot was Lennon's idea. "I suppose he just thought it would be effective. He took the picture himself with an automatic camera. It's nice. The picture isn't lewd or anything . . . We'd be the first to be embarrassed if anyone were to invite us to a nude party."

Such protestations of modesty left many detractors unconvinced. At the time, the sleeve was generally regarded as either exhibitionist, smutty or pornographic. The participants' insistence that they were 'very shy' was greeted with equal scorn. Perhaps the best summation of this media derision can be seen in the footage of their later bed-in at Montreal, where cartoonist Al Capp sarcastically waves a cover of the album in the air and announces: "If that isn't a picture of two shy people, I'd like to know what shyness is . . . I think everybody owes it to the world to prove that they have pubic hair. And you've *done* it. I applaud you for it . . . and I tell you that's one of the greatest contributions to enlightenment and culture of our time."

Lennon had wanted to release *Two Virgins* at the earliest opportunity but his choice of artwork resulted in a six-month delay, while his record company considered the implications. In order to avoid prosecution, it was decided that the American edition of the album should be placed in a brown paper bag, a fate that had previously been considered for *Sgt Pepper's* when Brian Epstein panicked over possible litigation from its illustrious montage of cover stars. While controversy over the proposed sleeve continued, Lennon feigned an incredulous innocence about the fuss he and Yoko were causing. "We had known each other two years by then . . . The album cover of us naked was a way to show purity. Everybody was sort of upset that two people were naked. We thought it was insane that everybody was so upset about it." Elaborating on this point to B.P. Fallon, Lennon complained: "The reaction was typical of narrow-minded compressed heads. A few people understand it. What was it – just two people naked. It's not lewd or obscene and there's nothing wrong with it. It's just two people without any clothes on. They think that once you get past babyhood there's something sinful about it. It's time they woke up. We're all naked underneath."

One major obstacle they faced was the urbane chairman of EMI, Sir Joseph Lockwood. Not surprisingly, he was concerned about the impact that the album might have on the career of the Beatles, not to mention the reputation of his record company. What would the shareholders think? At one point, it was suggested that the record should be released solely under Yoko Ono's name, presumably to protect Beatle John's reputation. Another idea mooted was the employment of a pseudonym, although that would have meant not using the controversial artwork. Lennon was at least amused enough to suggest sarcastically that he and Yoko rechristen themselves Doris and Peter for the occasion. Under pressure, Ono admitted that if they were blocked from using their real names, she would promote the work independently as a limited edition artwork of 50 copies to be distributed to key people of their choosing. In the end, the couple's forthright appeals and counter arguments won some compromises, but they still faced an uphill battle. As John Lennon pointed out: "*Two Virgins* was a big fight. It was held up . . . Sir Joseph Lockwood was a nice, nice guy . . . He said he understood it and he'd do everything he could to help us. Then, when we tried to put it out, he sent a personal note to everybody saying, 'Don't print it. Don't put it out.' So we couldn't get the cover printed anywhere."

Lennon's ironic comments on Lockwood's 'nice guy' image were unfair on one level. In the moral climate of 1968, full frontal nudity on an album cover was bound to cause offence and probably prosecution, particularly in Britain. What should have irked Lennon even more was the appalling attitude that the EMI chairman betrayed towards Yoko Ono. His prejudices were regrettably consistent with the prevailing public and media view of the time. When later recalling his first meeting with Ono, he said: "I wasn't sure if *it* was a human being or an animal." At a second meeting he insulted her with the quip: "Why don't you show Paul [McCartney] naked. He's so much better looking than you."

McCartney may not have been entirely convinced by the merits of *Two Virgins* but he did his best to win over Lockwood and was supportive enough to contribute an extravagantly portentous and grammatically confusing sleeve note, which read: "When two great Saints meet it is a humbling experience. The battles [*sic*] to prove he was a saint."

Sainthood, real or imagined, was never likely to persuade EMI or Capitol to distribute the offending disc, irrespective of the protective brown paper bag, whose outside featured a pointed description of Adam and Eve's nudity taken from the Book of Genesis. "EMI killed our album *Two Virgins* because they didn't like it," Lennon concluded with cold disdain.

As the second release on Apple, *Two Virgins* gained lots of publicity, but few sales. In the UK, it was distributed by Track, the label run by the Who's managers, Kit Lambert and Chris Stamp. Coincidentally, Track was also handling the Jimi Hendrix Experience's *Electric Ladyland*, released in the UK on 25 October, which also featured some controversial nudity. On the original pressing of *Two Virgins* there were no banding or track listings, just two sides of 'Unfinished Music'. Stateside distribution was handled by the small independent Tetragrammaton, which suffered a setback when 30,000 copies of the disc were impounded in New Jersey for breaching parochial obscenity laws.

Lennon later came to regard the display of nudity as a political act, albeit one unappreciated by the proletariat. "Working-class people reacted against our openness about sex. They are frightened of nudity, they're repressed in that way, as well as others."

When the album finally appeared in November 1968, it reached the shops a mere week after the Beatles' celebrated double album. That same month, Yoko had a miscarriage and John pleaded guilty to a trumped-up charge of marijuana possession. It was the unhappiest of times. For its creators, *Two Virgins* was soon *passé* and they were already working on new projects. "It was a bum album," Yoko concluded with mischievous irony. Nevertheless, it remains a defining moment in Lennon's creative life and a testament to his love of improvisation, mixed with humour and childlike wonder.

Two Virgins was simultaneously released in the USA (Apple T 5001) in the same form as its UK counterpart but oddly there was an attempt by the record company to 'band' the tracks with the following titles: 'Two Virgins Nos. 1–10'; 'Together'; 'Hushabye'. In May 1997, *Two Virgins* was finally released on CD (Rykodisc RCD 10411), with a surprise bonus track:

Remember Love

Like its original A-side 'Give Peace A Chance', the credits tell us that this was 'recorded in Room 1742, Hotel La Reine Elizabeth, Montreal by Les Studios André Perry, 7585 Malo, Ville de Brossard, PQ, Canada'. Others speculate that it may have been done later at the Lennons' home studio although it seems more likely that, if this indeed occurred, it was simply a sonic 'tidying-up' of the original tape. Either way, it's a simple, uncluttered recording featuring Yoko's classically trained, professionally enunciated vocal in one speaker and John's delicately played acoustic guitar in the other. An affecting ballad and a disarmingly simple paean to love, it has an ephemeral charm, although its skeletal structure and absence of chorus (in contrast to 'Give Peace A Chance') ensured that it was largely ignored at the time of its release.

UNFINISHED MUSIC NO. 2: LIFE WITH THE LIONS

Released: May 1969

Original UK issue: Zapple 01. US issue: Apple ST 3357. CD reissue with bonus
tracks: Rykodisc RCD 10412 (UK/US)

While the Beatles' legend inexorably entered its final phase, the John
and Yoko saga continued to excite world attention. In addition to
the reams of newspaper print documenting their public appearances
and personal upheavals, the duo continued recording experimental
albums of 'Unfinished Music', which partly functioned as aural
diaries of their recent troubled history. During the month that Side 2
of this album was recorded, Yoko Ono suffered a miscarriage and
Lennon pleaded guilty to illegal possession of cannabis, for which he
was fined £150, plus 20 guineas costs. That charge would have
serious repercussions later in his career when US authorities threatened him with deportation. The sleeve of this album captures the
sadness and drama of both the above incidents. On the front, Ono is
pictured in a hospital bed, clutching an apple, while Lennon sits
patiently on some cushions spread on the ward floor next to her. The
back cover pictures them outside Marylebone Magistrates' Court
surrounded by police after "being dragged out of the police station".
The scene receives a further ironic commentary in the album subtitle
Life With The Lions, a playful pun on the cosy British wartime radio
show *Life With The Lyons*. There's a similarly sardonic tone in the
manufacturing note: 'Made in merrie England', plus a slight dig at the
conservatism of the Beatles' producer – "'No Comment' – George
Martin" placed above the album title.

Contemporaneous critics and public alike perceived these records
as akin to the ravings of a madman and a madwoman. Few appreciated that Yoko Ono had solid avant-garde credentials stretching back
to the Fifties, when she had studied music and art at the prestigious
Sarah Lawrence College, before dropping out to stage events at her

loft in Greenwich Village. After marrying her second husband Tony Cox, Ono wrote intermittently and staged many talked-about exhibitions and provocative films, which spread her fame in art circles around the world. What she brought to John Lennon was a knowledge of conceptual and performance art, heavily influenced by such key figures as John Cage, Andy Warhol, La Monte Young and that New York group of painters, poets and musicians collectively named Fluxus.

Unsurprisingly, perhaps, Lennon felt that avant-garde was a limiting adjective to apply to the work of his beloved. "Well, that's the only word you can use for it, but I think a label like avant-garde defeats itself. You learn to have avant-garde exhibitions. The fact that avant-garde can have an exhibition defeats the purpose of avant-garde because it's already formalized and ritualized, so it's not avant-garde. But that was the only word . . . that was the word that was applied to her and her ilk."

The improvisational records that Lennon and Ono produced during this period still sound eccentric, although they clearly borrowed from current avant-garde thinking. John Cage's belief in encouraging audience participation as part of the artistic event had already been demonstrated by Ono in her exhibitions. It is here too in these experimental records. Even the title of the first two Lennon/Ono albums suggested a work of art in flux. In explaining the idea behind the concept 'Unfinished Music', Yoko Ono told critic Jonathan Cott: "If you listen to it, maybe you can add to it or change it or edit or add something in your mind. The unfinished part that's not in the record – what's in you, not what's in the record, is what's important. The record is just there to stimulate what's in you, to make it come out."

For many listeners accustomed to pop and rock, these experimental albums were seen as inexplicable and indulgent. Today, the world has caught up with the ideas, if not the aesthetic appreciation. As *New York Times*' critic John Rockwell rightly observes: "It is difficult to explain or excuse vanguard art to those who don't know it or can't stand it. To them, it can seem like deliberate provocation, with its apparently tedious length, deafening volume, aggressive behaviour towards an innocent audience and other unpleasantries."

It is amusing to consider that most of the people who bought the 'Unfinished Music' albums were likely to be disgruntled Beatles collectors whose acquisitive mentality demanded that they own every recorded utterance by the Fab Four. For those interested in esoterica, the purchasing motive was more likely intellectual curiosity or novelty hunting rather than genuine enthusiasm. Of course, Lennon saw it differently. For him, avant-garde was another important new experiment, like folk rock, ragas, sound collages and all the other trends that the Beatles had helped to popularize during the second half of the Sixties. The newly created Zapple label, which issued this record and George Harrison's experimental *Electronic Sounds* on the same day, was intended as an outlet for all sorts of improvisational and spoken word recordings. Instead, the label ceased operation after its first two releases – an apposite enough comment on the public's reaction to these arcane pieces. Limited availability and a relatively small number of pressings have ensured that both volumes of 'Unfinished Music' remain collectors' items, but those that are still in circulation are likely to be near mint copies. Repeated listening was never high on the list of priorities for serious or casual purchasers and, given the topicality of the material coupled with notions of instant disposability, it is doubtful whether Lennon and Ono ever expected anyone to play these records too long after their release date.

Exact sales figures for these discs are not known but, judging from an interview with Barry Miles in September 1969, Lennon was informed that *Life With The Lions* had shifted 60,000 copies in America. "I'm very excited. It's nothing on Beatles sales but it's a lot of albums for that music. Maybe some of them were Beatlemaniacs who thought they were going to get something else, but I think they might have guessed by now after *Two Virgins*. I can't keep framing it in Beatles music to bring along the people. How many 'Revolution 9's am I going to get on an album? . . . Sixty thousand kids in America are having no trouble with *Life With The Lions*. There's always going to be people complaining because we left the Cavern and went to work in Manchester. That's all it is, really. How dare I leave the Cavern then jump into a bag in the Albert Hall?"

Clearly frustrated by the expectations still foisted upon him as an ex-Beatle, Lennon was determined to push ahead with his avant-garde experiments. "I'm just moving out or pressing the outer limits of whatever's going on and people say, 'Why don't you stay where we can recognize you?' There's no time to wait for people to understand why I've grown a beard or why I've shaved it off, or why I want to be naked, or why I want to stand on my head. If people waited for people to understand everything they did, nothing would ever get done."

Cambridge 1969

On 2 March 1969, two months before the release of *Life With The Lions*, Lennon and Ono performed before an audience of approximately 500 people at Lady Mitchell Hall, Cambridge. "I was invited to Cambridge to do a number, a sort of avant-garde number," Ono explained. "And they didn't realize we were together . . . They didn't realize then and they invited me, so I said, 'All right what shall I do?' And John was saying, 'Well, it's all right, why don't you go?' And they were saying: 'Well are you going to bring a band?' So John said, 'Well, I'm the band, but don't tell them. I'll be the band.'"

For Lennon the opportunity to appear onstage with Ono was irresistible. This was his first public performance since the glory days of the Beatles and the results could hardly have been more contrasting. Instead of adoring fans, he was faced with an avant-garde audience that regarded him suspiciously as an interloper from the unsavoury commercial world of rock music. It was salutary for Lennon to empathize with the feelings of Ono, who had suffered far worse criticism when daring to attend Beatles sessions.

The concert, which took up an entire side of this album, begins with Yoko quietly announcing: "This is a piece called 'Cambridge 1969'." Her familiar screaming vocal dominates the recording, while Lennon provides accompanying feedback through his guitar. As the performance progresses, Ono's screams undulate, then gradually become more intense. It's tough listening for non-avant-gardists, but there is a noticeable sense of calm in those more palatable moments when the feedback is lowered. Towards the end, the pair are joined by jazz avant-garde players John Stevens and John Tchakai. A cymbal is then used to vary the sound pattern before the listener is once more enveloped by the swirling feedback. It is just possible to hear Yoko intoning the words 'Free Hanratty', which emerge as a ghostly whisper through the speakers.

James Hanratty had been convicted of the 'A6 murder' at Dead Man's Hill in 1961 and subsequently hanged. Over the years there had been various campaigns protesting his innocence. Years later, the body was exhumed and the Crown's verdict exonerated through DNA evidence. At this time, however, John and Yoko were seemingly convinced that he had been 'murdered' by the state and subsequently expressed their support for his posthumous pardon in a meeting with Hanratty's parents on 10 December 1969.

As the Hanratty allusion passes through the audience's consciousness, a saxophone is introduced and the mood changes subtly once more. It leaves the listener wishing that the jazz musicians had joined the pair earlier in the piece to break up or vary the unrelenting scream/feedback routine . . . but that was no doubt the point of the exercise.

Lennon's recollection of the evening was suitably deadpan. "It was supposed to be an avant-garde jazz thing," he noted vaguely. "And there was this guy John Tchakai who was apparently a famous avant-garde sax guy, or jazz sax guy – I didn't know any of them. A few people that I don't remember the names of – they were there too. And I turned up as her band and the people were looking and saying: 'Is it? Is it?' I just had a guitar and an amp and that was the first time I'd played that style, just pure feedback and whatever is on the track. The audience was very weird because they were all these sort of intellectual, artsy-fartsies from Cambridge and they were uptight because the rock 'n' roll guy was there, even though I wasn't doing any rhythm. If you hear it, it's pure sound because what else can you do when a woman's howling? You just go along with it."

No Bed For Beatle John

This track, previously available on a flexi-disc in the March 1969 edition of the American arts magazine *Aspen*, documented the third week of November 1968, when Ono had her miscarriage at London's Queen Charlotte Hospital. Lennon had vowed to stay by her bedside throughout her stay, but a shortage of beds meant that he had to sleep on the floor, propped up by cushions. This track was akin to an elegy for 'John Ono Lennon II', the miscarried foetus whose remains were placed in a coffin and buried at a secret location.

The mood of the piece is predictably sombre and reflective, sounding not unlike a requiem mass. Ono reads or rather chants lines from the newspapers of that week, telling us how Lennon 'lost his hospital bed yesterday to a patient'. There is also an account of the furore surrounding the impending release of *Two Virgins* that same month. While Ono chants, Lennon provides a counter harmony with his reading, which is tantalizingly out of earshot for most of the piece. Overall, this performance is by far the most interesting and inventive track on the album and it is surprising that Lennon did not choose to repeat the idea of word chanting on one of his mainstream solo recordings. It is fascinating to consider what Phil Spector might have conjured if presented with this concept by Lennon.

Baby's Heartbeat
Towards the end of Ono's troubled pregnancy, Lennon taped a few seconds of the heartbeat of her unborn baby. Upon returning to the studio, he put this through a tape loop, creating a track in excess of five minutes. The result was this strange piece which sounds like a cross between a stereo test record and the soundtrack of an underwater adventure story. The baby's life force undulates eerily between the speakers, before suddenly stopping. This track was probably the most extreme example to date of John and Yoko's determination to document every episode of their lives together. As Lennon told B.P. Fallon at the time: "It took me a while to realize the Beatles were doing a diary too on records. Everything everyone does is his own diary, but I became aware of it as a Beatle. I'm trying to get over as quickly as I can what is actually happening to me at this given time, and so we collect photos, tape it or make films of what's happening."

Two Minutes Silence

Borrowing the idea from John Cage's controversial concert piece *4'33"*, Lennon and Ono offer us two minutes of silence. This fits perfectly in the context of this album as a haunting requiem for the dead baby. Drama and expectancy are added to the listening process through the use of such a long silence, which also offers the chance to meditate on the couple's loss or, indeed, anything else that comes into the listener's mind. According to Lennon, the two-minute silence was "copyrighted for the baby, and for all violence and death".

Radio Play

This track was also previously premièred as a give-away flexi-disc with the arts magazine *Aspen*. The punning title refers to the concept which consists of 'playing with a radio'. A static screech is created by turning a radio on and off in rapid succession, accompanied by a muted conversation between Lennon and Ono, which is vaguely audible in the background. The 'radio-switch' effect predates the 'scratching' technique later employed in rap music. Along the way, we hear Lennon attempting to phone the Ambassador Hotel to reach his aide, Anthony Fawcett. The rhythm of the piece gradually changes as Lennon continues to fiddle with the radio set, making a more intense sound that resembles the screeching of a violin. There's a certain childlike wonder here in the way they attempt to create new and unexpected sounds from unusual sources. Inevitably, though, the track goes on for far too long, by which time curiosity is replaced by impatience. It's not a piece that easily invites repeated listening.

In May 1997, *Unfinished Music No. 2: Life With The Lions* was finally released on CD (Rykodisc RCD 10412) with the following bonus tracks:

Song For John

Committed to tape on the same day as 'No Bed For Beatle John', this Yoko Ono composition was also known as 'Let's Go On Flying'. On the original tape it was part of what appeared to be a Yoko Ono medley, featuring a minute of 'Let's Go On Flying', followed by a fragment of 'Listen, The Snow Is Falling'. A prototype version of 'Don't Worry Kyoko (Mummy's Only Looking For A Hand In The Snow)' also featured on the tape but was later excised from the rest of 'Song For John' on Ono's solo CD reissues. The 'original' 'Song For John' can also be heard on the flexi-disc given away with *Aspen* in the summer of 1969.

Mulberry

Another recording from November 1968, this featured Yoko Ono intoning the word 'mulberry' in her inimitable style, backed by Lennon on acoustic guitar. The track was completed at the same time as 'No Bed For Beatle John', 'Baby's Heartbeat', 'Radio Play' and 'Song For John'.

WEDDING ALBUM

Released: November 1969

Original UK issue: SAPCOR 11. US issue: Apple SMAX 3361. CD reissue with
bonus tracks: Rykodisc RCD 10413 (UK/US)

The wedding of John Lennon and Yoko Ono, two weeks after the
nuptials of Paul McCartney and Linda Eastman, symbolized the final
severing of a musical partnership that had once seemed inseparable. It
would be several months more before the world realized that
Lennon/McCartney was a dead brotherhood. In the meantime, John
and Yoko continued to transform the circumstances of their daily
lives into aural events. Not surprisingly, their marriage provided a
living documentary that served as a romantic but salutary saga for the
world. The couple had intended to marry on a cross-channel ferry to
France, but they were denied access to the *Dragon* at Southampton
Docks due to passport irregularities. After consulting Beatles aide
Peter Brown, they flew to the Rock of Gibraltar on 20 March, where
they were married in the British Consulate building. They were in
and out of the country in an incredible 70 minutes. As Lennon
explained: "We chose Gibraltar because it is quiet, British and
friendly. We tried everywhere else first. I set out to get married on
the car ferry and we would have arrived in France married. But they
wouldn't do it. We were no more successful with cruise ships. We
tried embassies. But three weeks' residence in Germany or two
weeks in France were required."

The events that followed the marriage became international news.
After spending a couple of days at the Plaza Athenee Hotel in France,
during which they met painter Salvadore Dali, they announced their
intention to stage a 'bed-in' for peace to take place in Amsterdam.
One week later, the world's media descended on Room 902 of the
Amsterdam Hilton Hotel, eager to document a salacious story.
Instead, they found the Lennons sitting in bed, holding hands,
modestly clad in white pyjamas. Despite frequent derision from

various media pundits, Lennon sold the story of peace in the same way that he related more prosaic Beatles activities: "We're staying in bed for a week to register our protest against all the suffering and violence in the world . . . We're promoting peace for the whole world, but mainly aiming towards the youth. We are appealing to people with violent inclinations for change. We believe violent change doesn't really accomplish anything in the long term because in the 2,000-plus years we've been going, all the violent revolutions have come to an end, even if they've lasted 50 or 100 years. Unfortunately, the few people who have tried to do it our way – Jesus, Gandhi, Kennedy, Martin Luther King – have been killed. The way we might escape being killed is that we have a sense of humour and the worst or the least we can do is make people laugh."

Throughout the week, the newly-weds were at their most engagingly humorous and won over several cynical reporters who saw some perverse logic in their bed-in. Cartoonists loved the event and newspapers were full of depictions of 'bed peace', usually featuring world leaders tucked up uneasily together. Newspaper pundits in search of new angles called in doctors and psychiatrists to analyse the implications. "Modern technique is to get even unfit people out of bed as soon as possible so that they can recover their strength," a medic suggested. "I should think they will feel very wonky when they get up." This prediction proved accurate. Upon their return to England, Lennon admitted he was still feeling the after-effects of the elongated bed-in. "Mentally we are both still very alert, but physically we are exhausted. In fact, we're going to bed for a week to recover."

Psychiatrist Dr Ellis Stungo admitted that he was baffled by the logic behind the bed-in: "I can't get a firm line on their behaviour." Despite this, he was clearly willing to have a stab at explaining their hidden motivations. "It is sheer exhibitionism but one would have thought that they had had so many opportunities to publicize themselves that their need would be satisfied by now. Perhaps it may be they feel their acclaim is waning, they need to feel acclaimed and this exhibition is a way of restoring security to them. On the other hand, it may be that they are both so unattractive and know that they are unpopular, so this is a way of trying to justify themselves – trying to show everyone that theirs is a tremendous romance of which they are not ashamed."

Oddly, no attempt was made to place Lennon and Ono's activities in the wider context of such leading art movements as the Dadaists or the Fluxus group, which had specific connections with Yoko. More puzzling was the media's failure to connect the bed-in with the work of the avant-garde *Internationale Situationiste*, a political movement founded in Italy in the summer of 1957, which had come to prominence during the Paris Riots in May 1968, only 18 months before the UK release of *Wedding Album*. The Situationists combined Marxist and Dadaist thought and sought to enlighten the proletariat by attacking the passivity of consumerism, deriding the mindlessness of work and exploiting the creative possibilities of enforced unemployment and increased leisure time. Situationist doctrines were espoused through sharp, provocative slogans such as 'culture is the inversion of life', 'the more you consume, the less you live', 'be reasonable – demand the impossible' and 'it is forbidden to forbid'. The sloganeering recalled Ono's use of placards with cryptic messages and Lennon's occasional lyrical aphorisms.

In addition to the countless commentaries from brow-creasing columnists on the rights and wrongs of the bed-in, there were numerous letters to the press from Joe Public. Some were scathing, some conciliatory and a few featured a tongue-in-cheek humour which appealed to Lennon. "The seven-day lie-in by John Lennon makes sense, not as a means of achieving world peace, but as a rest cure," one reader suggested. "This is the way to get away from the madding crowd unless it calls at your bedside. I am convinced that the health of the nation would improve if every husband and wife had three days in bed in turn – waited on hand and foot. The only time we get a three-day lie-in is when we go down with 'flu. The Government should cancel a Bank Holiday and introduce a Bed Holiday. Or why not a national lie-in?"

Lennon remained upbeat about the ridicule. "We are not laughing at you any more than you're laughing at us," he said at a press conference after the event. "It was just our protest against violence.

30

Everybody has their bags. In Paris, the Vietnam peace talks have got about as far as sorting out the shape of the table they are going to sit around. Those talks have been going on for months. In one week in bed, we achieved a lot more. A little old lady in Wigan or Hull wrote to the *Daily Mirror* asking if they could put Yoko and myself on the front page more often. She said she hadn't laughed so much for ages. I wouldn't mind dying as the world's clown. I'm not looking for epitaphs."

The selling of peace was also promoted through the distribution of acorns to various world leaders ("We want them to plant them for peace") and 'bagism', another Yoko-influenced concept which required the pair to hide away in a white bag while conducting a press conference. Startled and sceptical interrogators at the Hotel Sacher in Vienna were reduced to asking such teasing questions as "How do we know it's you?"

There was further proof of Lennon's enduring commitment to Yoko soon after when, in a fit of disenchantment with British imperialism, he elected to change his middle name from Winston to Ono. Although he would shortly deny faith in all belief systems, Lennon, at this point, still saw some significance in numerology, stressing: "Yoko changed her name for me. I've changed mine for her. One for both; both for each other. She has a ring; I have a ring. It gives us nine 'O's between us, which is good luck. Ten would not be good luck."

While the newspapers continued to document the bed-ins and the Acorns For Peace campaign, the Lennons were systematically filming their own lives. The Amsterdam Hilton bed-in had been regarded as a pivotal moment in their public lives – not just as a cry for peace but as a celebration of marriage. A cinéma-vérité film of the event was captured in documentary form on *Honeymoon*, while the audio equivalent was this commemorative *Wedding Album*.

In addition to a two-sided record, this ornate box set featured various items of marital memorabilia, including a copy of their marriage certificate, a photo of a slice of wedding cake, four passport sized photos taken in a booth, a poster featuring scenes from the wedding, a black and white postcard of the bed-in at the Amsterdam

Hilton Hotel and a booklet of press cuttings detailing, in both amusing and gruesome reportage, the ridicule and condescension heaped upon them in the name of journalism. As Lennon explained to the BBC: "It was our way of sharing our wedding with whoever wanted to share it with us. We didn't expect a hit record out of it. That's why we called it *Wedding Album*. You know, people make a wedding album, show it to the relatives when they come round. Well, our relatives are what you call fans, or people that follow us outside. So that was our way of letting them join in on the wedding."

What Lennon failed to mention was that the fans had already savoured the wedding story on record six months earlier, courtesy of the Beatles' chart-topping 'The Ballad Of John And Yoko', which humorously and poignantly detailed the tribulations of the pair at the hands of the authorities and the media. Intriguingly, the excellent single that documented John's union with Yoko was recorded by himself and Paul McCartney. At this point, Lennon was still willing to use the Beatles' name to document his and Ono's trial by media, which meant that a well deserved number 1 record could be achieved in the UK, a statistic never to be accomplished by the later Plastic Ono Band. Using Paul McCartney as a creative foil to relate the ballad of John and Yoko was an irony that few noted, then or since. Clearly, though, John felt it was appropriate that he and Yoko should release their own avant-garde version of recent events for posterity.

Wedding Album retailed at £3 10s, twice the price of a normal LP record in 1969. Needless to say, the work was never likely to be a best seller but it remains a prized collectors' item. It was largely ignored by record reviewers, with the notable exception of *Melody Maker*'s Richard Williams who wrote a surprisingly lengthy appraisal headlined 'Memento Of Our Time'. Describing the package as "possibly the most lavish production yet conceived in the medium of popular music," Williams concluded: "This album will make interesting listening in 20 years' time. What will we think of it then?" In his analytical zeal, however, Williams made a famous blunder which won sympathy from every critic who has ever taken a fatal gamble on an over-clever theory. Williams had been sent a test pressing of the album on two separate discs, the blank flip-sides of which contained a 'test signal'. Never one to underestimate an avant-gardist, Williams assumed that the work was a double album and actually reviewed all four 'sides'. "Sides Two and Four consist entirely of single tones maintained throughout, presumably produced electronically. This might sound arid, to say the least, but in fact constant listening reveals a curious point: the pitch of the tones alters frequently, but only by micro-tones or, at most, a semi-tone. This oscillation produces an almost subliminal, uneven 'beat' which maintains interest."

Williams' mistake endeared him to the Lennons who sent back a telegram saying, "This is the first time a critic topped the artist." The review served a purpose, however, confirming that almost anything attempted by John and Yoko could safely be classified under the description 'conceptual art'. As Lennon admitted: "Yoko calls her work 'concept art'. Take the 'cept' off and you've got 'con art' and you're near the point. We're here to give people laughs as well." Although *Wedding Album* was the last of their avant-garde albums trilogy, Lennon was determined that more should follow. "We're trying to do these things at the time they are happening. We'd like to be able to produce them as fast as newspapers and television can. It will be a constant autobiography of our life together – and it will go on for the rest of our lives."

John And Yoko

After incorporating Ono as part of his middle name, Lennon celebrated his new bonding by recording this experimental piece with her. Employing a microphone in the shape of a stethoscope, they taped several seconds of their respective heartbeats. John then consigned these to a mastertape, making a loop by which the sounds were repeated for 22 minutes. These were then played back while the Lennons added a mantra, intoning their names 'John And Yoko' for the duration of the recording. Drawing an analogy between Ono's film-making and this performance, Peter Doggett noted: "In the same way that the purity of Yoko's film *Bottoms* has been spoilt by the inclusion of semi-humorous voice-overs, so the beauty of the original statement – the two hearts pounding together to create a womb-like, mysterious pattern of sound – was subverted by the

33

addition of the couple's voices. Having made the transition from 'Baby's Heartbeat' to their own, the experiment wasn't repeated."

Whether the two voices detract from the power of the two hearts beating is debatable. The track actually begins with the scrunching of an apple, after which the chants continue for an entire album side. Lennon and Ono manage to convey a variety of emotional responses while uttering their names, sometimes sounding petulant, loving, quizzical, frustrated and agonized. They whisper, shout, scream, purr, yearn and plead, while alternating the speed of their intonation to suggest everything from complete desolation to orgasmic joy. The major problem in appreciating the piece is not the combination of voice and sound, which works reasonably well, but the interminable length of the exercise which strains the listener's patience and attention span after the first few minutes have elapsed. At the end, they finish off the apple they had begun eating some 20 or more minutes before. It is tempting, and probably quite correct, to find symbolism in the Lennons devouring an Apple, given the fortunes of the company at the time of the recording.

Amsterdam
The famous John and Yoko bed-in at the Amsterdam Hilton attracted journalists from all over the world and the Lennons decided to capture the event on record. For an entire 25-minute side of an album, the listener is allowed to eavesdrop on an audio-vérité best of the bed-in. It commences with John announcing, "OK, Yoko," after which his spouse sings 'John John (Let's Hope For Peace)'. The performance is chanted in traditional Japanese style, with instrumentation and background effects which, overall, sound much more impressive than the later 'rock' version performed by the Plastic Ono Band on *Live Peace In Toronto 1969*. Its major weakness is Lennon's interjections, which sound as intrusive as some of Ono's contributions to his rock numbers. Developing the song, Yoko implores "Oh John, let's hope for peace for our children, for our countries, for our world, for our future . . ."

Ono's performance is followed by an interview about the peace campaign, which manages to mix hippie left-wing rhetoric with

34

fleeting examples of Lennon's humour. Recorded in London after the Amsterdam bed-in, it displays Lennon in confident mood, sounding articulate and persuasive. Ono enters controversial territory, blaming the world, as much as Hitler, for the persecution of Jews. They then discuss political history, with references to various acts of imperialism and peace attempts through the ages. Lennon eventually interrupts with the admission: "I'm as violent as the next man . . . we're violent people. I prefer myself non-violent. I prefer my friends when they're non-violent . . . I prefer to live in peace."

Suddenly, the scene switches and after hearing seagulls and other sound effects we're taken back in time to Amsterdam, as John strums and sings 'Day In Bed'. In this section, we eavesdrop on the Lennons waking up for their bed-in. "Good morning," John yawns, as journalists gather. He orders tea and brown toast from room service and is presented with a dog from a peace-loving visitor. He then reads some humorous extracts from the newspapers spread before him, while a sitar is played in the background. Photo shoots and interviews follow. One reporter attempts to return to the early Beatles' days and, failing to remember the correct title 'Love Me Do', asks John about their first record 'Do You Love Me'. "Not particularly," Lennon replies sardonically.

John next strums and sings 'Goodbye Amsterdam' and Yoko replies with an impromptu song 'Stay In Bed . . . Grow Your Hair'. The acoustic backing closely resembles the melody line of the Beatles' 'Because'. As the side reaches its close, Lennon intones the traditional nursery rhyme, 'Goodnight, sleep tight . . .', leaving Yoko to sum up the event. "What a beautiful day," she observes. "Very tiring though." A final bash at a new anthem follows as they chant 'Grow Your Hair. Bed Peace. Hair Peace'. The track ends with what sounds like an aeroplane revving up. Overall, 'Amsterdam' works reasonably well as an aural extract from the bed-in and is suitably varied and entertaining in its contents to warrant more than a cursory listen.

In May 1997, *Wedding Album* was finally issued on CD with the following bonus tracks, originally premièred as B-sides:

Who Has Seen The Wind?

Originally the B-side of 'Instant Karma!' and credited to 'Lennon/ Ono with the Plastic Ono Band', this song came with the advice 'Play Quiet' on the vinyl single. Sounding like a tone poem, this very short track was most notable for its unusual backing which appears to combine harpsichord and woodwind, creating a parlour music ambience seemingly intended to transport the listener into a different musical age.

Listen, The Snow Is Falling

Oddly out of chronological sequence as a belated addition to this 1969 album, 'Listen, The Snow Is Falling' was originally included as the B-side to the 1971–72 single 'Happy Xmas (War Is Over)'. Its inclusion here seems even odder when you consider that the startling 'Open Your Box', which was the B-side of the preceding 'Power To The People', appeared nine months earlier in the USA and over one-and-a-half years before in the UK, yet it is conspicuous by its absence as a bonus track. Presumably, Yoko Ono sanctioned this song's inclusion on the grounds that she had written the composition, in part, some years before, although if you applied that same logic to Lennon's work, many bonus tracks would feature in decidedly strange surroundings.

Credited to 'Yoko Ono and the Plastic Ono Band', the original single of 'Listen, The Snow Is Falling' featured a then innovative photographic montage of Lennon/Ono on the record label in which John's face gradually metamorphosed into that of Yoko's over five different images. By Ono's experimental standards, this song was almost mainstream and unexpectedly commercial. The perfect complement to 'Happy Xmas (War Is Over)', it begins and ends with the sound of somebody trudging through the snow. Chiming sleigh bells and wind-blown snowflakes add to the festive imagery. Some of these aural images were borrowed from a sound effects record which included the titles 'Feet In The Snow' and 'Strong Wind'. During the session, Yoko marshals the musicians, sternly telling John: "I asked you to play the organ – I've been asking you to do that all along." Pianist Nicky Hopkins is also given some pointers: "Pretend

36

that it's snowing – that snow is melting on your fingertips, not that banging." There is even a disagreement with Klaus Voormann over the placing of specific chords, but finally the take is completed.

Yoko's voice has never been this attractive or radio-friendly before or since and it is regrettable that the song failed to secure airplay or sympathetic comment from her former critics. Lyrically, she tracks the trail of ubiquitous snow from Trafalgar Square to the Empire State Building via Tokyo, Paris and Dallas, although it also lodges between Lennon's head and her mind and is used as a metaphorical conduit for their love. Snow, of course, was a dominant image in Yoko Ono's work, as evidenced by her *Snow Piece For Solo* and, most famously, in the chilling subtitle to 'Don't Worry Kyoko'.

Don't Worry Kyoko

Originally released as the B-side to 'Cold Turkey', this song was sub-titled '(Mummy's Only Looking For A Hand In The Snow)' whereas on the later *Live Peace In Toronto 1969* it was listed as '(Mummy's Only Looking For Her Hand In The Snow)'. There is a case for either title. In her book *Grapefruit*, Ono included *Three Snow Pieces For Orchestra* which include the words 'Find a hand in the snow'. Listen closely to the Toronto concert, however, and she seems to sing 'her hand'. The argument is not settled by the original version on which there is no reference to the subtitle in the actual song. Instead, Yoko endlessly repeats 'Don't worry' until it becomes a des-perate mantra. By any standards, it's an extraordinary performance and arguably her most arresting on record. The vocal extem-porization begins as a scream of exorcism, far more frightening than the Janov-inspired utterances heard on *John Lennon/Plastic Ono Band*. Ono's keening, banshee wailing continually shifts tempo as she howls, bleats, gurgles and ultimately transforms feral sounds into cathartic release, culminating in a speaking-in-tongues resolution, at which point the name 'Kyoko' is finally heard. Despite the frantic plea 'don't worry' there is nothing reassuring in Yoko's words. On the contrary, her vocal sounds so frighteningly intense that Kyoko appears to have very good reasons for worrying. What transforms the song, however, is the menacing accompanying electric guitar. Here, late Sixties, blues-based rock music collides with something more primal and alien to form a synthesis that still sounds radical and innovative several decades later. Not that anyone was quick to credit Yoko Ono for allying avant-garde and rock music in such brutal and breathtaking fashion. As she later admitted: "I was pretty upset at the time, because it was totally misinterpreted, like saying, 'Yoko's screaming.' When you really listen to it, you know that it's very kind of musical – musical is a very strange word – but adding a kind of dimension in music, rather than just some Oriental woman screaming."

LIVE PEACE IN TORONTO 1969

Released: December 1969

Original UK issue: Apple CORE 2001. US issue: Apple SW 3362. CD reissue:
Apple CDP 7 90428 2 (UK/US)

The live début of Lennon's Plastic Ono Band as part of the Toronto
Rock 'n' Roll Revival Festival at the Varsity Stadium on 13 September 1969 proved one of the most spontaneous and unlikely happenings of the era. Co-promoter John Brower had phoned Apple
Records at the last minute and invited Lennon and Ono to attend, no
doubt in the hope of drumming up some publicity. His request
seemed over-optimistic but there were sound reasons for assuming
that Lennon might look favourably upon the event. A few months
before, John and Yoko had flown to Montreal for a celebrated bed-in
at the Queen Elizabeth Hotel, during which a star-studded guest list
had sung along to a new anthem, 'Give Peace A Chance'. Even the
country's president Pierre Trudeau had spoken of Lennon with toler-
ance and respect. After receiving an invitation to plant acorns for
peace the minister said: "I don't know about acorns, but I'd like to
see him if he's around. He's a good poet."

The recording of 'Give Peace A Chance', credited to the Plastic
Ono Band and released in the summer of 1969, was a defining
moment that provided further evidence of Lennon's intention to
forge a separate identity from that of the Beatles. His concept of the
Plastic Ono Band offered a new musical freedom to be relished.
However, the story almost ended at this point. While driving in
Scotland, the Lennons were involved in a car accident that could
easily have resulted in something more serious than a brief period in
hospital, where they were treated for cuts, bruises and shock. During
their convalescence, 'Give Peace A Chance' was released and
climbed to number 2 in the UK charts. Its success encouraged John
and Yoko to develop the Plastic Ono Band concept and consider
more projects and happenings. Fond memories of their recent visit to

Canada, and the fact that 'Give Peace A Chance' was due for release in the USA during the same month as Brower's Toronto festival, ensured that the promoter received a positive response. His cause was assisted by the acts he had already secured. Lennon was intrigued by the rock 'n' roll legends set to appear, a formidable list that included Chuck Berry, Jerry Lee Lewis, Little Richard, Gene Vincent, Bo Diddley and Fats Domino. As Lennon's PR Anthony Fawcett recalled: "He had hardly said hello before he was agreeing to go – on the condition that he and his band could play live at the Revival."

The decision was a testament to Lennon's love of Fifties rock 'n' roll and his willingness to create instant happenings. Remarkably, he had not even formed the band who would play their first gig the following night. With extraordinary rapidity, he pulled together a seemingly makeshift group comprising bassist Klaus Voormann (the Hamburg pal who had contributed the front sleeve of *Revolver*), session drummer Alan White, celebrated guitarist Eric Clapton and the ubiquitous Yoko Ono. The following day, Lennon slept in and threatened to pull out of the concert and send some flowers instead. Luckily, he changed his mind and joined the assembled crew on a later flight.

The trip to Toronto was memorable in more ways than one. Much to their astonishment, Lennon revealed to the musicians that he was leaving the Beatles and offered them the chance to work with him on future projects. It was clear, however, that the Plastic Ono Band would always be a fluid unit without a formal line-up. "The Plastic Ono Band is a conceptual band that never was," Lennon later insisted. "There never had been any members of it . . . It wasn't like a Wings or whatever, where you had a name and you belong to it. There's nobody ever in this band, there are no members."

For 'the band that never was', there remained the problem of selecting a suitable set list. Lennon had jotted down some rock 'n' roll evergreens that they could all perform, but their attempts at rehearsing on the plane proved desultory at best. "We tried to rehearse which was stupid," Lennon recalled, "because with electric guitars you can't hear anything. Luckily it was a rock 'n' roll festival because I don't know the words to any songs except the ones from when I was a kid."

While Lennon prevaricated, the Canadian media was blasting out news of his imminent arrival and starstruck kids were heading for Toronto in the hope of witnessing a historic event. By late afternoon, there were over 27,000 spectators in the stadium. On arrival, Lennon conducted a press conference, laced with fist-thrusting political rhetoric, proclaiming: "The power doesn't belong with Mr Trudeau, Mr Wilson or Mr Nixon. We are the power. The people are the power. And as soon as people are aware that they have the power, then they can do what they want. And if it's a case of they don't know what to do, let's advertise to them to tell them they have an option. They've all got a vote. Vote for peace, folks."

Backstage at the Varsity Stadium, the Plastic Ono Band barely had time to continue their rehearsal before they were due onstage. Lennon was already vomiting at the prospect, as pre-performance nerves and heroin withdrawal took their toll. As the song annotations below explain though, the show was not the disaster it might have been, but a modest success. Shortly after the concert, Lennon told Barry Miles, "I dug performing in Toronto and I didn't have that Beatles' mystique to live up to, which is a drag about performing with the Beatles. You've got to *be* the Beatles. But performing is a groove, I enjoyed it like mad." A decade on, in one of his final interviews, nostalgia made him even more enthusiastic about the event. "It was fantastic. It was getting dark. The lights were just going down. This was the first time I ever heard about this, I'd never seen it anywhere else – they all lit candles, or lights, and the sun was going down. There was 50–60,000 people. All these candles lit up and it was really beautiful. The vibes were fantastic, and we did the string of rock 'n' roll stuff."

Lennon's determination to release the concert as a live album initially met steely resistance from his record label. "Capitol didn't want to put it out. They said, 'This is garbage. We're not going to put it out with her screaming on one side and you doing this sort of live stuff.' And they just refused. But we finally persuaded them that people might buy this. Of course it went gold . . ."

The Toronto show was also filmed, but D.A. Pennebaker's movie of the event (provisionally titled *Sweet Toronto* and later renamed *Keep*

On Rockin') was not completed until the following year, by which time it was decided that the Plastic Ono Band's performance should not be included. It was another 19 years before the set finally appeared commercially on home video, complete with a number of additional Yoko Ono squeals that had been deleted from the album recording.

Blue Suede Shoes

The spontaneity of this opening number contributed to the concert's unfolding drama. "Get your matches ready, the Plastic Ono Band . . ." announces compere Kim Fowley as Lennon and friends take the stage.

"We're just going to do numbers we know because we've never played before," John explains, after which they begin tentatively with this Carl Perkins' classic. The metallic rasp of Clapton's lead guitar set against Lennon's confident vocal works well and the feel is reminiscent of the old BBC sessions during the early days of Beatlemania. "We just wrote this list," Lennon said of their impromptu set. "I hadn't even got the words to any of the songs . . . 'Blue Suede Shoes' and a couple I hadn't done since Liverpool in the Cavern, and that's all we could do. We went on and we were so nervous because we didn't know what we were doing." Evidently, 'Blue Suede Shoes' had first been suggested by George Harrison, who was a big fan of Carl Perkins and had already sung 'Everybody's Trying To Be My Baby' as a Beatle. "I'd given it to George before the Beatles got big," Lennon countered. "So it was George's song, but it was originally mine. I liked Carl Perkins and Elvis too." Clearly, all the Beatles were Perkins' fans. During sessions for the BBC in 1963, Harrison was the featured vocalist on 'Glad All Over' and McCartney had sung lead on 'Sure To Fall (In Love With You)'. Even Ringo had offered an exuberant rendition of 'Honey Don't' on *Beatles For Sale*. In order to provide a visual accompaniment to 'Blue Suede Shoes', Yoko disappeared into a white bag while it was played.

Money

Memories of early Beatles performances, not least their doomed

Decca audition, are reinforced as the group tackle the Berry Gordy song that so brilliantly closed *With The Beatles*. Here, Lennon's vocal is unaccompanied and you miss McCartney and Harrison's distinctive harmony and familiar reply line, 'That's what I want'. It's also odd to hear the guitar rather than the raucous piano that punctuated the Beatles' thrilling version. Although Lennon will soon be undertaking primal therapy, he studiously avoids the screeching that characterized the previous recording, preferring a more restrained approach. Discussing the decision to include 'Money', Lennon noted: "It's simply a matter of what songs I knew and which would be easier for a band who'd never played together before. So we pretty much stuck to 12-bars, which most musicians can gig along with. And that's why I vaguely knew 'Money'. I knew a couple of verses and I had Yoko holding up the words for me. I didn't use them. If I didn't know the words I just made them up. Obviously, it's a matter of necessity for four people who have never played together to pick songs that are pretty easy to play."

Dizzy Miss Lizzy

After finishing 'Money', Lennon recalls turning to Eric Clapton in a vain attempt to decide what to play next. The guitarist responded with a shrug of the shoulders, but John recovered his memory sufficiently to kick-start another rock 'n' roll favourite. He had played this 1958 Larry Williams song many times during his youth, and it was previously the closing track on *Help!* This version is understandably uncertain in places as the group gradually attempts to find its way into the performance. Despite some nervy moments, Lennon responds well to the challenge of playing without a proper rehearsal. "I knew this one because the Beatles did it on every tour," he exaggerated. "We knew it was a cinch, especially if you were nervous, because the backing was so solid. I always enjoyed singing it though because it just grooved along. You can hear I'm more relaxed on that track than the others." The Beatles had previously performed the song on their 1965 US tour, most famously at the Hollywood Bowl, and were obviously fans of Larry Williams' material as evidenced by their versions of 'Slow Down' and 'Bad Boy'.

Yer Blues

Lennon sounds more expressive here as he resurrects one of the
darker moments from *The Beatles*. He had previously performed the
song in a line-up with Eric Clapton, Keith Richard, Mitch Mitchell
and Yoko Ono on the Rolling Stones' then unreleased film *Rock 'n'
Roll Circus*. Clapton's familiarity with the composition ensures that
this searing version is memorable, with 'Revolution' style guitar
work to the fore. "I can't remember when I had such a good time,"
Lennon later enthused. "We did all the old things . . . Yoko, who
you can say was playing bag, was holding a piece of paper with the
words to the songs in front of me. But then she suddenly disappeared
into her bag in the middle of the performance and I had to make
them up because it's so long since I sang them that I'd forgotten most
of them. It didn't seem to matter."

Cold Turkey

"We've never done this number before, so best of luck," announces
Lennon, after which they tackle his harrowing account of heroin
withdrawal. Taken at a slightly faster pace than the single version, the
song features some jagged guitar work interspersed with effective
vocal interjections from Yoko Ono. At the end, Lennon berates the
audience for not responding enthusiastically enough to his new composition, although this was edited out of the released recording. Once
more, the decision to perform the song was spontaneous. "I hadn't
decided upon an arrangement," Lennon admitted. "I just sang it to
the group. Because it was basically a three-chord song they picked it
up quite well. It was just verse/chorus/verse/chorus. Here too, Yoko
was holding the words but just out of sight. I had to dodge off the
mike to try and get one of the verses. It's entirely different than the
single, but you can see where the single came from. A more professional version of this would be more commercial but that's how I
wanted the song to go." The performance proved as uncompromising as the subject matter, which is hardly surprising in view of
Lennon's physical state. "I just threw up for hours until I went on.
Nearly threw up during 'Cold Turkey'. I could hardly sing any of
them. I was full of shit."

By the time *Live Peace In Toronto 1969* was released, the harrowing studio version of 'Cold Turkey' had already reached the UK Top 20, establishing the Plastic Ono Band as the new vehicle for Lennon's most challenging work. "There isn't enough outlet for me in the Beatles," he informed journalist Alan Smith that same month. "The Plastic Ono Band is my escape valve. And how important that gets, as compared to the Beatles, I'll have to wait and see. You have to realize that there's a peculiar situation in that if 'Cold Turkey' had had the name Beatles on it, probably it would have been a number 1. 'Cold Turkey' has got Ringo and me on [the studio single version], and yet on half the Beatles' tracks of *Abbey Road*, I'm not on, or half the tracks on the double album [*The Beatles*] – and even way back. Sometimes there might be only two Beatles on a track. It's got to the point where if we have the name 'Beatle' on it, it sells. So you get to think: 'What are we selling? Do they buy it because it's worth it, or just because it says 'Beatles'?"

Give Peace A Chance

This spirited version of Lennon's peace anthem was particularly memorable for its humorous ad-libbing ('masturbation, castration, United Nations and Teddy Roosevelt'). At one point, Lennon pays passing tribute to British comedian Tommy Cooper, a name presumably unfamiliar to his Canadian audience. The comedy was appropriate, given Lennon's view of himself and Yoko as the world's clowns. But beneath the elongated wordplay the song's sentiments were bitingly insistent. "I wanted to write something that would take over from 'We Shall Overcome'," Lennon explained. "I don't know why. Maybe because that was the one they always sang. I thought, 'Why doesn't somebody write one for the people now?' The songs that they go and sing on the buses even, and not just love songs."

Don't Worry Kyoko (Mummy's Only Looking For Her Hand In The Snow)

"And now Yoko's going to do her thing all over you," Lennon announces. An extraordinary version of this anthem to Yoko's daughter Kyoko follows, complete with the references to 'mummy's only looking for her hand in the snow' missing from the single recording issued as the B-side of 'Cold Turkey'. The composition's inclusion in concert was appropriate considering that Kyoko was also involved in the auto accident in Scotland two months before and had suffered small lacerations to the face requiring stitches. As the song reaches agonizing pitches of intensity, Lennon and Clapton lock into an instrumental groove, which reinforces Ono's intense vocal exhortations. They seem likely to develop the song into an elongated jam but, regrettably, it ends after 4 minutes 16 seconds. Nevertheless, its power as a live spectacle – which was later bettered by a rendition at the London Lyceum featured on *Some Time In New York City* – was undeniable. Lennon never doubted the importance of the composition which he claimed was a glimpse into rock's strange future. "Yoko's whole thing was that scream," he enthused to *Rolling Stone*. "Listen to 'Don't Worry Kyoko'. It's one of the best rock 'n' roll records ever made. Listen to it and play 'Tutti Frutti' . . . you'll see what she's doing . . . It's as important as anything we ever did . . . She makes music like you've never heard on earth."

John John (Let's Hope For Peace)

The audience barely has time to recover before Yoko segues into this eerie, cascading exhortation for peace. Intriguing in parts, the mantra continues for almost 12 minutes, sustained by constant feedback. "We finished with Yoko's number because you can't go anywhere after you've reached that sort of pitch," Lennon explained. "And to end the show I just said, 'Look, at the end, when she's finished doing whatever she's doing, just lean your guitars on the amps and let it keep howling, and we can get off like that.'" Lennon's instructions were fully heeded, leaving the audience to bathe in a full minute of speaker reverberation before roadie Mal Evans turned off the equipment, ending this memorable exercise in musical spontaneity.

JOHN LENNON/PLASTIC ONO BAND

Released: December 1970

Original UK issue: Apple PCS 7124. US issue: Apple SW 3372. CD reissue with
bonus tracks: EMI 5 28739 2 (UK)/ Capitol 5 28739 2 (US)

It is intriguing to consider that the most groundbreaking and accomplished album of John Lennon's career might never have happened had he not received a book in the post. The tome in question was *The Primal Scream* written by Arthur Janov, a psychologist who was to have a profound influence on Lennon's thinking in the immediate wake of the Beatles' break-up. With the possible exception of Brian Wilson's mentor Dr Eugene Landy, no psychologist has ever had such a startling effect on a rock performer's writing and musical direction. As soon as Lennon began paging through the book, he realized that the contents were deeply relevant to his troubled life. He was particularly impressed by the case studies of patients who testified to having discovered a cure for their adult neuroses by belatedly confronting their childhood nightmares.

Janov's theories made exciting reading. He believed in the therapeutic value of regression techniques as an aid to restoring a patient's ability to feel. His central thesis was that man's alienation and inability to form fruitful personal relationships stemmed from infant rejection and childhood trauma. As he explained: "The single most shattering event in the child's life is that moment of icy, cosmic loneliness when he begins to discover that he is not loved for what he is. . . ." What his therapy offered was a systematic removal of the layers of conditioning by which the individual masks his pain. By facing the monsters of his imagination and embracing that primal moment of darkness, the patient could then exorcize the original source of the pain. This catharsis was ultimately realized through the uttering of what Janov called the 'primal scream', after which the individual would emerge reborn and ready to enjoy life in a more healthy psychological state.

Lennon was astounded by the implications of the book, which offered the chance to cut through to the very root of his life's problems. He already knew that the traumas he had suffered as a child had left deep scars and unresolved feelings of bitterness. When his parents' marriage had ended, he was eventually faced with the terrible dilemma of choosing between them. Oscillating in emotional confusion between his father and mother, he finally turned to Julia Lennon, only to be abandoned by her soon after and placed in the custody of his aunt. During his adolescence, he re-established a close relationship with his mother, only to lose her again when she was killed in a road accident near his home in July 1958. "He just went to his room into a shell," his Aunt Mimi recalled.

His wayward father, who had lost contact with John over the years, did not reappear until the emergence of Beatlemania. Nor did the pain end there. The sins of the father were repeated in the next generation when John Lennon left his wife Cynthia and son Julian. By his own admission, he had spent little time with the boy and since pairing off with Yoko, regular contact between father and son had all but ceased.

Although the impressionable Lennon still felt the stings of disillusionment following his brief involvement with transcendental meditation guru the Maharishi Mahesh Yogi, he could not resist the lure of Janov's message. What particularly appealed was the notion that he could unleash a lifetime's neurosis in one great cathartic scream. As he later admitted: "I would never have gone into it if there hadn't been the promise of this scream, this liberating scream."

Lennon's effusive endorsement was, of course, media shorthand for a more sophisticated system of therapy. As Janov later wrote in clarification: "Primal therapy is not just making people scream. It was the title of a book. It was never 'Primal Scream Therapy'. Those who read the book know that the scream is what people do when they are hurt. Others simply sob or cry. It was the hurt that we were after, not mechanical exercises . . ."

If Lennon had good reason to feel empathy with Janov's theories, then the same could be said of Yoko Ono. Although the daughter of wealthy and successful parents, her upbringing was not without its share of suppressed feelings of rejection. She had not even met her father until the age of two and, for much of her childhood, her mother was an aloof, distant presence. With two broken marriages and her child Kyoko now in the hands of her ex-husband Tony Cox, she seemed another likely Janov case study. What probably clinched the matter was her now stormy relationship with Lennon. During this difficult period, their romantic fantasies had been undermined by bickering and domestic tension.

Lennon's aide Anthony Fawcett documented, with notable perception, the seriousness of a marriage in crisis: "Early in 1970, in addition to his despair that the Beatles really were finished, there were mounting tensions in his relationship with Yoko, which became more destructive day by day. He retreated into passivity and inertia . . . John and Yoko took the only escape they knew from pain and anxiety and hid in each other's love. But rapidly it became an obsessive, possessive love; without realizing it they were stifling each other . . . Living with them became harder by the day . . . I was acutely aware of the rapid deterioration of their relationship . . . John escaped from his problems by watching television. It seemed as if he didn't really care where he was as long as there was a colour television at the foot of the bed . . . John and Yoko isolated themselves, communicating with no one. In part, I saw their withdrawal as a reaction to the frantic pace of the year before, the continual dialogue with the media, the peace efforts, all the travelling. Also, although he didn't realize it at the time, John desperately needed somebody else to turn to, someone to help him besides Yoko, who acted as his only outlet. It was obvious to me that their relationship could not continue much longer the way it was going."

In March 1970, the Lennons enrolled in Arthur Janov's primal therapy programme. At first they were treated at home in Tittenhurst Park, the sprawling Georgian mansion in Ascot that Lennon had bought the previous year for £150,000. It was then decided to relocate temporarily to the Primal Institute in California for more intensive sessions. Over the succeeding months, John worked through his childhood pain in search of catharsis. During the therapy, designed to strip him of psychological defences, he could be observed sitting on the floor, rocking back and forth, then screaming like an infant as he tore away at the falsities that blighted his ability to express his true self. As he said: "In the therapy you really feel every painful moment of your life. It's excruciating. You are forced to realize your own pain, the kind that makes you wake up afraid with your heart pounding."

Despite the rigours of the therapy, Lennon persevered and was astounded by the early effects. "It was the most important thing that happened to me besides meeting Yoko and being born," he gushed. At one point, he got so carried away with the programme's healing properties that he threatened to convert the world.

"John was really taken with primal therapy," Janov stressed. "He wanted to rent the QE2 and have us sail around the world doing primal therapy. He wanted to buy an island and found a primal nation. He was pretty serious. I put the kibosh on it."

After five months with Janov, Lennon was finally obliged to terminate the treatment and concentrate on his ongoing battle with the US immigration authorities, which had already petitioned for his deportation. He had no choice. "He was forced to leave," Janov regretted. "It really botched the whole process."

Despite Janov's understandable regret, the primal therapy sessions were far from worthless or unsuccessful. Lennon emerged not only with a new attitude, but a head full of remarkable lyrics. Through the summer of 1970, he underwent an inner voyage of discovery, composing an album of songs that were among the finest and certainly most intense of his entire career.

In transferring his ideas on to record, Lennon felt he required minimal embellishment. For the rhythm section, he turned to two old friends, Klaus Voormann and Ringo Starr, who offered a pared-down sound that perfectly complemented the material. Another inspired choice was legendary producer Phil Spector who had previously worked on the Beatles' *Let It Be* and, more recently, on the magnificent 'Instant Karma!', an exuberant and spontaneous single, written, recorded and mixed within a day. It had reached number 5 in the UK charts and number 3 in the USA, confirming the twin commercial and aesthetic validity of the Plastic Ono Band. Spector's major contribution was precisely the opposite of his early Sixties'

'Wall Of Sound' experiments. Instead of drowning Lennon's voice in Wagnerian orchestration, he ensured that the stark and raw texture of the vocal was captured with perfect fidelity. Yoko Ono, meanwhile, busied herself working on a companion album, which would be released on the same day as her husband's, complete with almost matching cover artwork.

The extraordinary *John Lennon/Plastic Ono Band* album that emerged from the primal period was the most naked, self-analytical work ever released by a popular recording artiste. It confronted, unflinchingly, every area of his personal and public life, with revealing and often harrowing commentaries on parental rejection, sex, class exploitation, the hollowness of fame, the death of God, the demise of the Beatles, and much more. It was, as *Rolling Stone* writer Stephen Holden later claimed, "a masterpiece that by its very nature could never be repeated . . . eloquent in its careful simplicity and radically honest to a degree perhaps never before attempted in Western music."

Mother

The death of Lennon's mother Julia was one of the most traumatic events of his life. It hardened his cynicism as a teenager and, according to the testimonies of close friends, made him an intolerable and bitter companion subject to outbursts of cruelty. Uncloaking that most painful moment was a crucial part of Lennon's primal therapy and it was no coincidence that two confrontational songs on the subject book-ended this album. The opening track commences, appropriately enough, with the sound of a funeral bell. "It's a church bell which I slowed down to 33, so it's really like a horror movie and that was like the death knell of the mother/father Freudian trip," Lennon explained.

Ringo Starr's drums are upfront in the mix, a dull metronomic thud in which the metre is frozen like a death march. The sparse piano reinforces the funereal mood created by the tolling of the bells as Lennon laments the passing of a mother who didn't want him around. There is Oedipal wish-fulfilment in the ambiguous line about never having *had* his mother, an interpretation which might sound extreme until you consider the underlying languid eroticism in his previous tribute 'Julia'. It was significant that he later called his wife Yoko Ono 'mother', even using the name in the interviews they conducted together.

Having addressed his mother, Lennon uses the second verse to concentrate on his father's abandonment. The tale of the wayward Freddie Lennon, who left his family and went to sea, was a familiar saga to Beatles' followers, although the extent of his culpability may have been exaggerated. In the end, of course, John lived with neither of his parents and was brought up by his mother's sister, Aunt Mimi. "I soon forgot my father. It was like he was dead." Lennon Snr later re-established contact with John and even recorded a self-congratulatory single, 'That's My Life'. Although the rapprochement between father and son was awkward at best, they remained in touch. The lyrics of 'Mother' suggest that John retained enough emotional distance to exorcize his bad feelings and bid his father a stoical farewell.

By the end of the song, Lennon attempts to break the circle of inherited pain by warning future generations of the need to confront and work through parental death. His message to both his mother and father is one of final reconciliation and acceptance, after which he tells his audience (patronizingly referred to as 'children' in the rock parlance of the period) that he is now ready to move on and all he has left to say is 'goodbye'. But this can only be achieved by re-enacting and releasing his pain. Thus, he concludes by growling, pleading and at last screaming his suppressed feelings in a childlike wail, imploring his mama not to leave and his daddy to come home.

Despite the harrowing theme, Apple elected to release an edited version of 'Mother' as a single, just after Christmas 1970. Predictably, it failed to reach the US Top 40. Nevertheless, it remains an exemplary track with an exceptional production. At times Lennon's voice seems to emerge from oceanic depths and although Phil Spector successfully unleashes the Janov-inspired scream in all its intensity, he also succeeds in containing it. More importantly, Spector somehow manages to conjure music from the pre-Beatles' era while making it sound engagingly radical and modern. This brilliantly complements

Lennon's theme, in which past and present are locked in a therapeutic battle. Memory is the fountainhead of an Edenic state, rapidly usurped by feelings of fear and loss. Lennon realizes that it is only by confronting his neuroses in song that he can achieve catharsis.

Hold On

The intense mood is temporarily alleviated by this affecting and tender ballad. Lennon offers hope, protesting that the good fight can be won. He once said that back in Liverpool he was simply known as 'Lennon', a name that was often spat out with rough contempt. Here, however, he references himself more gently as 'John'. Midway through he sings 'Kookie', briefly his pet name for Yoko Ono. This should not be confused with the catch-phrase popularized on the *Andy Williams Show* nor with the teen idol immortalized by Ed Byrne in the Sixties' television series *77 Sunset Strip* and certainly not, as some critics regrettably heard, the word 'cocaine'.

The composition's fragmented tune, complemented by Ringo's jittery drumming, emphasizes the tentative nature of Lennon's assertions, which provide hopeful assurances without any certainties. As the singer explained: "I'm saying 'Hold on John' because I don't want to die . . . I don't want to be hurt and please don't hit me . . . Hold on now, we might have a cup of tea, we might get a moment's happiness any minute now. So that's what it's all about, just moment by moment. That's how we're living now, and cherishing each day, and dreading it too. It might be your last." In the final verse he momentarily forgets John and Yoko and addresses the world, externalizing the sentiments and emotions with a utopian vision of everyman seeing the light.

I Found Out

Although Lennon would later embrace New York radicals as kindred spirits in the fight for world peace, his attitude towards the counterculture in 1970 was one of evident impatience. Here, his feelings pour forth in a vitriolic outburst against the politically hip who dare to pester him on the phone or casually call him 'brother'. Explaining the genesis of the song to *Rolling Stone*, he complained: "I'm sick of those aggressive hippies . . . being very uptight with me, either on the street or anywhere, or on the phone, demanding my attention as if I owed them something. I'm not their fucking parents . . . They come to the door and expect to just march around the house or something like an old Beatles fan . . . I'm sick of them, they frighten me, a lot of uptight maniacs going around wearing fucking peace symbols."

After venting his rage in the first verse, Lennon continues with the hard-edged, sinewy guitar arrangement and Starr's powerful drumming to attack all manner of creeds, institutions and belief systems. Eastern and Western religions, macho sexuality and poor parenting are vilified in turn as Lennon catalogues his disillusionment and warns us to be more vigilant and discriminating. Typically, there's a heretical comparison between saviour and pop star, recalling his controversial remark about the Beatles being bigger than Christ. Here that contention is restated in the line about having seen religion 'from Jesus to Paul', with McCartney earning a backhanded compliment in passing. Interestingly, Lennon's disillusionment with religion produces sadness rather than anger, allowing him to cry out once again. Although the song advocates personal revolution, there is a constant recognition that the tearing down of belief systems and idols must be accompanied by tears and pain. The unrelenting rock rhythm concludes with a couplet that neatly fuses Karl Marx's comments on the opiate of the masses with Janov's beliefs in the therapeutic value of confronting one's demons. Addressing both himself and his audience, Lennon warns of the deadening effects of dope and cocaine and the liberation that can come from feeling your own pain.

Working Class Hero
Here, Lennon extends the theme of 'I Found Out' to document, with pained ferocity, society's infliction of pain on the individual, from the cradle to the grave. It serves both as a song for everyman and as an intensely personal statement. Indeed, the power of the composition emanates from the subdued, reflective acoustic setting, which conveys a sense of bitter autobiography, as well as offering a sustained denunciation of socialization, punctuated by swear words

omitted from the lyric sheet 'at the insistence of EMI'. There's great acerbic irony in the song's languid last line in which Lennon invites potential heroes to follow his lead. Far from affirming heroic credentials, the song actually testifies to the fundamental loss of self that the proletariat suffers in securing societal acceptance and recognition. Explaining his theme to the left-wing journal *Red Mole*, Lennon reflected on the tendency to siphon talent for propagandist effect. "They allowed the blacks to be runners or boxers or entertainers. That's the choice they allow you – now the outlet is being a pop star, which is really what I'm saying on 'Working Class Hero' . . . It's the same people who have the power, the class system didn't change one little bit. Of course there are a lot of people walking around with long hair now and some trendy middle-class kids in pretty clothes. But nothing changed except that we all dressed up a bit, leaving the same bastards running everything." ·

In less polemic mode, Lennon saw the song as a thoughtful comment that might appeal to workers, affluent or otherwise. "I just think its concept is revolutionary and I hope it's for workers and not for tarts and fags . . . It might just be ignored. I think it's for the people like me who are working class, whatever, upper or lower, who are supposed to be processed into the middle classes, or in through the machinery, that's all. It's my experience, and I hope it's just a warning to people."

Lennon was correct, inasmuch as the song transcends the purely political to comment on the unchanging nature of the human condition. Significantly, there are no screams on 'Working Class Hero'. Whereas other songs on this album caused Lennon to rant and rave, his voice on this track is consistently in the lower register and such a painful yet restrained reading makes the statement even more disturbing and convincing.

Inevitably, several critics used the phrase 'Dylanesque' when describing the song, although its sentiments bore only passing comparison to Zimmerman's early protest songs. Lennon was unimpressed with the analogy and rightly argued that, "Anybody that sings with a guitar and sings about something heavy would tend to sound like Dylan . . . The only folk music I know is stuff about miners up in

Newcastle, or Dylan. So in that way I've been influenced, but it doesn't sound like Dylan to me."

Isolation

Musicologist Wilfred Mellers called this "an English, 1970 equivalent of the negro blues, which was an urban folk art of the solitary heart". Viewed more prosaically, it's a frighteningly impressive combination of words and melody to express a sense of isolation. The arrangement, consisting of sparse instrumentation with bare open fifths on the piano, conveys a mood of solitary rumination. In the first two verses, Lennon details the vulnerability and pariah status of himself and Yoko, ridiculed for their wealth and put down by everybody, simply for wanting to change the world through their peace initiatives. Significantly, they are portrayed as just a 'boy' and a 'little girl' in an almost Blakean image of childhood innocence and wisdom. By the end of the third verse, such reflection provokes an eruption of pain and anger, emphasized by a change in tempo, a thud of the piano keys and a viciously intense vocal double tracked for emphasis. As the music reaches a crescendo, Lennon starts shouting at an imagined 'you' – the bringer of pain who is incapable of understanding the hurt they have caused. The line is devastating in its intensity and seemingly directed at every figure of authority he has encountered in his life. Yet the 'you' sounds so personal in its accusative tone that it is difficult to believe that Lennon was not thinking of a particular individual when singing the words. The triumph of the lyrics lie in the impassioned phrasing. In the end, there is the chilling realization that Lennon may be addressing his own audience and the much maligned 'you' who suffers the bulk of his wrath is not simply everyman or his mother Julia, but the album's listener. Bitterness overtakes Lennon in the next couplet when he sarcastically informs that mysterious 'you' that they are ultimately not to blame on the grounds that they are merely human and thereby a victim of the insane.

The hyperbole over, Lennon reverts to the contemplative mode of the earlier stanzas, acknowledging that everyone is alone and afraid. But he cannot quite rid himself of an encroaching misanthropy as he meditates on humanity's extinction. Only the end of the world, it seems, can negate universal isolation. Like a Sun King, he posits the questionable notion of the Sun as an eternal celestial body, while suggesting the likelihood of an imminent apocalypse on Earth. The song ends on a note of dramatic cessation.

Remember

Arguably, Lennon's most effective song of remembrance since 'Strawberry Fields Forever', this was markedly different in construction, both musically and lyrically. Stripped of the rich imagery of its great predecessor, it displays none of the self-interrogative wordplay, complex production and mystifying effects that characterized the Beatles at their apotheosis. Similarly, there is a distinct absence of the stately nostalgia offered on Lennon's finest autobiographical reflection 'In My Life'. Instead, he concentrates on the process of memory itself, employing a simple, chugging rhythm to enliven this trip back into the joys, innocence and fantasy terrors of childhood. The album's rear sleeve features a photo of John as a child, a clear enough indication of the subject matter of several of the songs on this album. Unlike 'Isolation' or 'Working Class Hero', there is no attempt here to veer into political or religious argument. The early reminiscences are of a simple world of black and white morality in which heroes and villains play specifically defined roles with inevitable consequences. This role playing extends to parents who are portrayed as constantly acting and displaying absolute authority over their children. Referring to their self-deluding dreams of celluloid stardom, Lennon reiterates the wish-fulfilling fantasies of 'I Found Out' in which his parents were described as never having wanted him – and, as a result, they made him a star. In a telling reference to his feckless father Freddie, Lennon describes the world of his childhood as a paternalistic society in which the man is always likely to leave everyone 'empty-handed'. He approaches the past with a sense of spatial distance, noting not only the tendency of the child to see the world as disproportionately large, but also acknowledging the way in which revisiting places and observing objects alters over time so that they become smaller and less significant than once assumed. Memories are exposed as potentially deceptive and chimerical, a thought that prompts him to stress the importance of remembering *today*. Like an obsessive documentarian, Lennon sees the possibility of capturing truth within the present which can then be remembered at a later date as a panacea for whatever sadness or madness is thrust upon time's victim. This is his final solution and sanctuary from the neuroses that currently overwhelm him.

The uptempo feel, with forceful piano playing and prominent drums, mirrors his racing imagination, which takes full flight in the amusing and dramatic conclusion. As his mind once more commutes back to childhood, Lennon recalls the refrain 'remember, remember the Fifth of November', a street song chanted on Guy Fawkes' Night. Fawkes' failure to blow up the Houses of Parliament in the Gunpowder Plot later prompted annual celebrations in England, but in Lennon's fantasy the radical succeeds and the final sound we hear is a great explosion.

Love

Phil Spector plays parlour piano here, conjuring an anachronistic musical mood for a song whose message of universal love is unbound by time. According to Lennon: "I wrote it in the spirit of love. It's for Yoko. It has all that connotation for me and it's a beautiful melody, and I'm not even known for writing melody." The short lines and three-word aphorisms recall Ono's own writing, but there is a crucial difference in Lennon's lyric which is completely devoid of imagery. There's a key moment at the end of both the first and final stanzas of the song when Lennon defines love as an insatiable infantile hunger for affection; love is both *wanting* and *needing* 'to be loved'. As he pointed out: "The worst pain is that of not being wanted, of realizing your parents do not need you in the way you need them. When I was a child, I experienced moments of not wanting to see the ugliness, not wanting to see not being wanted." Elaborating on the definition of 'love', he observed: "Well it means Yoko to me, God and people. I think love's a gift. You can't just sit on your back with it – you have to nurture it like a rare flower. You have to water it, make sure the flies don't get to it, don't let the dog crap on it. You have to work on it to help it grow. It's a full-time occupation, being in love."

Well Well Well

Jagged guitar work and a thumping bass drum make this the heaviest and loudest song on the album. Wilfred Mellers described it as a "voodooistic nightmare", citing the line 'she looked so beautiful I could eat her' as evidence of a "cannibalistic impulse". Judging from Lennon's lithographs, however, it is more likely that he was referring to the sensual pleasures of oral sex. In this sense, the frantic tribal screams at the close of the song imply orgasmic delight as much as impending violence. It might also be worth noting that in an earlier version of the lyric, Lennon wrote the line, 'She looked so beautiful I could wee'.

Lyrically, the song begins with an account of an after-dinner conversation between John and Yoko during which they discuss such subjects as revolution and women's liberation. The desultory chorus of 'well, well, well' sounds suspiciously like an ironic, self-deprecating comment on their radical musings. Later, the scene shifts to the English countryside, but this is no Romantic pastoral. There is something decidedly non-idyllic about the way they feel nervous and guilty without knowing why. The extended coda sounds like a perverted 'Hey Jude', the la-la-la singalong replaced by Lennon's scary wailing. It is as if he is determined to scream his way out of the dilemmas presented in the song. The stoical 'well, well, well' chorus grows more shrill with each passing minute until it resembles a cry of impotent despair. Initially his fellow musicians were taken aback by the intensity of his railing. As Ringo Starr remembers: "We'd be in the middle of a track and John would just start crying or screaming, which freaked us out at the beginning."

Look At Me

This sweet, reflective, self-questioning ballad sounds strangely out of place amid the intensity of the surrounding material, although it works well as a pacific counterpoint. It comes as no surprise to learn that the composition dates back to pre-primal therapy days, having been attempted in 1968 during the recording of *The Beatles*. The melody recalls 'Julia' from that same work, thereby providing another oblique link to Lennon's troubled childhood and mother fixation. While it lacks the harshness of the primal therapy songs,

59

it shows Lennon attempting some serious self-examination in the immediate aftermath of his transcendental meditation course with the Maharishi Mahesh Yogi. There is a sense of amazement in the lyric, as if the narrator is looking in a mirror and seeing a new face for the first time. 'Who or what am I supposed to be?' he asks himself. At the heart of the song is a narcissistic confusion that barely allows any contact with the outside world. It is only the qualifying 'you and me' that provides a crucial addendum to his thinking, with Yoko Ono now inextricably linked to his notion of self.

God

The climactic moment on the album is one of Lennon's greatest songs. Phil Spector creates a wide expanse between vocal and instrumentation to add depth to the meditation, while Billy Preston's Floyd Cramer-style piano flourishes serve as a mild sweetener to the secular and spiritual tergiversation. The opening maxim about God being a concept by which people measure their pain, is carefully stretched across three short lines so that the listener can savour each and every word. Indeed, Lennon is so struck by the ingenuity of his phrase that he informs us like a pedagogic preacher, 'I'll say it again', and proceeds to do precisely that. His emphasis is important, not only because it forces us to concentrate on a key hypothesis, but for the way it expresses Lennon's sense of wonder in coining such a conjecture for public consumption. Elaborating on his favourite axiom during an interview with *Rolling Stone*, Lennon postulated: "Pain is the pain we go through all the time. You're born in pain. Pain is what we're in most of the time. And I think the bigger the pain, the more gods we need."

After a short piano interlude, Lennon denies every belief system, icon, anti-hero, dictator and cult figure that his imagination can conjure. Even his 'walrus' image has to be discarded. That Lennon's litany is an expression of denial rather than an act of devotion makes this anti-prayer even more effective and enlightening. It is only through the extinction of godhead and the realization of self that he can achieve redemption.

In explaining the composition's construction, Lennon confirmed that the mantra was very much like a stream of consciousness out-pouring produced through word association. "A lot of the words, they just came out of my mouth," he marvelled. " 'God' was stuck together from three songs almost. I had the idea 'God is a concept by which we measure [our] pain'. When you have a phrase like that you just sit down and sing the first tune that comes into your head . . . I don't know when I realized I was putting down all these things I didn't believe in. I could have gone on. It was like a Christmas card list. I thought, 'Where do you end? Churchill? . . . and who have I missed out?' . . . I thought I had to stop . . . I was going to leave a gap and say, 'Just fill in your own and put whoever you don't believe in.' It had just got out of hand."

Significantly, Lennon moves from religious denial (Buddha, Mantra, Gita) to conclude with the modern day deities of the rock world, notably Elvis and Zimmerman. "I don't believe in Dylan. I don't believe in Tom Jones either in that way. Zimmerman is his name. My name isn't John Beatle, it's John Lennon."

Saving the best heresy for last, Lennon concluded that he no longer believed in Beatles, adding a pregnant pause for dramatic effect. Making this sort of statement in the same year that the Beatles had split was bound to cause critical comment. The public had yet to come to terms with the realization that the Fab Four was history. Hearing Lennon's emphatic denial of their mythic importance blighted any illusions of a cosy reunion. When questioned on that epochal line, Lennon casually retorted: "I don't believe in the Beatles, that's all. I don't believe in the Beatles' myth. 'I don't believe in Beatles' – there is no other way of saying it, is there? I don't believe in them, whatever they were supposed to be in everybody's head, including our own heads for a period . . . Beatles was the final thing because it's like I no longer believe in myth, and Beatles is another myth."

After 15 instances of denial, Lennon provided a postscript, 'I just believe in me', belatedly adding, 'Yoko and me', as though she was an extension of himself. The pronouncement was the same as that previously voiced on 'Look At Me'. This was his new 'reality'. Even after all this, Lennon still has another shock in store for his listeners.

Having denounced the Beatles as mythical entities and affirmed his self-awakening to a new reality, he proceeds to toll the death knell for an entire era. The myth of the Sixties as expressed through a decade of extravagant headlines, groundbreaking artistic achievements, self-congratulatory hype and youth-conscious idealism is washed away in four short words: 'The dream is over'.

Those iconoclastic words are spoken in such an insouciant manner that it is as if the era had never mattered in the first place. Appropriately, there is no anger or remorse in Lennon's exercise in self-realization, just acceptance. "It was a dream. I don't believe in the dream any more . . . I don't believe in it, the dream is over. And I'm not just talking about the Beatles, I'm talking about the genera-tion thing. The dream is over. It's over and we've got to – well, I have anyway, personally – get down to so-called reality."

At the last, he speaks to the listener like a nurse comforting the bereaved. All he can offer to us 'dear friends' is the hard but practical advice that we'll just have to carry on without our illusions. But what is man without his dreams? This is the question that he does not con-sider, let alone answer. But he does leave us with the lingering suspi-cion that there might be more to his faith than the solipsistic 'me' or its variant 'Yoko and me'. Not long before he wrote 'God', Lennon spoke at a press conference and betrayed a point of view that, although suitably vague, hardly attested to an unconditionally atheis-tic point of view. "I believe that God is like a powerhouse," Lennon suggested, "like where you keep electricity, like a power station. And that He's a supreme power, and that He's neither good nor bad, left, right, black or white. He just is. And we tap that source of power and make of it what we will. Just as electricity can kill people in a chair, or you can light a room with it. I think God *is*."

My Mummy's Dead

The album's short postscript was this macabre elegy whose tune was borrowed from the nursery rhyme 'Three Blind Mice'. It's like listening to a poorly recorded 78 rpm record on an ancient phonogram. As in the opening track, Lennon confronts his relation-ship with his mother, thereby cleverly book-ending the album and reiterating one of its most important motifs. The song captures the menace of childhood fears through adult remembrance in a most disturbing fashion. "It was almost like a haiku poem," Lennon said. "Obviously, when you get rid of a whole section of illusion in your mind you're left with great precision. Yoko was showing me some of these haikus in the original." There is a strong sense of temporal dislocation in the song as Lennon travels back in time to confront the root of his adult neuroses in the form of his mother's death. Like a muted George Formby singing through a megaphone, Lennon expresses in eight terse lines the lingering pain that he could never properly show to the world or vanquish from his psyche.

In October 2000, *John Lennon/Plastic Ono Band* was reissued on CD with two bonus tracks.

Power To The People

Originally released as a single in March 1971, three months after the appearance of *John Lennon/Plastic Ono Band*, this sounds strangely out of place as an addendum to this famous album. Although chronologically close, the composition bears no relation to the unique material herein. The pained, introspective Lennon, evident throughout the primal album, is nowhere to be seen. Instead, we see the songwriter turned political pundit, with an instant slogan for his followers and left-wing friends. His previous ambiguity on the Beatles' 'Revolution' is replaced by cast-iron conviction as he urges listeners to get the revolution started immediately. Like several of Lennon's political songs, 'Power To The People' offered a slogan rather than a solution. Producer Phil Spector's use of a gospel choir, combined with Bobby Keyes' fierce, rasping saxophone, brought a much needed drama to an otherwise straightforward melody, creating an impressive, anthemic single. Although the lyrics were essentially simple sloganeering, there was at least an awareness of women's issues hidden away in the verses, anticipating Lennon's later work on *Some Time In New York City*.

But it was the song's title alone that most people heard blaring from radios. Lennon was largely responsible for turning the words 'power to the people' into a modern-day cliché. "I remember that was the expression going round in those days . . ." he remarked from a more jaundiced perspective in 1980. "Tariq Ali had kept coming round wanting money for the *Red Mole* or some magazine . . . I used to give anybody money, kind of out of guilt . . . I was thinking, 'Well, I'm working class and I am not one of them, but I am rich so therefore I have to.' So any time anybody said something like that, I would fork out . . . I kind of wrote 'Power To The People' in a way as a guilt song . . . It's like a newspaper song – when you write about something instant that's going on right now. I don't call it a well-crafted song or anything, just that was the news headline with misprints and everything. But the B-side was 'Open Your Box', which is worth a play."

Do The Oz

It was not Yoko Ono's B-side 'Open Your Box' that provided the second bonus track but a song that originally appeared in July 1971 as the B-side to Bill Elliott And The Elastic Oz Band's 'God Save Us'. Again, it all seems a long way from *John Lennon/Plastic Ono Band*, but as a bonus track 'Do The Oz' is a reminder of a time when Lennon had passed through his Janov-period and was emerging as a new radical with a campaigning conscience. 'Do The Oz' is a soaring anthem, propelled by Ono's banshee wail and a tonsil-ripping vocal from Lennon which still sounds primal therapy fresh. At one point, he attempts to rival his partner with orgasmic effusions which end up sounding like a playful companion piece to the harrowing harangues on 'Cold Turkey'. Amid the screaming and exhortations are some satirical moments, not least the adaptation of the Cockney dance the 'hokey cokey' into a political parody with Lennon urging us to put the 'left-wing in' and the 'right-wing out'. Given that this song had already appeared on 1997's *Anthology*, it might have been more appropriate to include some of the rehearsal tapes or alternate takes from *John Lennon/Plastic Ono Band* in preference to material issued after the event.

IMAGINE

Released: September (US) October 1971 (UK)

Original UK issue: Apple SAPCOR 1004. US issue: Apple SW 3379. CD reissue
remix: EMI 5 24858 2 (UK)/Capitol CDP 5 24858 2

Although *John Lennon/Plastic Ono Band* was a commercial success,
peaking at number 6 in the US and number 11 in the UK, its sales still
lagged behind the first post-Beatles releases of Paul McCartney and
George Harrison. Lennon could reasonably claim that he was recording by far the most adventurous material and additionally had allowed
his popularity to be compromised by a series of wilfully experimental
works with Yoko Ono, which had left potential purchasers suspicious
of his product. Whether Lennon felt intimidated by the superior sales
of his former colleagues is debatable, but in 1971 he decided to record a
more accessible album, aimed directly at the pop masses. In many
respects, *Imagine* was a watered-down version of its predecessor, with a
sprinkling of sugared melodies to make it a little more palatable for
former Beatles lovers. Although recorded very quickly, it was a finely
crafted album and remains Lennon's most well-known solo work.

Four months before the release of *Imagine*, Paul and Linda
McCartney issued *Ram*, which topped the UK charts and spawned a
US number 1 single, 'Uncle Albert/Admiral Halsey'. Lennon was
appalled by the mediocrity of the material and took surprising offence
at several of *Ram*'s innocuous tracks, which he regarded as thinly
veiled criticisms of himself, Yoko and the other Beatles. While
McCartney had been coy in his criticisms, Lennon was brutally frank,
damning his former partner on the devastating character assassination,
'How Do You Sleep?' The employment of George Harrison on
Imagine and a free photo inside featuring a send-up of the cover of
Ram, with Lennon playing with a pig, reinforced the attack. With
the dispute over Apple having recently been the subject of High
Court proceedings, the public was left in no doubt about the enmity
between the two leading ex-Beatles.

McCartney offered an olive branch of sorts by praising Lennon's achievement on *Imagine*, while adding "but there was too much political stuff on the other albums". Lennon was unimpressed and responded: "So *you* think 'Imagine' ain't political, it's 'Working Class Hero' with sugar on it for conservatives like yourself!! You obviously didn't *dig the words* . . . Your politics are very similar to Mary Whitehouse's — saying *nothing* is as loud as saying *something* . . . Join the Rock Liberation Front before it gets you . . . No hard feelings to you either. I know basically we want the same, and as I said on the phone and in this letter, whenever you want to meet, all you have to do is call."

Lennon's imperiousness and competitive ire were punctuated by the enormous success of *Imagine*, but he was the first to admit that it was mediocre compared to its groundbreaking predecessor. With the assistance of Phil Spector and the Plastic Ono Band/Flux Fiddlers (basically, George Harrison, King Curtis, Nicky Hopkins and Badfinger's Tom Evans and Joey Molland, along with Klaus Voormann and Alan White), Lennon constructed an engaging and professional album that achieved its purpose. For those who preferred Lennon's message undiluted by over-sweet melody, it was a little anti-climactic, but how else could he possibly have followed the brilliant *John Lennon/Plastic Ono Band*?

Imagine fulfilled one crucial objective by re-establishing Lennon with the record-buying masses. This time around, he was rewarded by reassuring Beatles' sales figures as *Imagine* topped the charts on both sides of the Atlantic, a statistic that had yet to be achieved, however narrowly missed, by either McCartney, Harrison or Starr.

One week before the release of *Imagine*, the Lennons relocated to New York, temporarily settling in Greenwich Village. "Yoko and I were forever coming and going to New York, so finally we decided it would be cheaper and more functional to actually live here," John explained. He would never return to the country of his birth.

Imagine

This is undoubtedly Lennon's most famous post-Beatles song, a moving anthem that has come to define the innocent hope for world peace that he propagated during the latter part of his life. Although it was obviously the most crafted melody on the album, its impact was not immediate but grew with generational radio play, reinforced by minor cover versions and a keener public sympathy towards Lennon's quixotic views.

Researching the origin of the song and its development from demo form to completion, Peter Doggett observes: "There are countless takes and mixes of 'Imagine' in existence, but all of them simply document the painstaking path to the finished arrangement, without shedding any fresh light on the song. Initially, Nicky Hopkins filled out the backing with a harmonium, and then attempted to double Lennon's keyboard part on electric piano, before John realized that this was a song which would benefit from extreme simplicity. Before the strings were added in New York, however, and Spector pumped up the piano echo, 'Imagine' sounded stark and strangely sinister, with the piano, bass and drums left dry on the tape, casting no shadow . . . To increase the audience for his message, Lennon chose to allow Spector his head, coating the basic tracks with a thin veneer of sweetness which bridged the gap between cult acceptance and mass commercial appeal."

In America, the single 'Imagine' peaked at number 3, but in Lennon's homeland it was only played as an album track until its belated release in 1975. Four years on, its impact was inevitably lessened, although it still rose to an impressive number 6. The chart statistics are a revealing comment on the gradual ascent of the song towards the status of a standard. It was not until after Lennon's murder that the composition finally earned its evergreen status, completing a climb to number 1 in the UK almost a decade after its first appearance on vinyl.

Along the way, there had been a subtle but significant change in public attitude towards the song, so much so that even some religious groups were not averse to chanting its chorus. Back in 1971, though, the composition was not greeted with universal approbation. Many religious listeners were disturbed that Lennon's imaginary Eden was a paradise without a heaven. In putting society to rights, Lennon envisaged a world without territories or possessions, but his first line of attack was religious beliefs – imagining no heaven was his opening line. In interviews Lennon toned down the message, pointing out, "If you can imagine a world at peace, with no denominations of religion – not without religion, but without this 'my God is bigger than your God' thing – then it can be true."

It was not only those sympathetic towards institutionalized religion who felt uncomfortable with 'Imagine'. Radical politicos were unimpressed by Lennon's wishy-washy utopianism, which they felt paraded naïve and palpably unattainable ideals without once suggesting how they might be realized. Lennon had attempted to counter such criticism in advance with the song's humble conclusion in which he portrayed himself as a solitary dreamer inspired by the optimistic hope of witnessing world peace in his lifetime. Evidently, he believed that those people he was addressing in song might help him achieve that impossible dream. The utopianism, sweetened by strings, sounded like a musical précis of Martin Luther King's 'I have a dream' speech. But hadn't Lennon the 'dreamer' just told us on his last album that the dream was over and angrily dismissed the proletariat as 'peasants'?

Some of the peasants clearly felt misgivings, which were mainly directed against the bourgeois Lennon pontificating on the dangers of materialism. *Rolling Stone*'s postbag included one sarcastic letter which crowed: "Imagine John Lennon with no possessions!" It was a pertinent criticism although, in fairness, Lennon had at least hesitated over the subject of surrendering possessions. Imagining no heaven was 'easy if you try'; imagining no countries wasn't hard to do; but imagining no possessions was a more difficult challenge, forcing Lennon to enquire of his listeners: 'I wonder if you can'.

The dreamy idealism at the song's core was largely due to the influence of Yoko Ono. Indeed, Lennon was greatly indebted to her poetry for the composition's framework. During the first onslaught of Beatlemania in the spring of 1963, she had published *Drinking Piece For Orchestra*, which opened with the line 'Imagine letting a goldfish swim across the sky'. Her *Tunafish Sandwich Piece* from the following year commenced with the words 'Imagine one thousand suns in the sky at the same time', while *Rubber Piece* asked readers to 'Imagine your body spreading rapidly all over the world'. While the liner notes of *Imagine* credited the sleeve design, carefully acknowledging "cloud piece on cover by Yoko Ono from *Grapefruit* paperback", there was no mention of any literary contribution to the title song. Never mind that her lyric *Cloud Piece* featured another inspirational line, 'Imagine the clouds dripping . . .'

When discussing 'Imagine' many years later, Lennon admitted: "Actually that should be credited as a Lennon/Ono song. A lot of it, the lyric and the concept, came from Yoko. But in those days I was a bit more selfish, a bit more macho and I omitted to mention her contribution . . . The song was originally inspired by Yoko's book *Grapefruit*. In it are a lot of pieces saying, imagine this, imagine that. Yoko actually helped a lot with the lyrics, but I wasn't man enough to let her have credit for it. I was still selfish enough and unaware enough to sort of take her contribution without acknowledging it. I was still full of wanting my own space after being in a room with the guys all the time, having to share everything."

Crippled Inside

In lighter mood, Lennon penned this attack on the spiritual bankruptcy of straight society. Lyrically, it's a simple, unilluminating observation of hypocrisy sung without venom or passion. One musicologist traced the melody back to the days of the black and white minstrels, and there is a touch of music hall frivolity as Nicky Hopkins plays barrel-house piano, laced with honky tonk styling. George Harrison plays dobro which again emphasizes the old America influence. But there is also a skiffle shuffle brought to the fore by Steve Brendell's upright bass, taking the place of the drums. The homely message is completed by the acoustic guitar ensemble playing by Ted Turner, John Tout and Rod Linton. Inevitably, the song's slightly taboo title ensured that radio play was limited, the more so in recent years when political correctness has led to greater sensitivity.

Students of Lennon's artwork were all too aware of his morbid fascination with the physically deformed. It is a subject that has attracted the attention of all his biographers and is backed by several first person testimonies. His former girlfriend at art college, Thelma Pickles, recalls: "Anyone limping, or crippled or hunchbacked, or deformed in any way, John laughed and ran up to them to make horrible faces. I laughed with him while feeling awful about it. If a doddery old person had nearly fallen over because John had screamed at her, we'd be laughing. We knew it shouldn't be done. I was a good audience, but he didn't do it just for my benefit . . . He had no remorse or sadness for these people. He just thought it was funny."

Gerry Marsden also remembers the 'cripple' routine, revealing that Lennon would not only mock them but sometimes pretend to be crippled himself. Even Lennon's most sympathetic biographer, the urbane Ray Coleman, admits: "He quickly developed a bizarre obsession for cripples, spastics, any human deformities, and people on crutches."

At the height of Beatlemania, Lennon was regularly using the word 'spastic' to interviewers and complaining about seeing wheel-chairs in the audience, although he put a positive gloss on his squeamishness: "I'm not hung up about them. I feel terrible sympathy for these people. It seems to be like the end of the world when you see deformed spastics, and we've had quite a lot of them on our travels. In the States, they were bringing hundreds of them . . . I can't stand looking at them. I have to turn away. I have to laugh or I'd collapse from hate of the situation . . . You got the impression the Beatles were being treated as bloody faith healers. It was sickening."

By the time of *Imagine*, of course, the 'obsession' with physical deformity had turned inwards, a likely by-product of his recent immersion in primal therapy. Yet, he never quite lost his flippant use of the term 'cripple'. Tape snippets from his closing years reveal him singing a parodic cover featuring the line, 'you're a cripple in disguise'. It's also worth noting that he originally suggested 'Crippled Inside' as a possible single, seemingly unaware of its contentious title.

Jealous Guy

'Help!' may have been the first song in the history of popular music to use the word 'insecure', but it pops up once more in the second verse to this memorable composition. The song begins with Lennon announcing that he has been 'dreaming' of the past, a meditation that does not bring nostalgia but insecurity and loss of control. In focusing on the past, he neatly balances the utopian dreams of the future voiced in 'Imagine'. It's a revealing admission that beneath the idealized love of John and Yoko lies darker feelings and hidden fears. "I was a very jealous, possessive guy," Lennon later admitted. "A very insecure male who wants to put his woman in a little box, lock her up, and just bring her out when he feels like playing with her."

"Jealous?" exclaimed Yoko Ono to biographer Philip Norman. "My God! He wrote a song, 'Jealous Guy', that should have told people how jealous he was. After we were together, he made me write out a list of all the men I'd slept with before we met. I started to do it quite casually – then I realized how serious it was to John. He didn't even like me knowing the Japanese language because that was part of my mind that didn't belong to him. After a while, I couldn't even read any books or papers in Japanese."

Despite the song's *mea culpa* tone, the tune is surprisingly jaunty, having been adapted from the composition 'Child Of Nature', which Lennon had written during his visit to India in 1968. Beneath the cleanly produced performance, images of darker days can be detected. In the final verse, there are visceral images of pain being swallowed and a shivering inside that recalls the withdrawal symptoms previously documented in more chilling detail on 'Cold Turkey'. There is a similar contrast between high romance and earthy realism in the engaging coda where Phil Spector's lavish orchestration clashes head on with Lennon's prosaic, carefree whistling, a likely tribute of sorts to the ending of Otis Redding's 'Dock Of The Bay'.

'Jealous Guy' gained a wider audience in the wake of Lennon's death, when Roxy Music hit the top of the UK charts with their own over-faithful reading. Years later, Yoko Ono, interviewed by Paul Trynka, admitted that she was nonplussed by the extent of Lennon's emotional negativity. "Before I met John I was always saying jealousy is one of the emotions that is so irrelevant. I never had any sort of strong jealousy. I never experienced it . . . John might have been killed because of that . . . it could kill people."

It's So Hard

This straightforward 12-bar blues workout allowed Lennon to relax without any need to provide a significant statement. Still recovering from his primal analysis, his lyrics here seldom evolve beyond the song's simple title. The familiar blues refrain 'know you got to run, know you got to hide', already popularized by Stephen Stills on 'Carry On' and 'Know You Got To Run', is adapted to provide the song's base. Phil Spector adds some orchestration to the mid-section, but at 2 minutes 22 seconds, the track passes quickly without making too much impression. Lennon's attempt to show his worth as a potential bluesman might have been embarrassing but for the presence of guest alto saxophonist King Curtis, whose contribution is exemplary. Well known for his sax work on such hits as the Coasters' 'Yakety Yak', a Lennon favourite, Curtis provided the perfect accompaniment. Regrettably, he did not live to hear the work on vinyl, for he was fatally stabbed on 15 August 1971, two months before the album's release.

I Don't Want To Be A Soldier

Musically, this has some interesting shades, with Spector drowning Lennon's vocal in echo, George Harrison providing some impressive slide guitar, Nicky Hopkins adding piano, Jim Keltner and Klaus Voormann taking up the rhythm, and King Curtis prompting a short jam towards the end involving Badfinger's Joey Molland and Tommy Evans on acoustic guitars, abetted by Steve Brendell on maracas and Mike Pinder on tambourine. At six minutes, this was the longest track on the album. Given its length, it was a pity that more attention wasn't paid to the words, which let the song down badly. Lennon appears to be emulating 'God' through his use of repetition, but this is a mantra without a meaning and a lyric with nothing to say. The rhyme scheme (a, a, a, a) merely alternates the words 'die', 'fly' and 'cry' producing some of his most banal lines. In Lennon's lyrical land-scape, rich men, failures, and churchmen cry; lawyers lie; beggars and soldiers die; and – presumably for lazy rhyming convenience – sailors, poor men and thieves all fly!

Lennon's sepulchral cry 'oh no' (a probable pun on 'Ono') takes us into the extended jam, which meanders at times but offers a reasonably climactic close to the first side of the album. The song's title came as no surprise to Beatles' fans who had been aware of Lennon's anti-militarist stance since his interview with Barry Miles, published in September 1969. Recalling how he had avoided National Service, which ceased to be obligatory just as he was coming of age, Lennon came across as a confirmed teenage pacifist. "I wouldn't fight at all . . . I'd always had this plan about Southern Ireland. I wasn't quite sure what I was going to do when I got to Southern Ireland, but I had no intention of fighting. I just couldn't kill somebody. I couldn't charge at them. I don't know whether I could kill somebody who was actually trying to kill me." Those Liverpool contemporaries who recalled his fierce temper and penchant for violent outbursts during his teens had less trouble conjuring a vision of Lennon as a soldier of retribution.

Gimme Some Truth

This passionate rant against hypocrites, pig-headed politicians and chauvinists was one of the highlights of the album. Lennon's bile pours forth in polysyllabic splendour. There's a gasp of celebration ('Whoo!') as he savours every one of his sneering, gleeful put-downs. In different circumstances, this might have become a Beatles song, having been first attempted in primitive form at the end of one of their sessions back in January 1969. It is appropriate, therefore, that George Harrison should be on hand to play a searing guitar solo that transforms the track, channelling Lennon's anger into self-righteous passion. "Did you know that George wanted to redo his guitar solos on 'Gimme Some Truth' and 'How Do You Sleep?'" Lennon asked critic Richard Williams. "That's the best he's ever played in his life, and he'd never get that feeling again. But he'd go on forever if you let him."

As the song careers through each new verse, Lennon piles on the adverbs as if there aren't enough words in the dictionary to express his disgust and contempt. He even uses the nursery rhyme character Mother Hubbard as a verb. Richard Nixon's underlings become the 'son of Tricky Dicky' and there's an odd reference to 'mommie's little chauvinists'. Against a drum barrage from Alan White, Lennon finally hits his adversaries over the head with a psychiatrist's medical text book, branding them all 'schizophrenic, egocentric, paranoiac prima donnas'. Even by his most venomous standards, this took some beating.

Oh My Love

This beautiful melody again harks back to Beatles' times, having been previously played as a guitar-based composition in 1968. Musically, the keyboard line dominates, with Lennon on acoustic piano and Nicky Hopkins on electric piano, while Alan White adds some evocative Tibetan cymbals, complemented by Harrison's guitar and some delicate orchestration from Spector. The credits diligently point out that Yoko Ono is claiming a joint credit for the work, a matter then in dispute with impresario Lew Grade, whose company, ATV, had recently acquired Northern Songs from publisher Dick James. Reading the lyrics, the Ono influence is self-evident, most notably in the nature imagery, which features her familiar allusions to trees, sky and clouds. "Yes, the chords too," she agreed. "The music side of it. The white piano was brought in. It was a birthday present to me. I said, 'I always wanted to use this chord, John . . .' The chords are rather interesting, and so he was saying, 'Oh yeah, we can do that.' He just worked with it. The lyrics are mostly his."

The song's lyrics obviously inspired the rear cover artwork which shows Lennon lying on the ground, staring at the sky. While the line 'everything's clear in our world' recalls the Beatles 'nothing's gonna change my world' from 'Across The Universe', other phrases betray Ono's metaphysical musings. In an otherwise naturalistic lyrical landscape, Lennon conjures a wind that can be seen and a mind that can be felt. Even Yoko's youthful classical training can be detected in the stately use of piano and carefully enunciated vocal.

How Do You Sleep?

Arguably the highlight of the album, this forthright attack on Paul McCartney may have offended some commentators, but it was undoubtedly one of Lennon's most compelling and passionate songs.

74

"It was like Dylan doing 'Like A Rolling Stone'," Lennon explained, "one of his nasty songs . . . venting my anger or frustration . . . and using Paul as the object of it." As the documentary film *Imagine* reveals, the studio rehearsal was even more irreverent and vitriolic, with Lennon sneering: "How do you sleep, you cunt?" Although his feud with McCartney was raging at the time, the song was more a release of suppressed spite than a final comment on a fragmented friendship. "I used my resentment and withdrawing from Paul and the Beatles to write 'How Do You Sleep?' I don't really go around with those thoughts in my head all the time. I wanted a funky track and this was a good way to make it."

When asked whether it was appropriate to make public his quarrel with McCartney, Lennon bristled with indignation. "Oh, hell's bells! Listen to *Ram*, folks! The lyrics weren't printed, just listen to it. I'm answering *Ram*. When I heard *Ram*, I immediately sat down and wrote my song . . . It's as simple as that. It's also a moment's anger. But it was written down on paper and . . . it wasn't as angry as when I sang it in the studio, because it was four weeks later . . . It was like a joke. 'Let's write this down.' We don't take it that seriously."

The song begins with a string section warming up in obvious imitation of *Sgt Pepper's Lonely Hearts Club Band*. Lennon then bursts through with his first line of attack – the contention that *Sgt Pepper's* took McCartney by surprise. It's an audacious opening, not least because it seems so blatantly unfair. The implicit suggestion that McCartney was somehow taken aback or even intimidated by the Beatles' most famous album is unwarranted. As Lennon certainly knew, the *Sgt Pepper's* concept was originally McCartney's and he also contributed more songs to the finished product than his accuser. The point is worth making as it indicates Lennon's willingness to interpret events to his rhetorical advantage.

Lennon next addresses, in oblique fashion, the crazy rumours about McCartney's death, the 'proof' of which had reached absurd levels of ingenuity among American conspiracy theorists. The artistic death that Lennon imagines his partner has suffered is only mildly contentious in comparison to the proposition that he never had any talent in the first place. Taking a line appropriately coined by

McCartney's adversary Allen Klein, Lennon derides Paul's artistic value to the Beatles, while insisting that his sole contribution was the sentimental 'Yesterday'. The use of the lower-case 'yesterday' simultaneously suggests that his present work is worthless – a point rammed home by denigrating his first solo single, 'Another Day'. This attack is preceded by the claim that McCartney is surrounded by sycophants and, apparently worst of all, 'straight' people. Revealingly, it was those criticisms that McCartney focused on while defending his reputation. When asked for his reaction to Lennon's gibes by Chris Charlesworth, he replied: "I think it's silly. So what if I live with straights? I like straights. I have straight babies. It doesn't affect him. He says the only thing I did was 'Yesterday'. He knows that's wrong . . . He knows and I know it's not true."

Then again, Lennon seemed more than willing to stretch the truth for propagandist effect. One of the more outlandish lines in the song is Lennon's innuendo that his partner is being henpecked (jumping to attention when his 'momma' asks him anything). Given Lennon's own reliance on Yoko Ono and the vitriol he had received from the media for allowing her to dominate his life, this was a surprisingly cheap shot. It also sounded hypocritical coming from someone who professed a strong affiliation with women's rights. Viewing such sentiments from a more charitable angle, one is tempted to argue that Lennon, ever the self-analyst, is projecting his own feelings outwards. At the time of the album's release, he said: "I could have been writing about myself." The tendency to see McCartney as his mirror opposite, a view intensified by years of face-to-face songwriting, performing and friendship, may have blurred Lennon's vision. Moreover, in recognizing McCartney's artistic decline, he must have been aware of his own susceptibility to falling standards now that the Beatles' quality control could no longer be called upon.

By the final verse, his attacks become more pointed as he accuses McCartney of surviving on his pop star looks, then dismisses his latest work as mindless 'muzak'. The song ends with a rhetorical question, more despairing than sarcastic in its exasperation. Surely, Paul must have learned *something* during all those years.

Lennon's inflammatory lyrics and awesome vitriol dominate any reading of the song, but special commendation must be given to Phil Spector's sweeping orchestration, courtesy of string arranger Torrie Zito, which heightens the drama immeasurably. The presence of another Beatle at the session adds to the tension, and when George Harrison lets rip with an invigorating slide solo at the end of the second verse, the stage is set for a gripping conclusion. Lennon saw many of his songs from this period as news despatches from the front of a private war, and never cared that their topical venom might make uneasy listening at a later date. It is regrettable that the composition's subject matter precluded its revival on later media tributes to the singer.

How?

The structure of this composition, with its series of rhetorical questions, recalls the stark self-analysis of Lennon's previous album, but the music is richer. Again two pianos dominate, reinforced by a solid backbeat and Spector's atmospheric use of echo. Lennon's plaintive vocal combines particularly well with the orchestration. The descending scale is interrupted by dramatic stops as Lennon's enquiries end in stasis. After three verses and eight long questions, there is some resolution in the consideration that life is a struggle that has to be endured. In the last verse, Lennon performs the familiar trick of transferring his feelings outwards to embrace everyman, just as he had done in 'Imagine'. But such platitudes are not enough to pacify the songwriter's troubled spirit and the song ends by repeating the key questions voiced in the first stanza.

Oh Yoko!

Lennon celebrated the joys of dependent love with this upbeat tribute to his wife. One of the older compositions on this album, its existence was first mentioned during an interview with *NME*'s Alan Smith printed on May Day 1969. "I think I'm going to make a pop record with Yoko," Lennon enthused. "I've got this song we were singing last night, and I think it'll be quite a laugh for her to do a pop record. It's one I've written myself and it's about Yoko, but I'll just change the word 'Yoko' to 'John' and she can sing it about me."

Interestingly, the song was first demoed as a slow ballad in the same key as the mournful 'Mother' before Lennon perfected a rearrangement for his band. There is a childlike glee in the lyrics as John describes the all-embracing nature of his love and the perceived ubiquity of Ono in his life. He relishes singing the words 'Oh Yoko!', seemingly transfixed by the beauty of the internal rhyme. Images of domesticity dominate as she infiltrates his mind while sleeping, bathing and dreaming. During the final lines he pays tribute to her personal symbolism by imagining himself calling her while in the middle of 'a cloud'. A veritable musical romp, the song has some lovely moments, not least the exuberant piano solo, Spector's falsetto on the chorus, and the playful Dylanesque harmonica break at the end, which also subtly references the Beatles' 'Love Me Do'.

"It was a very popular track," Lennon concluded. "Everybody wanted it as a single, but I was sort of shy and embarrassed, maybe because it didn't represent my image of myself, of the tough, hard-biting rock 'n' roller with the acid tongue."

SOME TIME IN NEW YORK CITY

Released: June 1972 (US) September 1972 (UK)

Original UK issue: Apple PCSP 716. US issue: Apple SVBB 3392. CD reissue with
bonus tracks: EMI 5 40978 2(UK)/ Capitol 5 40976 2 (US)

After arriving in New York, the Lennons were embraced by the local
radical community, including Jerry Rubin, Abbie Hoffman and street
musician David Peel. John and Yoko even joined some of their new
friends in the whimsically titled Rock Liberation Front, a group
"dedicated to exposing hip capitalist counter-culture rip-offs and
politicizing rock music and rock artistes". Although they clearly had a
lot of fun, much of their time was spent on more serious issues such as
fighting city hall, attending deportation hearings and engaging in
immigration and custody battles.

The politicization of the Lennons has sometimes been dismissed as
'chic radicalism', as if they were merely posing to impress America's
hard-line New Left grandees. Such cynicism ignores John Lennon's
more complicated evolution as a political animal. His interest in
revolutionary politics, which culminated in the recording of *Some
Time In New York City*, could be traced back at least four years. In
1968, Lennon first aired his political conscience in song on the
Beatles' 'Revolution'. The original take was agonizingly ambivalent,
with Lennon uncertain if he wanted to be 'in' or 'out' of the 'revolution'. But when the song appeared as the B-side of 'Hey Jude' in a
brilliant, hard-rocking arrangement, propelled by shards of searing,
distorted guitar work, Lennon unambiguously counted himself 'out'
of destructive action and openly criticized the followers of Chairman
Mao. Subsequently, the *New Left Review* dismissed 'Revolution' as "a
lamentable petty bourgeois cry of fear", while another radical paper
Black Dwarf saw the song as evidence that the Beatles "are deliberately
safeguarding their capitalist investment". In an open letter to Lennon,
they asked: "Come and join us!" He responded with his own 'open
letter', defending the setting up of Apple ('western communism' as

79

McCartney said), concluding: "I'll tell you what's wrong with the world: people. So do you want me to destroy them? Who fucked up Communism, Christianity, Capitalism, Buddhism, etc? Sick heads and nothing else . . . You smash it, and I'll rebuild it."

Throughout 1969, John and Yoko preferred to pursue their own pandemic peace initiatives, with bed-ins in Amsterdam and Montreal, and the release of 'Give Peace A Chance'. During 1970, their agenda was dominated by the personal politics of Janov-inspired therapy. The sole evidence of any radical activity was a donation to Michael X's Black House. But Lennon was already moving towards the hard Left. By January 1971, he felt sufficiently confident to submit to a no-holds-barred interview with the International Marxist Group-affiliated *Red Mole*, conducted by Robin Blackburn and Tariq Ali. It was an extraordinary confrontation during which Lennon espoused a new-found commitment to socialist principles and even apologized for his faint-hearted views in 'Revolution'. "I made a mistake . . . The mistake was it was anti-revolution . . . I didn't really know much about the Maoists but I just knew that they seemed to be so few and yet they stood in front of the police waiting to get picked off." Over the succeeding months, Lennon busied himself with causes, championing the defendants in the *Oz* trial and even supporting Scottish workers made redundant at the Upper Clydebank shipyard. Once in America, he emerged as a vociferous opponent of the Vietnam War, appearing at various marches and protests. In December 1971, the peace anthem 'Happy Xmas (War Is Over)' was released. That same month, Lennon played a concert in support of the imprisoned radical John Sinclair and performed at Harlem's Apollo Theatre in a benefit for the families of the prisoners shot at Attica State. Not long after, Lennon appeared on *The Michael Douglas Show* in the company of Black Panther, Bobby Seale.

Any of the above activities might have attracted the passing interest of subversive hunting spooks, but it was one of Lennon's more fanciful ideas that caught the attention of the FBI. During a radio interview, he announced his intention to tour America as part of a radical revue whose aim was to prevent the re-election of Richard Nixon. The plan was also mentioned when he met various political pals, including yippie Ed Sanders and poet Allen Ginsberg. Nothing substantial emerged from those talks, but the authorities dutifully logged Lennon's involvement. Even FBI Director J. Edgar Hoover expressed an interest, seemingly convinced that Lennon and his acolytes would attempt to disrupt the forthcoming Republican National Convention. When Lennon appeared on television and complained that his phone had been tapped, most viewers considered him paranoid or self-obsessed, but his instincts proved sound. FBI files have since confirmed that the former Beatle was spied upon, despite the fact that one informant had advised that he was not a threat "since he is constantly under the influence of narcotics".

The surveillance continued sporadically until he received his green card in 1976. By then, of course, Lennon's role as an American radical was long over. Lengthy legal battles over his immigration status, the need to maintain a positive image and, fatally, the re-election of Nixon, combined to rob Lennon of his political will. After the watershed year of 1972 when he released *Some Time In New York City*, Lennon retreated from radical politics with the same speed at which he had arrived.

The USA's Freedom of Information Act has allowed public access to the FBI files pertaining to Lennon. Clearly, their interest lay in his possible subversive activities in relation to the American government. There is no mention of his wider movements or possible links with the Irish Republican Army. Whether the British authorities noted any such involvement remains classified information. In the countless books on the history of the Troubles, no informant or IRA member has ever come forward to clarify matters. That said, the worlds of popular music and Irish political commentary seldom dovetail. It can now be revealed that Lennon did indeed meet a senior IRA man at a crucial stage in his political education.

Gerry O'Hare was a well-known Irish Republican who started off in the civil rights' organization, the People's Democracy, then joined the Provisional IRA. After setting up Radio Free Belfast as a propaganda vehicle, he was arrested and interrogated at Long Kesh, before being instructed by his superiors to resume his pirate radio propaganda after his release. "I was held for 48 hours and got the shit kicked out of me like everybody else," he recalls. "It was fucking hard enough, I can tell you. I was pinned, two fingers against the wall, feet spread out, and they'd put a foot out and bring you down. They were saying things like, 'You won't be telling any more lies,' and all that old shite. I was bollixed by the end of it." Later nick-named 'Lucky' Gerry, O'Hare was, as one colleague noted, "the only man I know who has been in every prison on this island of Ireland, north and south." At his militant peak, O'Hare took on the mantle of 'S O'Neill' (the northern equivalent of 'P O'Neill', the IRA's nomenclature for public pronouncements). "There weren't many of us involved in PR at that time . . . There was a great mistrust of the media. There were guys like myself and later times Danny Morrison who saw the value of using the media. The media wanted to get stuff from us and we wanted to get stuff across so there was a little two-way agreement. So I became 'S O'Neill' and the media would know how to confirm any statement by that name. I would have to talk to the BBC, UTV, ITV – and if they saw a statement coming in, there was a confidential way of checking it out. There were bogus statements going out and we had to stop people from claiming responsibility for things. So we set up a system and the media were delighted about it." Later, during one of his jail spells, O'Hare became involved in the famous helicopter escape from Mountjoy Prison and subsequently edited the Republican newspaper *An Phoblacht*.

Like John Lennon, Gerry had a wife whose exploits and aspirations threatened to rival his own. Rita O'Hare was one of the few women to achieve prominence in the overwhelmingly male world of Irish Republicanism. She was shot amid a gun battle with British soldiers in Andersonstown, imprisoned, then released for Christmas on compassionate grounds due to the severity of her injuries. Fleeing south to the Republic, she remained actively militant and, amazingly, while still on the run, she was caught attempting to smuggle a stick of gelignite inside herself while visiting an IRA prisoner in Portlaoise jail. The Special Criminal Court in Dublin sentenced her to three years' imprisonment. Rita later relocated to America, emerging as one of the most powerful and influential figures in the Sinn Féin party. Interestingly, her former husband Gerry never became a member: "In my time the editor of *An Phoblacht* was always an army person, not a Sinn Féin person. In those days the army ruled the roost. Loads of guys who would have been IRA guys wouldn't have wanted to be involved in the political side. It's completely different today because Sinn Féin has taken over the mantle of the political wing."

In common with many Irish Republican sympathizers of the period, John Lennon first became affected by events in Northern Ireland during the summer of 1971 when internment was introduced. It was on the morning of 9 August that British troops began Operation Demetrius. Under the Special Powers Act, the government was able to arrest, detain and imprison members of the public indefinitely without trial or recourse to legal representation. As a means of defeating terrorism, the policy proved disastrous. The intelligence gathering, based on outdated lists supplied by the Royal Ulster Constabulary, was appalling. Provisional IRA personnel were young, mobile and still largely unknown to the forces. Farcically, they knew of the intended sweep in advance and remained untouched by the operation. Those rounded up consisted of some old Official IRA men, long out of service, and a number of civil rights activists, socialists, and nationalist supporters whose only crime had been to question the status quo. The rest were political innocents, relatives of Republican sympathizers or those unlucky enough to be living at an address or a street where the army turned up at daybreak. Many others were dragged in for no apparent reason whatsoever. The heavy-handedness of the forces provoked much bitterness, made worse by the realization that the arrests were sectarian in intent.

That summer the UK charts had been dominated by Middle Of The Road's singalong 'Chirpy Chirpy Cheep Cheep'. Loyalist supporters now adopted its chorus as a chant and stood outside Catholic houses singing 'Where's your daddy gone?' to distraught children. These macabre singalongs appealed to Loyalists on the rampage. A couple of years before, a brigade of drunken RUC officers had invaded the Bogside area of Derry, frightening locals and damaging property, while singing a chilling adaptation of '(Theme From) The Monkees': 'Hey, hey, we're the Monkees, and we'll monkey you around . . . till your blood is on the ground.' One woman later told a British government enquiry that they were chanting outside her window, "Come on, you Fenian, 'til we rape you." It was only when she telephoned the authorities to complain that she discovered that it *was* the police who were parading the streets, smashing windows and spoiling for a fight.

Internment soon provoked full-scale rioting and fatalities. Within days, 22 were dead in Derry's Bogside area alone. There were more casualties in the 96 hours following internment than there had been in the whole of 1970. Attitudes hardened as news filtered through of police brutality during interrogations. A number of the detainees were subjected to routine beatings, forced to run barefoot across ground covered with broken glass or thrown blindfolded and screaming from helicopters, which they assumed were hovering in the clouds of Belfast rather than three feet from the ground. Others had liquid funnelled into their ears, their heads held under water, their testicles agonizingly squeezed, objects inserted into their backsides, plastic bags placed over their heads and their bodies burned on radiator pipes or electrically shocked with cattle prods. Deep interrogation techniques were also employed, with prisoners forced to stand spreadeagled against a wall for hours, sometimes days, while being bombarded with white noise and assaults upon their person at the first sign of any movement. Sleep and food deprivation were accompanied by bizarre rituals. Interrogators climbed aboard men's backs and rode them like horses, some were forced to wear soiled underpants on their heads or subjected to sudden manic dramas such as the appearance of an aproned butcher, complete with bloodied cleaver. Families were targeted as part of the interrogation process, and some women detainees claimed they were threatened with rape. Five years later, the European Commission of Human Rights found Britain guilty of torture. An appeal to the European Court of Human Rights overturned that charge but upheld a decision of "inhuman and degrading treatment".

While much of the above was downplayed or completely ignored

in the mainstream media, more militant broadsheets were documenting the inequities of internment, and Lennon was quick to act. The
same month that internment was introduced, 1,500 marchers turned
out in London's Oxford Street to protest about British involvement
in Northern Ireland. At the centre of the crowd Lennon could be
seen carrying a placard which read: 'For the IRA Against British
Imperialism'. When asked later to reconcile his twin support for
pacifism and the IRA, Lennon responded: "I don't know how I feel
about them because I understand why they're doing it and if it's a
choice between the IRA and the British Army, I'm with the IRA.
But if it's a choice between violence and non-violence, I'm with
non-violence. So it's a very delicate line."

Soon after moving to America, Lennon and Ono wrote 'Luck Of
The Irish' as a catch-all comment on British imperialism. It might
have ended there but for the tragic events of Bloody Sunday. On
30 January 1972, British soldiers shot dead 13 unarmed Catholic men
during a demonstration in Derry in protest against internment. The
soldiers later claimed that they shot civilians aiming bombs at them, a
charge completely unsubstantiated by forensic tests. At the end of the
inquest into the deaths, Derry City coroner Major Hubert O'Neill
reached the chilling conclusion: "I say without reservation – it was
sheer, unadulterated murder." In the poorer areas of Northern Ireland,
Catholic communities rioted, while in the House of Commons the
firebrand MP Bernadette Devlin landed a punch on the person of
Home Secretary Reginald Maudling. The murders even inflamed
moderate opinion in the south of Ireland, prompting a crowd to burn
down the British Embassy in Dublin. Unsurprisingly, the newly
politicized John Lennon was soon drawn into the fray. Again taking
to the streets, this time in New York, he led the demonstrators with a
rousing rendition of 'Luck Of The Irish'. Proudly proclaiming his
Irish roots, Lennon reminded those present that Liverpool was the
uncrowned capital of Ireland and immediately set to work on a new
song 'Sunday Bloody Sunday'. Recalling the demonstration, he gave
a wonderfully insouciant description of the day, using vocabulary that
sounded as though it had been specially commissioned by a radical
lexicographer. "The mood of the crowd was a happy one under the

circumstances, considering we were all there to show our sympathy for the 13 people who were mercilessly shot down by British imperialists."

While the FBI concerned themselves with Lennon's comments on the Republican party, they ignored his tacit support of the IRA. Even prominent politicians in New York, Boston and Chicago frequently played the 'Irish card' when necessary, so Lennon's 'rebel' stance on this issue prompted minimal interest from the authorities. But what were the IRA thinking? Did Lennon's activities register on their radar? Within the IRA high command was there any comment made about Lennon? Was contact made with the singer to enlist his support? Amazingly, the answer to these questions was 'yes', as Gerry O'Hare (the IRA's former 'S O'Neill' operator) revealed to me in an exclusive interview.

Were you aware that Lennon was protesting about Bloody Sunday?
Yes. We were up to speed with him all right because he was very interested. You see in New York there were Irish Americans who kept him briefed. I was over on a speaking tour and a guy said to me, 'Would you like to meet John Lennon?' Within two days I was in his presence.

Lennon released political agitprop songs like 'Sunday Bloody Sunday' and 'Luck Of The Irish', donated royalties to the Civil Rights Movement, joined marches and said he supported the IRA and was protesting about the victims slaughtered "by British imperialists". How did the IRA high command react to this? Would his words and songs have been considered significant in any way, or would the IRA think it was just a joke?
No! He was taken very seriously because he offered to do a concert – one in Dublin and one in Belfast. When I was in New York I met him briefly through a contact whose name I do not want to divulge. I went up to the apartment and I asked Lennon was he serious about all this. He said he was, but his problem was that if he left America he might not be able to get back in again and he was frightened about this . . . So I came back and told the people on our side, 'He wants to do it but this is his big problem.' And then, of course, it faded from

our priorities. But I did speak to him myself. He knew who I was and where I was coming from. He said he'd do it all right.

But how seriously would somebody like him be taken? Wouldn't some of you have seen him as a joke?
I don't think so. He was already writing all his protest stuff like 'Working Class Hero' and things like that. Paul McCartney wrote one as well, 'Give Ireland Back To The Irish'. But I think he stood back from it very quickly, didn't he?!

Were any of these comments or songs about Ireland of any value?
Oh, of course they were at the time. You have to think of the time. There was nobody bigger than the Beatles, and John Lennon was espousing his working-class values. With me, he was the first guy to use the word 'fuck'. Didn't he use that in 'Working Class Hero'? We were thinking, 'This is brilliant, how did he get away with it?' . . . Whether they [Lennon & McCartney] were [just] caught up in the emotion, I don't know, but they were powerful people to have on your side [as far as championing Irish unity] or to be able to say, 'Well, they're on our side.' Then, of course, in America we had the Kennedys and that dynasty [as supporters of civil rights in Ireland].

Did you think John Lennon was genuine?
Yes. He gave me the impression he was genuine. I said, 'That's fine.' The upshot of it was that he said he'd love to do a concert but if he did it he insisted on doing one in Belfast too. I got the impression that he was very anxious to do one for the Protestant community as well. In the end he just explained to me, 'I have a difficulty, my lawyers are fighting this. There's a lot of things I want to do and I badly want to go back home.' He kept saying 'back home' and I presume he meant London or Liverpool or whatever. Finally, he said, 'Until such time as that, this will have to be put on the long finger.' So it was left to the guy who introduced me to him, that if it was ever going to happen then he would be the contact and we would do what we had to do on this side. But nothing ever happened.

87

After trawling through Lennon's press archives, I found confirmation of O'Hare's story in a 1972 interview conducted by Roy Carr, in which the singer said: "Yoko and I thought about going over to Ireland to do something, but until we've cleared up this immigration thing, we can't leave America. We're kind of trapped. It might prove difficult for us to re-enter the country." As well as writing 'Luck Of The Irish' and 'Sunday Bloody Sunday', Lennon made a donation to an unidentified Irish Civil Rights organization, which some detractors claim may have been an IRA front for obtaining funds. This may explain why, according to former intelligence officer David Shayler, MI5 allegedly had a note on file tenuously linking Lennon with IRA funding.

As ever with Lennon, the everyday circumstances of his life, personal and political, permeated his music and songwriting and this was made manifest on *Some Time In New York City*. During a period when introspective singer songwriters were in vogue, he was emerging as a cause-seeking protest singer, a species that had been commercially redundant since Dylan waved farewell to the radical left in the mid-Sixties. Potential purchasers needed only to inspect the packaging or read the song titles to realize the extent of Lennon's political dogmatism. The front cover was a pastiche of *The New York Times*, using song titles as headlines and lyrics as news stories. The US version included a postcard depicting the Statue of Liberty raising a clenched fist and a British Army recruitment ad from the pages of *The Sun*, filled in with John Lennon's signature and the words 'Fit To Die' scrawled across the page. International rock fans recently accustomed to songs about Yoko Ono, now had to embrace such names as John Sinclair and Angela Davis and, ideally, show some interest in US prison riots, British foreign policy, the IRA, Free Derry, and women's liberation. They also had to swallow the promise of a free live album, only to be confronted by a retail price that was somewhat higher than expected.

Those grown used to the craftsmanship of *Imagine* had a rude awakening in the form of backing group Elephant's Memory, a former bar band specializing in Chuck Berry riffs and lively performances whose sole claim to fame was providing some backing music to the film *Midnight Cowboy*. It was, of course, most appropriate for Lennon to use a relatively unschooled bunch of musicians to play his and Yoko's political street poetry, but many critics and a large proportion of record buyers were alienated by the results. *Rolling Stone*'s Stephen Holden described the album as "incipient artistic suicide" and in a lengthy overview complained that the work was essentially puerile propaganda, adding, "The tunes are shallow and derivative and the words little more than sloppy nursery rhymes that patronize the issues and individuals they seek to exalt. Only a monomaniacal smugness could allow the Lennons to think that this witless doggerel wouldn't insult the intelligence and feelings of *any* audience." Taking an overview of John and Yoko's career, Holden praised them for their willingness to pursue avant-garde ideas: "Such commitment takes guts. It takes even more guts when you've made it so big that you don't need to take chances to stay on top. The Lennons should be commended for their daring. What is deplorable, however, is the egotistical laziness . . . that allows artistes of such proven stature, who claim to identify with the 'working class hero', to think they can patronize all whom they would call brothers and sisters."

Of course, *Some Time In New York City* was never intended as an artistic statement in the vein of 'Imagine' or the personal/political songs on *John Lennon/Plastic Ono Band* but a brand of pure polemic in which the music was subservient to the message. The idea was first posited by Lennon during the Beatles' era when they rush released 'All You Need Is Love' and 'The Ballad Of John And Yoko' into the marketplace within days of their recording. "This was like news," Lennon explained, "like there would be spelling mistakes in the paper the next day or 500 dead when there was only 460. I didn't have time to work out other people's reaction to things. I just had to get it out." Getting the message on to the streets in the form of a bulletin was the main aim. This was Lennon attempting to use the album format as a newspaper, which is quickly read, digested and discarded. The cover of the album said as much. "It's not like the Bible," he quipped. "It's all over now. It's gone. It's finished. There is no more. My songs are not there to be digested and pulled apart like the *Mona*

Lisa. If the people on the street think about it, that's all there is to it really – except to say to those people who might be thinking along the same lines as me and Yoko, 'You're not alone' . . . When we made that album we weren't setting out to make the *Brandenburg Concerto* or the masterpiece everyone tries to write, paint, draw or film. It was just a question of getting it done, putting it out, and the next one's coming up soon. We needn't have done it. We could have sat on *Imagine* for a year and a half. But the things on *Some Time In New York City* were coming out of our minds and we just wanted to share our thoughts with anybody who wanted to listen. It was a quicker decision to make *Some Time In New York City* than any other album. And for that reason it only took nine days to complete."

A publishing dispute between Northern Songs and Ono Music over whether Yoko could reasonably be credited as a co-writing partner delayed the album's release in Britain by several months. By the time it appeared, most UK critics tended to follow the American line, with *Melody Maker* complaining of "glib politicizing", "mindless over-kill, cheap rhetoric and appallingly bad lyrics". *NME*'s reviewer Tony Tyler constructed a review in the form of an open letter head-lined: "Lennon, you're a pathetic, ageing revolutionary." Tyler was reasonably kind to the music, which he described as 'excellent' and he also praised certain tracks, notably 'Attica State' and 'New York City'. Evidently, it was Lennon's lyrics ("insulting, arrogant, rigid, dogmatic. . . .") that irked most. Two paragraphs were wasted taking the singer to task for his supposed shortcomings as a historian, includ-ing the allegation that he was ignorant about the role of the Scots in Ireland in key lines on 'Sunday Bloody Sunday'. In fact, Lennon's argument here was impressively accurate as any book on the history of the Troubles will testify. Tyler concluded: "You've still got important things to say so *say* them. Don't rely on cant and rigidity. Don't alienate. Stimulate. You know, like you used to."

Most of the reviews missed the point of *Some Time In New York City* and failed to appreciate the potency of Lennon's agitprop. A few years later some of its critics would be championing the sloganeering of punk, which used similarly direct lyrics for maximum impact. Lennon was initially defensive about the album, which he rightly felt was a stimulating commentary on his experiences in New York. As he explained to *NME*'s Roy Carr: "I tried to make my songs uncomplicated so that people could understand them . . . There was one criticism that said, 'Please write us some images, not the way you're saying it now.' Well, all I've got to say to people like that is, 'Get drunk or whatever it is you do. Lay on your bed. Make your own images.'" Elaborating on this point, he concluded: "The songs we wrote and sang are subjects we and most people talk about. It was done in a tradition of minstrels – singing reporters – who sang about their times and what was happening." In later years, he looked back at the work with a more jaundiced eye, seemingly worn down by all the critical disapprobation. Highlighting the album's limitations, he suggested: "It almost ruined us in a way. It became journalism and not poetry. And I basically feel that I'm a poet . . . I was making an effort to reflect what was going on. Well, it doesn't work like that. It doesn't work as pop music or what I want to do."

Lennon was correct, inasmuch as his topical songs consisted mainly of simplistic sloganeering, but such is the nature of most agitprop. What was refreshing and exciting about the album was his willingness to release a work so out of place in the rock market. In a period where staid studio work was the norm, *Some Time In New York City* was a brave and uncompromising album that displayed Lennon's egotism and altruism in equal measure. His determination to use Fifties' style musicianship to rugged effect emphasized the wide-eyed innocence and eagerness of a performer who saw himself as a reformer and political protester, seemingly immune to the gibes of an uncaring public. Like Lennon, Yoko Ono also went through a period of denial about the value of *Some Time In New York City* only to change her mind after a key event. As she told *Mojo*'s Paul Trynka: "It became such an incredible mistake on our part to make that album. Not because of the songs themselves, but what we had to deal with afterwards. But then I was invited by Gorbachev to Moscow with 200 other artists and, of course, in the communist world the one they like the most is *Some Time In New York City*. I felt like saying, 'John, are you listening?' It was only then that I knew it was an album that had some merit."

Some Time In New York City was a difficult album to love if
you did not share Lennon's political or humanitarian sympathies. In
short, non-liberals, patriotic Englanders, Protestant unionists, anti-
revolutionaries, and those with a particular distaste for American
hippie/yippie radicals were unlikely to sing along with Lennon.
However, this did not mean that it was necessary to support the
causes championed by the singer to appreciate the album. Just as
'Imagine' could be assimilated by the religious right and 'Cold
Turkey' could send shivers down the spine of somebody who'd
never even sampled a cigarette, these songs required no political
understanding to be enjoyed. Indeed, even detractors could no doubt
find humour in Lennon's proselytizing, which included some hilarious one-liners and off-the-cuff insults.

One plausible criticism of these compositions might be that they
are too rooted in their time. While the simple, unaffected utopianism
of 'Give Peace A Chance' and 'Imagine' have made them anthemic
songs, ideally suited to any cause devoted to peace, the subject matter
of *Some Time In New York City* are street songs seemingly cemented
in 1972. This, of course, is what Lennon intended and explained in
various interviews at the time. To my mind, this does not cheapen
their aesthetic currency. I would argue that there is greater 'relevance'
or 'meaning' in some of these songs than in a non-specific, catch-all
anthem like 'Power To The People' which sounds earnest, but ultimately says little or nothing beyond its rather vague title. Some might
counter that few now remember Angela Davis, John Sinclair or even
those slaughtered at Attica State, but how many of us knew the
stories of Tom Joad or Joe Hill or others immortalized in song? Then
again, the latter were arguably worthier recipients of sympathy or
reverence. One of the *NME*'s criticisms of Lennon at the time was
that Davis and Sinclair were peripheral figures, whose causes were
either irrelevant or else resolved by the time of the album's release.
What use was hearing 'Free John Sinclair' when he had long since
been freed by the authorities?

The answer, of course, was that the people and causes mentioned
worked on both a literal and metaphoric level. It was not necessary to
know who these characters were or what they did. All that was

required of the listener was to empathize on some level with the injustices mentioned or simply lose oneself in Lennon's passion for their plight. At a time when rock music was reacting against the earnestness of the Sixties by escaping into the fantastical, and generally glorifying artifice, Lennon's radicalism sounded jarringly out of place. It is instructive to consider Dylan's position during the same time period. A year before the release of *Some Time In New York City*, he had evidently turned back the clock to the protest days by releasing the single 'George Jackson', decrying the fate of the militant Black Panther. Cynicism was rife. Even Dylan's biographer Anthony Scaduto accused Dylan of bandwagon-jumping, maintaining that the master was throwing a sop to his former New York radical friends as a marketing device. Scaduto later recanted and told me that he felt he had misjudged Dylan and believed he had been sincere throughout this period. But it was symptomatic of the times to be suspicious. A few years later Dylan released *Desire*, partly co-written with Jacques Levy, and received even harsher criticism for daring to elegize the gangster Joey Gallo. Some weren't too pleased about Reuben 'Hurricane' Carter either, but that song had a thrilling tune that was difficult to dislike. The righteous mauling that 'Joey' received, mainly in the liberal American music press, underlined the dangers of eulogizing a figure of questionable morality with a song seemingly frozen in time. For those who dare say 'Joey' or 'John Sinclair' are static, forgotten figures, then the same must be said about the contemporaneous criticisms these songs suffered. The venom and outrage that the songs produced no longer seem appropriate or relevant. If we don't care about Joey Gallo or John Sinclair, then we care even less about the indignation of 1970s critics towards them. Distance has robbed these songs of relevance but in another crucial sense, it has freed them.

What Dylan and Lennon achieved in these compositions may have been questionable at the time, but now they survive in a different universe. Whether Gallo or Sinclair are 'worthy' does not matter because they live on as part of the modern rebel folk song. Flawed human beings they both may have been, but the specific details of their lives have now been transmogrified into myth. They exist as

93

part of the outlaw tradition in contemporary song and in approaching them we suspend our disbelief in the same way that we appreciate tales of Jesse James, Billy The Kid and Ned Kelly without considering the human suffering they inflicted. 'Pretty Boy Floyd' may have been an outlaw but when you listen to Woody Guthrie's song, the gangster becomes a humanitarian providing Christmas dinner for families living on welfare. I've no idea whether this ever really happened, nor do I care, for it is not the historical accuracy that I am responding to as a listener, but immersion in the propagandist passions of the songwriter. Agitprop creates its own black and white universe populated not by authentic flesh and blood figures, but idealized constructs who happen to share the name of real people. While operating in this part-fictional panorama, Lennon tells us more about his feelings of the moment rather than revealing any long-term commitment. In this sense, it does not matter whether he dismissed his songs about Sinclair, Davis *et al* or reverted to a perception of these characters as flawed figures in a more complex universe. He later criticized Janov, but that in no way detracts from the brilliance of *John Lennon/Plastic Ono Band* or lessens the doctor's role in inspiring the work.

Approaching *Some Time In New York City* anew, without the burden of having to understand or appreciate every nuance of Lennon's propagandist utterances, produces fresh and unexpected rewards. By projecting beyond the album's naturalistic landscape into the prism of myth, we can enjoy a work which is a remarkable achievement and, without doubt, Lennon's most curiously underrated work. In every respect, it stands up far better than any contemporaneous commentator could reasonably have expected. The passion that Lennon felt for specific causes, combined with the energetic, almost punk-like approach of Elephant's Memory, fashioned an album that thoroughly deserves a full-scale critical rehabilitation.

Woman Is The Nigger Of The World

When the arts magazine *Nova* interviewed Yoko Ono for their March 1969 issue, she expressed the view that "woman is the nigger of the world". The phrase stuck with Lennon who was determined to transform his partner's feminist slogan into a popular anthem. Like so many things in his life, he rushed to the feminist cause with the zeal of a new convert. The man who had condescendingly criticized pushy women in 'Girl' and exercised macho dominance in 'Run For Your Life' was now atoning for his chauvinist sins. On the record sleeve, the song was illustrated with a picture of a horned devil slicing a woman's stomach with a knife. The lyrics were equally direct and espoused the need for a change in male attitudes with firm conviction.

There is a discernible sense of wonder in Lennon's phrase 'Think about it', as he admonishes the listener to consider the inescapable logic of the song's title. He then tackles the selective apotheosis that men can employ in using the madonna/whore ideal – exalting women while denigrating them in the same breath. The proselytizing is similar to many of the songs on *John Lennon/Plastic Ono Band*, with Lennon pulling away a veil of false conditioning to confront the world's appalling treatment of women. His catalogue of abuse embraces sexism, psychological manipulation and enforced slavery to motherhood.

It is not Lennon's polemic that makes the song, however, but the rhetorical attacks on his audience to wake up to the realities around them. Like a father confessor, he demands an acknowledgement of guilt from the listener. If we do not believe his words then we need only take a look at the person we're with. In determining society's blame, he rightly cries for change, urging us to scream about it. The sheer force of Lennon's argument results in one of his greatest political songs. He handles the vocal line with sensitivity, building the tune around a sparse but effective arrangement, complete with 'invisible strings' not dissimilar to the sound of ELO.

The song's message proved anathema to the public and many critics of the period, but challenged head-on the prejudices of a testosterone-drenched rock world resistant to change. "It was actually the first women's liberation song that went out," Lennon claimed. "It was before Helen Reddy's 'I Am Woman' . . . It was talked about. It got the message across. The whole story is the title. The lyrics are just a fill-in. I felt the lyrics didn't live up to Yoko's title."

Inevitably, Yoko's aphorism caused concern to sensitive disc jockeys and a ratings-conscious media wary of causing offence. When the song was first performed on television on *The Dick Cavett Show* in May 1972, the host was obliged to voice a disclaimer prior to the broadcast. Lennon countered by winning the support of Ron Dellums, chairman of the Congressional black caucus, who issued the following statement: "If you define 'nigger' as someone whose lifestyle is defined by others, whose opportunities are defined by others, whose role in society is defined by others, the good news is you don't have to be black to be a nigger in this society. Most of the people in America are niggers."

With Lennon also appearing favourably in *Ebony* magazine, there was no doubting his point. Unfortunately, this proved insufficient to win the record a Top 40 placing in the US charts, or even a release on single in the UK, where a copyright dispute continued over Lennon/Ono compositions. Although disappointed by the single's lack of airplay ("It was banned in America because you couldn't say 'nigger'"), Lennon felt justly proud of the composition. "It's such a beautiful statement. What she [Yoko] was saying is true. Woman still is the nigger . . . You can talk about blacks, you can talk about Jews, you can talk about the Third World, you can talk about everything but underlying the whole thing, under the whole crust of it is the women and beneath them the children."

Sisters O Sisters
"Male chauvinist pig engineer," Yoko laughs at the start of the song.

"Right on, sister," jokes Lennon in response. The musicians' opening chords sound as if they're about to launch into the Beatles' 'Do You Want To Know A Secret?' Instead, we witness Yoko Ono embracing pop with some panache. At times, the song sounds like an early Sixties' girl group recording transposed through the avant-garde consciousness of Ono, via Phil Spector's signature production. Yoko demands wisdom and freedom for her sisters in an occasionally uncertain voice, buoyed by an arrangement that is impressively jaunty. Lennon later said: "Some people thought she was singing about nuns!" Detractors found the tune and lyrics trite, especially the utopian dream of building a brave new world, but these sentiments were not far removed from Lennon's 'Imagine'. Backing group Elephant's Memory were perplexed when Lennon encouraged them to respond to the lyric's rallying cry with a ska beat. "Elephant's Memory, all New York kids, were saying they didn't know what reggae was. I was trying to explain to them all. The only lick I knew to teach them was 'The Israelites', that Desmond Dekker thing . . . If you listen to it, you'll hear me trying to get them to reggae."

Attica State

On 13 September 1971, prisoners at the Attica Correctional Facility in upstate New York seized 50 hostages as part of a protest. The authorities responded by sending in 1,700 National Guardsmen and by the end of the siege the death toll read 28 prisoners and 10 guards, with 85 wounded. The following month, on the evening of 9 October, Lennon and Ono wrote this rousing protest song which firmly pointed the finger at Governor Nelson Rockefeller, who had refused to intervene by negotiating with the prisoners. 'Rockefeller pulled the trigger,' Lennon sang, adding to the political rhetoric with some sweeping views on prison reform, including the suggestion that all prisoners everywhere should be freed and offered love and care, while selected judges should be jailed. The breast-beating lyrics echoed specific lines from several other Lennon songs, including 'Revolution', 'Come Together', 'Give Peace A Chance' and 'Gimme Some Truth'. Musically, there were strong echoes of George Harrison's 'Old Brown Shoe'.

Emotionally, the song is not as angry as you might expect from the subject matter while the chorus is positively friendly with Lennon sounding like an Anglo-Australian as he tells us that we're all 'mates' with Attica State. The song worked spectacularly well as a rousing rant, perfect for live performance. On 17 December, Lennon appeared at a benefit for the prisoners' families staged at the Apollo Theatre, Harlem. He continued to promote the song energetically and even took to wearing a badge proclaiming: 'Indict Rockefeller For Murder – Attica'. The song was performed on both *The Mike Douglas Show* and *The David Frost Show*. During the latter the singer entered a heated debate with the audience. "We're like newspaper

97

men, only we sing about what's going on instead of writing about it," he explained in defence of his political material.

"Wait till they kill your son or daughter . . ." shouted a disgruntled audience member. "You are setting up thieves and murderers as heroes . . . I have to hold on to my purse. I have to be careful in the subway. I have to lock my doors because of people like these prisoners."

"They're that way because they never had a chance," Lennon replied. "We are society. We're all responsible for each other. We have to be." Responding to the criticism that he was making martyrs of the dead, Lennon concluded: "We're not glorifying them. This song will come and go, but there will be another Attica tomorrow."

Born In A Prison
Ono's second lead vocal on the album proves far more impressive than 'Sisters O Sisters', combining a beautiful high register reading with some off-mike yelps. Her lyrics, set against a compelling waltz-time arrangement, reiterate the sentiments of 'Working Class Hero', perceiving life as one long prison sentence. The imagery is a trifle convoluted, with extended lines used to convey Ono's arresting aphorisms in which bare wood can be transformed into a flute and a broken mirror into a razor. Stan Bronstein's chafing saxophone dominates the piece creating a cocktail-lounge feel, abetted by strings, the overall effect of which sounds musically out of sync with the work of every other major performer of the period. It is an intriguing complement to the other material on the album and a fine example of Ono falling under the melodic spell of her husband. Whereas their respective recordings once seemed antithetical in almost every respect, 'Born In A Prison' is a good example of her successfully utilizing western pop sensibilities.

New York City
Employing the Chuck Berry influence in a lyric and tune redolent of 'Back In The USSR', Lennon transforms a political rant into a rock 'n' roll boogie with considerable success. The mood is exuberant, with a rollicking piano backing, some great tenor sax and a vocal of

excited abandonment. Melodically, there are echoes of 'The Ballad Of John And Yoko' which is reasonably apt as this is another auto-biographical diary. Among the strange people he encounters in the song is a preacher who presents the theologically dubious notion that God is actually a red-herring in drag. Lennon then relates his meeting with street musician David Peel, when they sang 'The Pope Smokes Dope' for startled onlookers. "We got moved on by the police," Lennon proudly recalled. "It was all very wonderful." The narrative also tells of visiting Max's Kansas City, meeting Elephant's Memory, performing at the Apollo and happily discovering that it was possible to live in New York City without being constantly mobbed by the public and press. "In New York, I could walk around, where I still couldn't walk around in London . . . If I'd lived in Roman times, I'd have lived in Rome. Where else? Today America is the Roman Empire, and New York is Rome itself." Lennon closes his song of street protest with the reverse compliment 'what a bad ass city', indi-cating that he has already swallowed the New York vernacular.

Sunday Bloody Sunday

After hearing that British soldiers had shot dead 13 unarmed Catho-lics during a protest march in Derry, Lennon immediately put pen to paper to produce his most embittered political anthem. A military beat opens the song, after which Lennon presents powerful images of martyrs, nailed coffins and the existence of 'Free Derry'. The latter refers to the famous slogan 'You Are Now Entering Free Derry' which was painted in black letters on the wall adjacent to the Bogside on the morning of 5 January 1969. "It was the only sentence I ever came up with in my life that has lasted," says Derry journalist and political commentator Éamonn McCann. "And I didn't really come up with it. The originator of the phrase was Lenny Glaser who was a big counter-cultural hero in the 1960s. He was associated with the Berkeley Free Speech Movement. I'd seen a photograph of Berkeley College where they'd written 'You Are Now Entering Free Berkeley' and that's where the slogan came from. It became a nationalist expression meaning freedom from British rule, but at the time it was an expression of internationalism. It's a good example of the way a slogan or a political intention can be set down in one context or one historical period and, over time, it can change meaning. And I don't complain about that. Now it means something quite different because the situation and the area around the wall is now very different – particularly after Internment, Bloody Sunday, and the IRA."

In the chorus, Yoko Ono screeches the song's title like a keening lamentation for the dead. Her performance ably expresses the horror of the incident and its aftermath. Lennon then goes on to denounce Stormont, the seat of government in Northern Ireland and the Unionist stronghold which held sway in Ulster in the 50-year period between 1921–72. While denouncing the inequities of Britain's Internment policy, Lennon viciously attacks the Unionist majority in the North, rightly pointing out that they are a minority on the whole of the 'sweet Emerald Isle'. Not only does Lennon disagree with Unionist rule but expresses the desire to see those 'mothers' burn. A powerful guitar break intervenes before the crucial third verse in which Lennon's contempt spills over into, presumably unintended, polemic humour. Wrongly taken to task in the *NME* over his gibes about 'Anglo pigs and Scotties', Lennon is correct in highlighting that many of Ulster's population were descended from Scottish settlers and concentrated in the North East of Ireland in a Machiavellian attempt to colonize the island. Attacking the Orange community, Lennon sneers at their parades in which they display their allegiance to the Crown by waving Union Jacks. In exasperation he demands to know how they dare hold the people to ransom and insists that the English should be put to sea. 'Keep Ireland for the Irish,' he submits, paraphrasing the words of Paul McCartney, whose 'Give Ireland Back To The Irish' had recently been banned by the BBC.

Like Lennon, McCartney had shown considerable courage in addressing a subject unlikely to win universal support from a mainstream audience. "You can't stay out of it if you think at all these days," he insisted. "We're still humans, you know, and when you wake up and read your newspaper, it affects you . . . I don't now plan to do everything I do as a political thing, but on this occasion I think the British government overstepped their mark and showed themselves to be more of a repressive regime than I ever believed them to be."

Lennon approached the 'Irish question' with the same passion and venom used when dealing with the 'McCartney question' in 'How Do You Sleep?' In both songs, vitriol and overstatement are employed as an artistic device to bludgeon Lennon's opponents into oblivion. Both combine hate and humour in disconcerting fashion to create a narrative in which justifiable hurt seems to have been transformed into a retribution beyond reason. The final verse of 'Sunday Bloody Sunday' perfects this tactic. Having built a reasonable argument, Lennon's froth of indignation spills over into hysterical hyberbole. Long Kesh is described as a concentration camp and, leaving himself open to accusations of sectarianism, Lennon advocates the compulsory repatriation of Protestants who ally themselves with English rule. Even the Provisional IRA never went that far. Lennon appears to qualify these statements in the last couple of lines when advocating that Ireland should be left to the Irish, not the mandarins in London or the papacy in Rome. Such sophistry would have made no sense to Unionists, as Lennon may or should have known. Their notion of Ireland for the Irish was summed up in their perennial slogan, 'Home Rule Is Rome Rule'.

The analogy with 'How Do You Sleep?' also offers a stark reminder of the fundamentally different approaches of Lennon and McCartney as political writers. With the overly polite 'Give Ireland Back To The Irish', McCartney provided a simple slogan and a singalong tune but the lyrics lacked passion or bite. By contrast, Lennon struggled with the melody of 'Sunday Bloody Sunday', but composed some of the most acerbic lyrics of his career, before allowing himself to be overwhelmed by his angry rhetoric. Would Lennon and McCartney have produced a more lasting anthem if they'd combined their talents to write a protest song about English involvement in Ireland? Possibly. McCartney would no doubt have pushed Lennon into composing a more memorable melody and perhaps toned down the excesses of the final verse of 'Sunday Bloody Sunday', while Lennon might have given his former colleague the necessary anger and polemic humour to add some 'Anglo pigs and Scotties' to the bare lyrics of 'Give Ireland Back To The Irish'.

Despite its occasional flaws, 'Sunday Bloody Sunday' is still a stirring piece of propagandist pop and a case study in the limitations of agitprop as artistry. Of course, the very nature of agitprop is to cause reaction and it is almost always built on subjective outrage rather than polite objectivity. Those who complain about Lennon's writings on Ireland fail to appreciate the power of agitprop as a political tool. This was certainly not missed by the IRA which recognized the power of Lennon's words and attempted to win his support in advancing their cause against imperialist Britain. Lennon also felt that many critics were short-sighted and did not understand the importance of simply getting an angry missive on record at the earliest opportunity. "Here I am in New York," he told the *NME*'s Roy Carr, "and I hear about 13 people shot dead in Northern Ireland and I react immediately. And, being what I am, I react in four-to-the-bar with a guitar break in the middle. I don't say, 'My God, what's happening? We should do something.' I go: 'It was Sunday Bloody Sunday and they shot the people down . . .'"

Beneath the anti-imperialist taunts, Lennon was also advocating his usual message of waking up the workers to the wonders of socialism. "They're dreaming someone else's dream, it's not even their own. They should realize that the blacks and the Irish are being harassed and repressed and they will be next. As soon as they can start being aware of all that, we can really begin to do something. The workers can start to take over."

Luck Of The Irish

Lennon and Ono's second Irish song on the album originally began as a folk tune and the retention of a flute and waltz-time arrangement indicates its transition into a more pop mode. The chorus, in which the legendary luck of the Irish is seen as bad enough to encourage fantasies of English nationality, may seem condescending to some, but sounds typical of Lennon's acerbic and ironic wit. Structurally, the verses are split between two perspectives, with Yoko presenting a naïve, picture postcard view of Ireland, complete with corny references to leprechauns and the Blarney Stone, not dissimilar to a Hollywood Glockamorra. Some of her similes and metaphors are over-ambitious and convoluted to the point of baffling. She conjures the making of chains with morning dew, the retention of voices like flowers in order to create a pandemic outbreak of shamrocks and a world as high as the Mountains of Mourne. Characteristically, Lennon counters with a harsher perspective, chronicling a thousand years of torture, hunger, and rape by the British brigands. He also reflects nostalgically about stories of Ireland heard during his youth in Liverpool.

The clever idea of alternating verses of sentimentality and stanzas of hard street rhetoric elevates the song from the limited confines of pure sloganeering. Despite some decorative imagery, this composition remains one of Lennon's most piercing political songs. During the fifth verse his vituperation turns to exasperation as he wonders what the hell the English are doing in Ireland anyway. He then takes on the mantle of a neo-radical Bob Dylan, fusing 'With God On Our Side' and 'Masters Of War' as he accuses the British authorities of black propaganda against the 'kids' and the IRA, while they freely commit 'genocide'. The outlandish genocide accusation is comparable to the overstated allusions to concentration camps in 'Sunday Bloody Sunday'. But who else but Lennon would then dare to offer the catchy punchline, 'Aye! Aye! Genocide', as if he was singing the carefree Beatles' refrain, 'Yeah, yeah, yeah'?

John Sinclair

The radical John Sinclair was a beat poet and founder of the magazine, *Guerrilla: A Monthly Newspaper Of Contemporary Kulchur*. He became Minister of Information for the White Panther Party and managed the MC5, whose controversial album *Kick Out The Jams* brought the rhetoric of the political/musical underground to the mainstream rock community. In 1969, Sinclair was arrested for selling marijuana to an undercover policeman. Although the haul consisted of a mere two joints, Sinclair was sentenced to an outrageous term of 10 years' imprisonment. He had already served two-and-a-half years before the intervention of John Lennon, who attended a 'Free John Sinclair' rally at the Chrysler Arena, Ann Arbor, Michigan on 10 December 1971. The event, which featured Stevie Wonder on the bill, was captured on celluloid, but the film, provisionally titled *Ten For Two*, was not released.

Lennon closed his segment of the show with 'John Sinclair', written specially for the evening. Sinclair was freed within 55 hours of the concert, which partly testified to the potency of the protest. Prior to the performance, Lennon recorded this studio version of the song, which was subsequently doctored by Phil Spector. Undercover agents from the FBI kept a vigilant eye on Lennon's political and musical activities during this period and one report noted that this track "probably will become a million seller . . . but it is lacking Lennon's usual standards". Alas, the FBI's resident rock critic failed to appreciate Lennon's wonderful dobro playing, which provides the song with a musical clout missing from some of the other tracks on this album. Lyrically, it's simple, provocative and thought-provoking with a catchy refrain contrasting the sentence with the offence and a grand finale in which Lennon chants 'gotta' 15 times before adding 'set him free'. Lennon rams home his point by using the rhetoric of revolution (Sinclair must be saved from the 'Man') and frequently mentioning the prisoner's name, while questioning the actions of the 'judges' who end up as 'bastards' in the final verse.

Angela

Lennon's next campaign concerned black radical feminist Angela Davis, who had allegedly supplied firearms which were used by 17-year-old Jonathan Jackson to free his Black Panther brother George Jackson and two associates. During George's trial the younger brother drew a gun, then kidnapped the judge, several jurors and the district attorney. The episode ended in carnage with prison guards besieging a van, resulting in the deaths of Judge Harold Haley and Jonathan Jackson, among others. Angela Davis was subsequently arrested and charged with conspiracy, kidnapping and homicide. She was later acquitted of all charges, but spent 16 months incarcerated in the Women's Detention Center in New York. Lennon and Ono completed this protest while she awaited trial. It's a pleasant melody enhanced by the sheen of Phil Spector's production, with Stan Bronstein's saxophone and Adam Ippolito's organ sound prominent. Yoko takes the lead vocal which is impressive enough, but the words sound rushed and unfocused. The Ono influence is evident in the reference to a wind that never dies, but elsewhere the lyrics shift from extravagant (Angela is one of *millions* of political prisoners) to amusingly banal (rhyming 'coffee and tea' with 'equality' and the 'jailhouse key'). During the same period, the Rolling Stones released their own tribute to Davis, 'Sweet Black Angel', on the double album *Exile On Main Street*.

Lennon's views on prison reform were becoming increasingly ambitious and eccentric. During this period, he enjoyed a playful rivalry with the Rolling Stones' Mick Jagger. While being filmed for the documentary *Aquarius*, Lennon combined both concerns, pro-claiming: "Our job now is to tell them there is still hope and we still have things to do and we must get out now and change their heads and tell them it's OK. We can change it. It isn't over just because flower power didn't work. It's only the beginning. We're just in the inception of revolution. That's why we are going out on the road. All our shows will be free. All the money will go to prisoners or to poor people, so we'll collect no money for the performance. We hope to start touring in America and then eventually go around the world, and possibly to China too. For instance, we'd go to, say, Chicago and then, in the Chicago prison, half or a quarter of the money earned will go towards releasing the first 500 people alphabet-ically who couldn't get bail . . . So wherever we go, the show will arrive and we will release people in each tour. So possibly when the Stones are touring America for money, we'll be touring for free. What are you going to do about that, Mick?"

We're All Water

Yoko takes lead vocal on her third solo composition on the album. The lyrics can be traced back to her 1967 poem *Water Talk*, which contained the aphorisms and pantheistic philosophy discussed in the song. There are also references to President Nixon and Chairman Mao stripped naked, an idea visualized in a mock-up picture on the album's sleeve. Ono also offers a macabre analogy between the decomposing bodies of Marilyn Monroe and Lenny Bruce. Although the tune is not particularly memorable, the backing is hilarious. Bronstein's rasping sax and Yoko's vocal exclamations combine to create a sound which reproduces nothing less than the spirit of the Coasters and Johnny And The Hurricanes. Ono's inspired imitation of the yakety-yak sound is a wonderful meeting of avant-garde and pop, spread over seven minutes. It's a suitable romp with which to close the studio segment of the package.

Cold Turkey

The bonus album *Live Jam*, begins with the two songs featured by the Plastic Ono Band at the UNICEF Benefit, staged at London's Lyceum ballroom on 15 December 1969. "This song's about pain," Lennon announces as his makeshift supergroup, including George Harrison, Eric Clapton, Billy Preston and Keith Moon, tackle the harrowing drug song that the Beatles once rejected. Lennon screams in paroxysms of pain as his players provide a solid unvarying backbeat. As the song progresses, Lennon's voice gets wilder, re-enacting a roar that can be traced back as far as the tonsil-torturing 'Twist And Shout'. For Lennon, the live performances of the Plastic Ono Band provided a perfect format for interacting with the audience in a way that was never possible during his Beatles' days. "The original idea was that *you* are the Plastic Ono Band," he stressed. "They're not permanent and the audience is the band . . . If Yoko and I went on with the so-called Plastic Ono Band, instead of the audience just sitting there and waiting for us to perform like seals – let them be the star. Let's all groove together. When we performed with George, Eric and Delaney & Bonnie and everybody at the Lyceum I didn't care what the pop press said. It was a funky show. Some of the audience were right there with us . . . It was an amazing high. A 17-piece band. It's great with four musicians grooving but when you've got 17, it's something else. And when you've got the audience as well . . . The day we go on and the audience is the rhythm section, that's what I want. So it wouldn't matter if I was onstage or if I got fed up and went down in the audience for a bit too. Let's take turns being the big superstar."

Don't Worry Kyoko

What probably mystified audiences in 1969 can now be seen as a stunning finale by a greatly underrated performer. Setting the scene,

Yoko emerges from her white bag and announces, "John, I love you", then accuses, "Britain, you killed Hanratty, you murderers". Backed by gut-wrenching feedback, she loses herself in the 'Don't Worry Kyoko' mantra, which builds in intensity. As her screams increase in volume, the Plastic Ono Band find an enthralling three-chord groove, reinforced by a counter melody from Delaney & Bonnie's brass section. No punches are pulled as the spectators receive the full Yoko Ono vocal treatment in excess of 17 minutes. Heaven knows what the audience must have made of the evening. "The crowd must have been absolutely flabbergasted because there were 15 or 18 people onstage, with two drummers," recalls Alan White, who partnered Keith Moon during the performance. "We just jammed this one riff that developed and developed, and then came to a climax. It was amazing."

NME reviewer Alan Smith miscalculated the song's length, reckoning that it went on "for 40 minutes", then complaining that it "gave me one of the worst headaches I've suffered since I don't-know-when". Lennon was thrilled by the extraordinary performance and announced at the end of the show: "I thought it was fantastic. We play 1984 music. The Plastic Ono Band plays the unexpected. It could be 'Blue Suede Shoes' or it could be Beethoven's *Ninth*. I don't do Variety any more. I stopped that when I was with the Beatles."

Well (Baby Please Don't Go)
The second side of the *Live Jam* features Lennon and Ono guesting with Frank Zappa's Mothers Of Invention at the Fillmore East on 6 June 1971. It was a fascinating meeting between three people whose work had proven consistently challenging and controversial. Zappa had famously parodied the cover of the Beatles' *Sgt Pepper's Lonely Hearts Club Band* on the sleeve of the Mother Of Invention's *We're Only In It For The Money*, pinpricking what he regarded as pop's pomposity. The often acerbic Lennon evidently took no lasting offence and was probably amused by the parodic 'tribute'. Nevertheless, the notion of these cultural anarchists sharing a stage seemed novel, if not revolutionary, at the time. No warning was given to the audience about the arrival of John and Yoko, who

appeared onstage at the end of the Mothers' set. Some of the crowd were already leaving the Fillmore, unaware of the surprise encore guests. When word filtered through that John Lennon was onstage, many turned around and attempted to get back in. Deciding what to perform seemed largely spontaneous, although Zappa and Lennon found common ground in their appreciation of doo-wop and early rock 'n' roll.

"Hey, sit down and cool it for a minute so you can hear what we're going to do," Zappa tells the audience, then turns to his fellow players and warns, "And for those of you in the band who have no idea what's about to happen – this is in A-minor, and it's not standard blues changes, but it's close."

"This is a song I used to sing when I was in the Cavern in Liverpool," Lennon adds. "I haven't done it since, so . . ." What follows is the B-side to the Olympics' 1958 US Top 10 hit 'Western Movies', composed by the group's founder Walter Ward. Lennon's lead vocal is exceptionally strong, while Ono uses her screams as backing vocals. Zappa's guitar solo is also impressive, allowing Lennon the freedom to show us his greatness as a rock 'n' roll singer. This fine opening song stands up against anything on the better known *Rock 'n' Roll* album.

Jamrag
This screaming session merges with a cacophonous backing and meanders into a jam, with pianist Ian Underwood providing the familiar Zappa flavour. It's very much a case of Yoko Ono meets the Mothers. Although Lennon/Ono take full credit for the piece, the backing appears to be adapted from Zappa and the Mothers' 'King Kong'. But is this section part of 'Jamrag' or the succeeding 'Scumbag'? It is difficult to decide where the Lennons felt 'Jamrag' actually ended on the album. On the inner sleeve the track is timed as 1 minute 50 seconds, although it actually runs for approximately 5 minutes 36 seconds. When Frank Zappa reissued the Fillmore collaboration with the Lennons on his album *Playground Psychotics*, he made no mention of 'Jamrag' but instead transformed the jam into two separate songs, 'Say Please' and 'Aaawk', the credits of which read Lennon/Ono/Zappa.

Scumbag

The jam continues as Lennon shouts 'Scumbag' approximately 34 seconds in. Again, there is some discrepancy about where this song begins and 'Jamrag' ends. The inner sleeve times 'Scumbag' as 15 minutes which suggests that the Lennons saw the song actually beginning not just before Lennon announces 'Scumbag', but much earlier, amid the cacophony of Yoko's wail on 'Jamrag', prior to the 'King Kong' section. This might explain why Zappa receives a co-writing credit for 'Scumbag' while the Lennons alone are credited for what they saw as a two-minute 'Jamrag'. On Zappa's *Playground Psychotics*, 'Scumbag' is timed at 5 minutes 53 seconds, commencing close to Lennon's shouting of the title. Zappa also extends the writing credits to include Howard Kaylan.

The track has its humorous moments, most noticeably when Zappa demands a singalong from the audience. "All you gotta do is sing 'Scumbag'," he suggests, adding sarcastically, "Right on, brothers and sisters". Yoko can be heard in the background wailing from within the canvas bag that she had entered during the song. Overall, it sounds like an indulgent romp and enjoyable jam, but lacks enduring appeal as a concert memento.

Au

Feedback and electronic effects mesh together as Yoko utters a sound that resembles a wounded animal. On Zappa's *Playground Psychotics*, this track was sarcastically retitled 'A Small Eternity With Yoko Ono'. It's at times painful listening as Yoko takes us into that familiar refrain 'Don't Worry Kyoko', which by now has become something of a personal anthem. It seems as appropriate a way as any to conclude this much underrated and still unfashionable double album.

Some Time In New York City was belatedly reissued on CD in November 2005. Normally with such releases, the album is longer and usually contains some bonus tracks. Here, Yoko Ono reverses that tradition by shortening the album. Three tracks from the *Live Jam* disc ('Jamrag', 'Scumbag' and 'Au') have been excised. Presumably, there were copyright problems preventing the reappearance of the material featuring Frank Zappa.

Given the aesthetic debate surrounding *Some Time In New York City*, it was interesting to read how younger commentators reacted to the album 33 years after its original release. Judging from *NME*'s review, the once harsh judgements about Lennon's political material had been reversed, but those old prejudices about Yoko Ono's voice were still in evidence. Reviewer Mark Beaumont concluded that *Some Time In New York City* was "Lennon's most sizzling, politically striking and controversial solo work (check the PC-confounding 'Woman Is The Nigger Of The World', the pro-Irish independence anthems 'Sunday Bloody Sunday' and 'Luck Of The Irish', and 'John Sinclair' . . .)" but added that those songs were "damned by proximity to Ono's mawkish avant doo-wop 'tunes' ('Sisters O Sisters' and 'Born In A Prison') and 'singing' which resembles an oven full of geese being slowly gassed." Reviewing her decision to delete the *Live Jam* segment, he concluded cruelly: "Had she instead taken the decision to edit *herself* out of the album she would have an instant classic." While the vilification of Yoko Ono was a little surprising (her work has been retrospectively championed by other critics), it was gratifying to read the words "instant classic" applied to Lennon's political compositions. Whatever else, it demonstrated that songs which had once been dismissed by critics as ephemeral and fatally trapped in 1972 had considerably longer lasting appeal.

In order to compensate for the loss of the Zappa collaboration on *Live Jam*, Yoko Ono might have raided the vaults for outtakes, such as her and Lennon's unorthodox attempts at the Elvis Presley hits 'Don't Be Cruel' and 'Hound Dog'. Instead, saving herself from additional castigation by *NME*'s young critic, she took the more conservative option of featuring both sides of a classic single.

Listen, The Snow Is Falling

The UK B-side of 'Happy Xmas (War Is Over)' was an odd addition to the work as it had already appeared as a bonus track on the reissue of *Wedding Album*. Presumably, this duplication was either the result of a failure of memory or a lack of Ono B-side material from the same period. 'Sisters O Sisters' had appeared as the flip of 'Woman Is The Nigger Of The World' but, of course, the former was already on *Some Time In New York City*. That left two other candidates, 'Open Your Box' and 'Touch Me' (the UK and US B-sides to 'Power To The People', respectively) but as they had been issued over a year before this album, they were presumably considered unrepresentative of the era in question. Such quibbles aside, 'Listen, The Snow Is Falling' is still a welcome addition, particularly as sales of *Wedding Album* were relatively slight. It remains one of Yoko Ono's most accessible B-sides and a beautiful Christmas anthem.

Happy Xmas (War Is Over)

One of the greatest Christmas songs ever written, this composition began life as a poster campaign. In December 1969, the Lennons bought billboard space in 12 cities, including London, New York, Hollywood, Toronto, Berlin, Paris, Rome, Tokyo and Athens. Their message proclaimed: 'War Is Over! If You Want It. Happy Christmas From John & Yoko'. Almost two years on, the duo decided to record a seasonal single, using the slogan as their theme. It was a remarkable record in many ways, not least because it allowed Phil Spector to show off the same production talents that had graced his 1963 festive celebration *A Christmas Gift To You*. With the Lennons, he provided the familiar sleigh bells and tight harmonies, even recruiting the 30-piece Harlem Community Choir to spectacular effect. The choir parts were completed at an afternoon session in order to accommodate the young singers, aged between four and 12. Lennon momentarily adopted the role of school teacher, patiently reciting the lyrics while pointing to a blackboard. Afterwards, the entire ensemble gathered around a plastic Christmas tree for a photo that later adorned the front cover of the single. Lyrically, Lennon revealed himself as a master of ambiguity with the arresting opening line to the song, which seemed both reflective and accusative: 'And so this is Christmas/And what have *you* done?'

The only regrettable feature of the record was the tardy release date. "As usual, we messed it up," Lennon admitted. "We recorded it a bit too late. We almost missed the Christmas market that year."

This was no exaggeration. Amazingly, the single failed to enter the US Top 40, which was a terrible injustice.

Equally disappointing was its delayed release in the UK due to the dispute over Ono's writing credit. As manager Allen Klein explained at the time: "John and Yoko were quite prepared to allow their Christmas single to be issued in Britain, and for the royalties to go into court, leaving the eventual distribution to the judge. But this compromise was not acceptable."

MIND GAMES

Released: November 1973

Original UK issue: Apple PCS 7165. US issue: Apple SW 3414. CD reissue with
bonus tracks: EMI 5 42425 2 (UK)/Capitol CDP 5 42425 2 (US)

Following the release of *Some Time In New York City*, John and Yoko
slimmed down their public appearances, although not before topping
the bill at Madison Square Garden for the celebrated One To One
concerts for mentally handicapped children. These were to be John
Lennon's sole full-scale shows following the break-up of the Beatles
and the last time he appeared onstage with Yoko. At one point a live
album was scheduled, but it was placed on indefinite hold and would
not be salvaged until as late as 1986 for the posthumous release, *Live
In New York City*.

With Lennon's immigration status increasingly dominating their
lives, the pair decided to curtail their political activities, although
there were fleeting appearances, including a solidarity showing at a
demonstration outside the South Vietnamese Embassy in Washington and the launching of a campaign for the reprieve of Michael X.
Lennon also attended the Watergate hearings and watched with fascination as the counter-culture's arch nemesis was unmasked before
the nation.

For most of this period though, Lennon retreated to the staid daily
regulation of apartment life, having moved into the Dakota building
on West 72nd Street in February 1973. Creatively, he remained in
the artistic doldrums. While Yoko Ono issued the double album
Approximately Infinite Universe, her most accomplished solo work to
date, John hit a dry writing patch, made worse by a singular lack of
motivation. "I either write songs or I don't," he blithely explained at
the time. "It's getting to be work. It's ruining the music. Every time I
strap on a guitar, it's the same old jazz. I just feel like breathing a bit."

Despite these protestations against the work ethic, Lennon felt
obligated to do *something* and roused himself sufficiently to enter

New York's Record Plant East studio in the hope of completing a new album. Initially the news was encouraging. It transpired that Lennon was abandoning the overt agitprop of *Some Time In New York City* and recording a more orthodox album without assistance from Yoko. Hopes were high for a return to the tuneful craftsmanship of *Imagine* or, even better, the stark soul searching of *John Lennon/Plastic Ono Band*.

Unfortunately, the new album proved severely anticlimactic. Most of the songs were written in the weeks prior to the sessions and lacked the depth and quality of his better studio work, without the concomitant merits usually provided by spontaneity. In interviews of the period, Lennon openly revealed that he was far from confident about the album's merits and betrayed a lack of enthusiasm for the project that was worryingly apathetic. Most artists 'talk up' an album on release, but Lennon seemed ready to throw in the towel, as if challenging reviewers to confirm that he was a spent force. *Melody Maker*'s Chris Charlesworth gleaned the following information from the world-weary ex-Beatle: "The album's called *Mind Games* and it's, well, just an album. It's rock 'n' roll at different speeds. It's not a political album, or an introspective album . . . There's no deep message about it . . . The only reason I make albums is because you're supposed to . . . I haven't really got into somebody's album since I was into Elvis Presley and Carl Perkins, and even then singles were always the best."

Although Lennon may have been attempting to shrug off his radicalism in the hope of regaining some of his mainstream audience, his comments testify to an overwhelming disillusionment with the entire music business. At different times, Lennon responded to such feelings with works of cynicism, introspection or lacerating rage. Here, he seemed largely numb to new ideas, an artiste going through the motions, as though under contractual obligation to complete a work that he knew was largely lacklustre. He later described the album as "an interim record between being a manic lunatic and back to being a musician again".

The album's cover artwork seemed to sum up Lennon's detached state of mind. His superimposed image is shown walking away, with

bag packed, from the mountainous face of Yoko, whose visage dominates the surrounding landscape. At the time of the record's release,
Lennon was staying in Los Angeles, but he insisted there was no rift
in their relationship. "We get a little tense in the studio together, but
that's not to say we won't ever do another album," he told Chris
Charlesworth. "If we do an album, or a film, or a bed-in or whatever,
that's just the way we feel at the moment. We're playing life by ear,
and that includes our careers. We occasionally take a bath together
and occasionally separately. Yoko has just started a five-day engagement in a club in New York. She's over there rehearsing and I'm
letting her get on with it in her own way . . . Now I know people are
calling from England suggesting we've split up. It's not so. All that
scares us about being apart is whether something happens to us. Our
minds are tied-in together . . . Her energy is so much greater than
mine that I just let her get on with things."

Mind Games was not a complete failure. Indeed, the title track
clearly showed Lennon at his best and many purchasers must have
bought the album on the strength of that song alone. There are some
other promising moments on the album, but overall the work sounds
disconcertingly half-baked, with little sparkle in the production. It
was difficult to avoid the conclusion that Lennon had allowed too
much filler to clog up the album, amid a general air of apathy. If he
had exercised greater quality control and attempted to compose
material to equal the power and beauty of the album's title track, then
this would surely have been a major release. As it stands, it represents
Lennon at his most frustratingly ordinary, an artiste adrift in the early
Seventies without an agenda. He was not alone. 1973 represented a
chilling watershed for many former counter-cultural heroes suddenly
faced with an uncertain future.

Two telling statistics from the period summed up the current state
of ex-Beatledom. It was no surprise that Paul McCartney's *Band On
The Run* topped the US/UK charts as the year closed, while Lennon
had to be content with US number 9 and UK number 13. What was
more revealing was watching Ringo Starr's *Ringo* outstripping
Lennon's effort on both sides of the Atlantic. With George Harrison's
Living In The Material World having topped the US charts and

climbed to number 2 in the UK several months before, the figures spoke for themselves. Lennon was now, unarguably, selling fewer records than any of the other Beatles and, this time around, critics could not blame Yoko Ono or radical politics.

Mind Games

Undoubtedly the stand-out track on the album and a fine single as well, this saw Lennon at his hippie apotheosis. In proclaiming that love is the answer he pointedly reaffirms the message of both 'The Word' and 'All You Need Is Love'. Originally, the track was to be titled 'Make Love, Not War' but as Lennon explained, "That was such a cliché that you couldn't say it any more, so I wrote it obscurely. But it's all the same story." In place of the 'make love not war' sloganeering, which is reduced to a coda here, Lennon introduces some of his most extravagant lyrical flourishes, including the metaphysical notion of mind guerrillas, whose 'soul power' is put to the 'karmic wheel'. He also speaks of the search for the Holy Grail and speculates upon projections into space and time, as though he were a science fiction writer. Some of the lyrics were clearly influenced by the prose of Robert Masters and Jean Houston's consciousness-raising *Mind Games*, which Lennon credited as one of three important books he had read in the last couple of years, along with Arthur Janov's *The Primal Scream* and Yoko Ono's *Grapefruit*.

The continuing influence of Yoko lay beneath the surface of the lyrics. Indeed, the very notion of 'mind games' in its later colloquial sense, aptly described their interaction, particularly during their first meeting on 9 November 1966 at London's Indica Gallery. In the programme notes to the 1967 exhibition *Yoko Plus Me (Half-A-Wind)*, which Lennon sponsored but was otherwise uninvolved in, Ono recalled a playful example of mind games: "When 'Hammer And Nail' painting was exhibited at Indica Gallery, a person came and asked if it was all right to hammer a nail in the painting. I said it was all right, if he pays five shillings. Instead of paying the five shillings, he asked if it was all right for him to hammer an imaginary nail. That was John Lennon. I thought, 'So I met a guy who plays the same game I played.'" In a 1971 re-enactment of that gallery event Lennon was filmed climbing a ladder to read a message on a card through a magnifying glass. It read: 'Yes'. The singer was strangely impressed by the positive sentiments, which convinced him that Yoko was worthy of his patronage. Now, in the title track of this album, he chose to confirm with emphasis: '*Yes* is the answer.'

'Mind Games' was among the strongest Lennon tracks of the decade. The lingering influence of Phil Spector was evident in the cascading rhythm and juxtaposition of simple riffs and harmonic changes, all of which echoed his familiar Wall Of Sound. "That was a fun track," Lennon noted, "because the voice is in stereo and the seeming orchestra on it is just me playing three notes with slide guitar. And the middle eight is reggae. Trying to explain to American musicians what reggae was in 1973 was pretty hard."

The only frustrating feature of 'Mind Games' is that it was used to head an album that it could not possibly carry alone. 'Cold Turkey' or 'Instant Karma!' never had this responsibility. They were considered solely as singles. In earlier times, 'Mind Games' would probably have been treated the same way, but by 1973 the idea of a pure single was old hat. This was bad news for Lennon whose grounding was in the production of classic singles, a process that had been carried through from the Beatles to the early Plastic Ono Band. Cynical changes in the record industry meant that artistes were no longer encouraged to issue singles separately, but instead use the format as a taster for the all-important album. Unfortunately, this also meant that they could lazily use a single as a promotional device to push a minor collection of songs in the same way that performers and record companies did in the pre-Beatles era. 'Mind Games' was not that exploitative, having only climbed to number 26 in the UK and reached number 18 in the US. But there is no doubt that many people bought *Mind Games* on the strength of a classic single whose quality promised an album of greatness. Ironically, the work in its entirety might have been better appreciated without the burden of its brilliant lead track which serves only to highlight the musical paucity of the meagre fare that follows. After 'Mind Games' everything sounds shallow and disappointing. Unfortunately, the temptation is to blame Lennon for failing to reach similar heights throughout. Perhaps if the title track had been placed at the end of the album rather than the beginning, in reverse of normal marketing procedure, it might have given the other songs herein a chance to breathe.

Tight A$

The pun in the title, complete with pointed typography, was typical Lennon. In case we failed to appreciate the humour he included a suggestive sketch to illustrate the anal aspects of the title. Musically, the song revisited Lennon's early rockabilly interests, anticipating the *Rock 'n' Roll* album that would be completed at a later date. In his mind, though, the song was closer to the Tex Mex sound popularized by Sir Douglas Quintet and others. The vocal is compressed through the use of echo in obvious tribute to Sam Phillips' Sun singles. Sneaky Pete Kleinow, formerly of the Flying Burrito Brothers, provides the steel guitar which adds a country blues tinge at a time when country rock was at its fashionable peak. Lennon's phrasing transforms a basic tune into a mildly pleasing romp.

Aisumasen (I'm Sorry)

Lennon's humble apology to Yoko Ono in Japanese recalled the sentiments of 'Jealous Guy', albeit with simpler lyrics. Lennon openly borrows from the Beatles' lexicon of song titles, fusing 'All I've Got To Do' and 'I Call Your Name' to fashion a chorus. There's also a reprise of the lyrics to 'I Found Out' in the references to the necessity of feeling your own pain. Lennon sounds vulnerable, guilt-ridden and spiritually lost, seemingly as detached from Yoko as the miniature figure on the album's front cover. It is fascinating to consider that this composition started as a testament to his resilience, but ended up with all such positive attributes reversed. By shifting the pronouns used on the original demo, Lennon turned a song about strength and independence into an admission of childlike dependence, with Yoko as the sole panacea to his malaise. Ken Ascher's attractive piano accompaniment and a sterling performance from guitarist David Spinozza retain listener interest throughout. On an otherwise patchy album, this was one of the stronger tracks.

One Day (At A Time)

Presumably directed at Yoko Ono, this paean to the paradoxical nature of their love had unintended dramatic irony, for we now know that she was about to be replaced in his life by a new companion, May Pang. The song's title recalled that of Lena Martell's hit 'One Day At A Time', which cried out to Jesus for spiritual assistance. It also echoed the mantra of recovering alcoholics. Unfortunately, Lennon's composition fails to live up to the promise of its title. The lyrics aren't exactly Cole Porter as Lennon's analogies frequently fall into comic bathos. At times he seems to be imitating Ono's writing style (the fish and sea references recall her use of nature imagery) but whereas she mixed cliché, aphorisms and clumsy word construction to create something unusual, Lennon never gets beyond the platitudinous here. By his standards, this was a bland tune with maudlin lyrics, made worse by an irritating falsetto, which sounds like a failed attempt to parody Yoko Ono's high register. Despite an uplifting saxophone break from Michael Brecker towards the end, it fails to enliven.

Bring On The Lucie (Freda Peeple)

"All right boys, this is it! Over the hill!" Lennon announces at the start of the track. It is almost as if he realizes that the album needs to be awakened from its slumber with a rousing anthem. No commentator, myself included, has ever explained what Lennon meant or was referring to in the word 'Lucie', but the parenthetic addendum to 'free the people' is self-explanatory. Fuelled by fears of deportation, Lennon responded to his detractors with a political broadcast directed at the US government. Paraphrasing the opening lines of 'Imagine', Lennon creates his own utopia in which there are no borders, immigration controls or restrictions placed on individuals. Using the famous catchphrase and title of yippie Jerry Rubin's autobiography, Lennon urges us to 'Do it!'

In the succeeding verses, Lennon addresses recent political events in what sounds like a vicious attack on President Richard Nixon. Lennon briefly attended the Watergate hearings before retiring to his apartment to watch the proceedings on television. Here, the reference to being caught 'with your hands in the kill' (a pun on 'till') suggests both dishonesty and carnage in the same breath. The allusion to sliding down the hill on the blood of people killed also combines Watergate with the aftermath of the Vietnam War. Yet, Lennon holds back from actually naming Nixon, leaving us only with some vague references to 'paranoia' and an unidentified evil presence ('666'). The following year Neil Young was credited with some similarly uncertain Nixon bashing when using the phrase 'I never knew a man could tell so many lies' ('Ambulance Blues'), even though he never identified the subject by name in the song or in interviews, despite having shown no such reticence in the finger-pointing 'Ohio'. In later years, Lennon admitted: "It was bell, book and candle against Mr 666 Nixon. We used magic, prayer and children to fight the good fight."

Lyrically, 'Bring On The Lucie' may have been naïve but the same could be said for most of Lennon's political songs. At least here he sounds as exhilarated and committed as the fist-raising rabble-rouser on 'Power To The People'. Musically the backing track recalls George Harrison's 'My Sweet Lord' via the Chiffons' 'He's So Fine' with some appealing steel guitar from Sneaky Pete.

Nutopian International Anthem
The first half of the album closes with the shortest track in the Lennon canon: six seconds of silence, no less. This was the second occasion on which Lennon had used silence as an artistic expression, having previously dealt with the concept at greater length on 'Two Minutes Silence' from *Life With The Lions*. The idea of a Nutopian International Anthem without a sound was appropriate, inasmuch as the Greek word for Utopia literally means 'nowhere' or 'no place'. Nutopia, like Thomas More's *Utopia*, is an unrealizable ideal, but rather fun to imagine. It was typical of John and Yoko to respond to the realities of Lennon's threatened deportation not merely by campaigning publicly but by escaping into the sanctuary of their imaginations. Coerced by the hard hand of officialdom, they called a press conference at which the Declaration of Nutopia (reprinted on the album sleeve) was read. Its whimsical conceit was mildly amusing:

"We announce the birth of a conceptual country, NUTOPIA . . . NUTOPIA has no land, no boundaries, no passports, only people. NUTOPIA has no laws other than cosmic." The notion of a 'conceptual country' owed much to Yoko Ono's conceptual art which required a similar leap of the imagination on the part of the viewer, while the 'nutopian' sentiments echoed Lennon's daydream theories in 'Imagine'.

"Imagine there was a time when you didn't need a passport to go from country to country," Lennon was still saying in his final interview in 1980. "Really! It used to be that you could go around, you know. What is this game that somehow this is America and just across the field is Canada, and that you have to have all kinds of papers and posters and stamps and passports?"

Intuition
This affirmation of the power of intuition alludes to Lennon's love of music as a lamplight in the darkness and the need to survive life's vicissitudes. Pleasant, catchy but insubstantial, it sounds suspiciously like filler on an album that urgently needs a higher ratio of strong songs. The bland, plinkety-plonk tune, set against an ersatz ragtime arrangement, underlines the song's sentiments. Ironically, Lennon's intuitive grasp of musical structure and composition lets him down here for although the craftsmanship is evident, nothing of substance emerges. The final verse in which he refers to himself as down and out with nothing to say sums up this song all too accurately.

Out The Blue
The theme of this song is summed up in Lennon's accompanying lithograph which recreates the album's rear cover in starker form. Lennon looks like a recalcitrant dog, hunched down in retreat from Yoko's giant scolding eyes. The song, which begins as a simple acoustic number, ends up using gospel, country and choral to support its slight construction. Lyrically, Lennon switches uneasily from gruesome metaphor (the description of his life as a 'long slow knife') to a wacky simile (comparing his loved one to a UFO). He seems thankful to have survived long enough to make Yoko his wife and

fulfil the dream of 'one mind, one destiny'. Despite some good ideas and an adequate production and band effort, the composition sounds very much like a song that has not been fully developed lyrically. Like other material on the album it gives the strong impression of work completed rapidly to order. Paradoxically, it might have been even better if the song had been left in a starker state without the gospel chorus and full-on production. Deconstructing the composition to its original demo state allows Lennon's vocal passion to emerge unobtrusively.

Only People

This song of optimism recalled Ono's adage 'Only people can change the world' and Lennon's mantra 'Nothing's gonna change my world' (from 'Across The Universe'). Unfortunately, the 'right on', Rubin-influenced 'Do it!' lyrics sound terribly dated and there is even a moment of comic camp radicalism when Lennon announces to his followers that they don't need 'no pig brother scene!' Similarly, the sound is very much like mainstream studio rock of the early to mid-Seventies and largely devoid of Lennon's distinctive imprint and musical edge. He later admitted that the song was a failure, adding: "It was a good lick, but I couldn't ever get the words to make sense."

I Know (I Know)

This reflective acoustic ballad is one of the better songs on the album. Lyrically, the *mea culpa* sentiments and admissions of guilt recall 'Aisumasen (I'm Sorry)' while the fears about failing to communicate with his loved one echo parts of 'Intuition'. More than simply a love song to Yoko, the composition testifies to Lennon's own vulnerability and insecurities in a series of convoluted lines. There's an acceptance of passing time and emerging wisdom ending in the same conclusion as 'God' that the only reality is belief in himself and Yoko, with whom he shares his mind. Not that Lennon expressed any great enthusiasm in the final interviews of his life where he dismissed the composition as "a piece of nothing". For those who feel that the Lennon of 1973 was merely a pop craftsman writing material not dissimilar to that of Paul McCartney during the same period, it might be worth noting that in the final two verses the lyrics mention both 'Yesterday' and 'It's Getting Better'.

You Are Here

Building on the John and Yoko myth, this attempts a spiritual fusion of East and West, as Lennon brings together the two cities of Liverpool and Tokyo as a grand symbol of his immemorial, romantic love. Along the way, he reverses Rudyard Kipling's adage 'East is East and West is West, and never the twain shall meet'. Steel guitar dominates, adding a Hawaiian air to the proceedings. The song's title came from *You Are Here: To Yoko From John Lennon*, the 1968 art exhibition that Lennon held at the Robert Fraser Gallery. Patrons were confronted by a number of charity collection boxes and a large white canvas on which the words 'You Are Here' were inscribed in small lettering. Students at the Hornsey College of Art mischievously despatched a rusty bicycle on which they attached the message: "This exhibit was inadvertently left out." Lennon subsequently included their 'work' in the show. He also released 365 white helium-filled balloons containing plain postcards addressed to himself care of the gallery. Many of the replies received contained disparaging remarks about Yoko Ono and castigated Lennon for leaving his wife. Critical reaction to the exhibition was lukewarm at best, but Yoko offered a sterling tribute saying, "I don't think he had done too much avant-garde artwork but, when he did, he was excellent [and] above the level of many so-called avant-garde friends." While the song 'You Are Here' betrayed none of the avant-garde daring of the show, it at least offered an attractive melody which would later provide the musical inspiration for 'Beautiful Boy'.

Meat City

The album ends with this playfully acerbic and rocky finale. Set against a stirring arrangement, with plenty of guitar, Lennon offers a parody of jive talking with a satirical view of American consumerism gone mad. In the final verse there's a surprise shift of place from West to East as he announces his wish to visit China. Those words were in sharp contrast to his interview quotes in 1969, when he said: "I'm scared of going to Vietnam or Biafra and, until I'm convinced that I'd do better there than I can do outside of it, I'll stay out. I'd go to Russia but I'd think twice about China because I don't want to be a martyr. I'd like to play it safe and be around." Three years later, he was voicing the pro-China views evident on 'Meat City': "I will take the opportunity to try and see Mao. If he is ill or dead or refuses to see me, too bad. But if I go there I want to meet people who are doing something important. I want to take a rock band to China. That is really what I want to do. To play rock in China. They have yet to see that."

The lyrics of 'Meat City' provide fond memories of the Beatles' 'Back In The USSR', albeit minus that song's wit, forceful melody or inspired arrangement. So ends a frustratingly erratic album which would surely have been better if only Lennon had been more discriminating in his choice of material and production values.

In November 2002, *Mind Games* was reissued as a digitally remixed and remastered CD with three bonus tracks:

Aisumasen (I'm Sorry) [home version]

The title of this track is a misnomer as at this stage in 1971 it was still titled 'Call My Name'. Significantly, the guilty sentiments evoked in the title have yet to be written. Instead of 'Aisumasen' Lennon sings about easing his lover's pain, taking on the role of protector and saviour. The pronoun change from 'you' to 'I' in the finished song transforms what was originally an assertive lyric into a song of submission. Hearing this early version is a revelation of sorts. Far more naked in its bleak, acoustic setting, it suggests that some of the slighter songs on *Mind Games* might have sounded superior in a less produced state.

Bring On The Lucie (Freda Peeple) [home version]

This one-minute home demo, minus verses, shows Lennon working on the 'free the people' chorus. In common with his work on *Some Time In New York City*, there's a suggestion that we should 'kill the judges', although this allusion was excised from the final version.

Meat City [home version]

Captured in its raw acoustic state, this was simply a couple of blues chords bathed in microphone echo, but the basic song is clearly there. In its earliest form, the composition was known as 'Shoeshine', in deference to its swishy, boogie rhythm. "Oh, it is on," Lennon remarks at the end, seemingly unaware that he was being recorded.

WALLS AND BRIDGES

Released: October 1974

Original UK issue: Apple PCTC 254. US issue: Apple PCTC 254. CD reissue
with bonus tracks: EMI 3 409712 3 (UK)/Capitol 3 409712 3 (US)

While considering a follow-up to the largely disappointing *Mind Games*, Lennon became deeply involved in a publishing dispute which was to have serious repercussions on his recording schedule for the best part of two years. Morris Levy, one of the most voracious collectors of US artistes' copyrights, owned many of the classic rock 'n' roll hits of the Fifties, including the Chuck Berry standard 'You Can't Catch Me', part of which Lennon had borrowed for the Beatles' 'Come Together'. In 1970, Lennon admitted plagiarizing the song in an interview, and Levy's publishing company Big Seven Music responded with a lawsuit, seeking damages for unlawful appropriation. The defendants, Apple, initially took a combative stance, arguing that the similarities between the songs were incidental, boiling down to "five non-consecutive words" and not much more. The indefatigable Levy was never likely to be shaken off and the legal fencing continued for the next three years until a court appearance proved inevitable.

Like everyone else in the music business, Lennon was well aware of Levy's awesome reputation and exotic history. As a night-club owner, record company executive, promoter and publisher, Levy was a one-man metaphor of the American music industry. It was well known in New York circles that he had entered into clandestine arrangements with various underworld figures. Among these was Tommy Eboli, acting head of the Genovese family and one of the most feared Mafia men in the city. Eboli had a fierce temper and once served a prison sentence for assaulting a boxing referee who had dared award a points victory against his fighter Rocky Castellaini. There was nothing subtle about the assault. Eboli had simply climbed into the ring and laid out the official in full view of the spectators and the police. Eboli had interests in various restaurants, night-clubs, vending machines, juke-boxes and even a record company Promo Records, which specialized in 'cut out' albums. He was not a man to be crossed, and neither was Levy.

Since the Fifties, when Levy received an unlikely co-writing credit on Frankie Lymon & The Teenagers' classic 'Why Do Fools Fall In Love?', he had fully demonstrated his understanding of the economics of song publishing. By establishing Roulette Records and expanding his empire, he made enough money to buy various publishing concerns ensuring that Big Seven was one of the most powerful independents of its time with an estimated 30,000 titles under its control.

With various legal matters pending, not least an elongated battle with US immigration, Lennon found himself worn down by the Levy issue and instructed his lawyers to barter an ingenious settlement. Rather than fighting the action to completion through the courts, Lennon agreed to record three tunes owned by Big Seven Music on his next album – 'You Can't Catch Me', 'Angel Baby' and 'Ya Ya'. For Levy, the likely financial windfall from this arrangement proved irresistible.

From a critical standpoint, the prospect of three rock 'n' roll songs on a Lennon album would probably have provoked accusations of artistic atrophy, especially coming after the relatively disappointing *Mind Games*. However, if Lennon went ahead with a complete album of cover songs, he could claim that the work was a special edition and a fully realized concept in itself. Other artistes of the era, most notably David Bowie, had released such work and enjoyed considerable success. With no prospect of progressing musically with his present output, a rock 'n' roll album might provide a happy distraction and rekindle his creative fire. Yoko Ono recognized as much, arguing that he was not yet ready to express his emotional turbulence in song.

Lennon always loved playing rock 'n' roll. Even his return to the stage with the Plastic Ono Band had taken place at a rock 'n' roll festival in Toronto. "I like rock 'n' roll, man," he insisted. "I don't like much else. That's the music that inspired me to play music. There is nothing conceptually better than rock 'n' roll. No group, be it the Beatles, Dylan or the Rolling Stones, has improved on 'Whole Lotta Shakin' Goin' On' for my money."

Although Lennon would not be recording any Jerry Lee Lewis material, he had enough classic songs in mind to begin the covers project in earnest towards the end of 1973. In order to create an authentic Fifties' sound, Lennon placed himself in the hands of producer Phil Spector, who was given full artistic control. What seemed an excellent idea subsequently backfired when the sessions degenerated into a drunken fiasco with Lennon regularly downing bottles of brandy. The fiasco ended when the increasingly erratic Spector absconded with the tapes. Months passed and, with no news forthcoming from Spector, Lennon decided to abandon the project and write some new songs. He had just entered the recording studio to work on a new album when the Spector tapes were belatedly retrieved. When Lennon played them back he was shocked by some of his drunken performances and, worse still, realized that Spector's Wall Of Sound method of recording meant that the worst moments could not be isolated and wiped.

Rather than re-record the songs from scratch, Lennon preferred to forget Phil Spector, Morris Levy and rock 'n' roll and forge ahead with his new work. The title *Walls And Bridges* was inspired by a phrase he heard on television one evening: "Bridges you get over, walls you walk into." In Lennon's mind, it was symbolic: walls suggested protection, bridges offered escape. And anybody who had witnessed Lennon's life over the previous year could testify to his entrapment between each state. He had split with Yoko Ono and moved to Los Angeles to pursue and suffer what he later described as his "lost weekend".

The separation was a mysteriously calculated affair masterminded by Yoko, who had even provided John with a working companion, her assistant May Pang. "Extraordinary circumstances call for extraordinary solutions," Ono explained. When the arrangement was first mooted, Pang was astonished. "I couldn't believe what I was hearing. I did not want Yoko to think I had anything to do with her problems and, almost as if she could read my mind, she said: 'May, it's OK . . . Don't worry' . . . From everything I knew of John and Yoko together,

Yoko had the uncanny ability to make him do anything she wanted. Yoko's coolness shocked me."

Once in LA, Lennon swiftly hit a downward spiral, drinking frequently and playing the boorish rock star in public. During one well-publicized evening at the Troubadour, Lennon confirmed that he was now romantically involved with May Pang, kissing her with evident relish. Yoko's reaction was not recorded. Tales of his wayward exploits filled gossip columns and, with fellow drinker Harry Nilsson egging him on, Lennon soon became a *cause célèbre*. "Suddenly I was out on my own," he recalled. "The next thing I'd be waking up drunk in strange places or reading about myself in the paper doing extraordinary things, half of which I'd done and half of which I hadn't. And finding myself in a mad dream for a year. I'd been in many mad dreams, but this was pretty wild." In more defensive mode, he pithily noted: "So I was drunk. When it's Errol Flynn, the showbiz writers say, 'Those were the days when men were men.' When I do it, I'm a bum."

Even as a bum, Lennon was surprisingly creative. He produced the album *Pussy Cats* for Nilsson and soon turned the darker moments of his lost weekend into a series of strong songs. Instead of the desultory material that had weakened *Mind Games*, Lennon found himself penning some of his best work of the decade. He recoiled in disbelief at his unlikely ability to forge such a well-crafted and consistent record amid the chaos of his personal life. "I'm almost amazed that I could get anything out," he later admitted. "But I enjoyed doing *Walls And Bridges* and it wasn't hard when I had the whole thing to go into the studio and do it . . . I'm just glad that something came out. It's describing the year, in a way, but it's not as sort of schizophrenic as the year really was."

Confronting his confused relationships and wayward antics, Lennon produced an album of contrasting emotional moods. It provided fascinating listening. Musically, it was a varied collection, which lent heavily on horn arrangements and revealed an affiliation with current trends in black music. Even the sleeve artwork was alluring, with a cover featuring paintings from John, aged 11. The record was accompanied by a lavish booklet, which included lyrics, more paintings and a genealogy detailing Lennon's Irish roots and tracing back his family tree to such illustrious predecessors as John Lennon (1768–1846), a sailor famous for his daring feats, and John Brown Lennon, a nineteenth century American labour leader.

Critical reaction to the album was not as favourable as expected. *NME*'s Charles Shaar Murray commented: "First, the good news. The playing is faultless, if a trifle pedestrian, and the production is as smooth and silky as any discerning hi-fi buff could want. Now get set for the bad news. The songs are mostly a drag and, worse, most of them are solidly rooted in the Lennon lore of old."

Even Ray Coleman, *Melody Maker*'s pro-Lennon critic and later biographer, shrouded his enthusiasm in an apologetic tone: "Really, you have to be as hooked as I am on Lennon's stance and his singing voice to want to own this album . . . Nobody should ever go for a Lennon album these days expecting re-runs of 'I Am The Walrus', 'Norwegian Wood' or 'Strawberry Fields Forever'. The man is 10 years older, not much wiser, but more introspective, and still an emerging artiste who has been forced to come face to face with reality. But the bite is untarnished and the verse is still exceptional. Lennon remains, for me, a quirky genius."

With the benefit of hindsight, Peter Doggett provided the most insightful short critique of the album: "The *Walls And Bridges* material was certainly as graphic and revealing as anything Lennon had written in the past . . . Autobiographical evidence aside, *Walls And Bridges* worked simply as a collection of pop songs – more sophisticated than *Mind Games*, and produced with infinitely more verve and imagination. In fact, Lennon never made a richer solo record, nor one which demonstrated such a wide mastery of styles. *Walls And Bridges* mightn't have been his strongest album, or his most durable; but it did represent his last entire album of new songs, and also the last time – almost – that his music would reflect the contemporary world around him. It hinted at a new maturity of sound to come, taking in elements of the black music mainstream just as the Beatles had done a decade earlier. In an imaginary future, Lennon might have followed his new buddy David Bowie into some hybrid of cutting-edge funk and rock. But things didn't quite work out that way."

With Lennon's record sales on the slide since the glory days of *Imagine*, there was no guarantee that *Walls And Bridges* would win back a mass audience. All that changed in November 1974 when the album and attendant single 'Whatever Gets You Thru The Night' both reached number 1 in the US charts. Although *Walls And Bridges* deserves acclaim as one of Lennon's finest albums, arguably equalling or even surpassing *Imagine*, its importance has been played down by its creator. In his 1980 series of interviews, he rarely mentioned the work and when he did he famously described its contents as "the work of a semi-sick craftsman," a seemingly harsh and inexplicable judgement, no doubt fuelled by unhappy memories of his 'lost week-end' and the knowledge that the album represented his break away from Yoko Ono. The credits reveal that May Pang was 'Production Co-ordinator' while Yoko's presence was restricted to that of a phantom, appearing as the subject of Lennon's self-flagellating and occasionally confrontational lyrics.

Going Down On Love

Walls And Bridges opens with a polished, insistent composition, most notable for Lennon's strident vocal, Arthur Jenkins' bongos, some enticing reggae rhythms, and a strong brass arrangement from Bobby Keyes and the attendant horn section. The title is sexually suggestive as Lennon pictures himself on his knees, abstractly 'going down on love'. Like 'Come Together', the words and title were too subtle to cause offence to innocent listeners, including myself at the time. Others were no doubt more attuned to the sexual connotations. Presumably written about his troubled relationship with Yoko, the first verse laments a tainted love, then advocates a 'love the one you're with' philosophy, before concluding that there is a price for such dalliance. By the second verse, Lennon sees himself drowning in a sea of hatred and pleading for salvation. Finally, he again acknowledges that something precious has been lost, leaving him sowing his oats, while complaining as if this is a penance. For all his apparent self-loathing, Lennon seems to protest too much, a view reinforced by the song's jaunty tone. While the lyrics suggest submission and stoical disillusionment, the performance is both irreverent and defiant.

Whatever Gets You Thru The Night

Bobby Keyes' tenor saxophone again dominates as Lennon lets rip with this catchy rocker. Elton John plays piano and organ and combines well with Lennon as second vocalist. As Lennon explained: "How that record came about was that Elton was in town and I was doing it and needed a harmony. He did the harmony on that and a couple more and played beautiful piano on it." Despite the enormous success of the collaboration, Lennon felt its chart position was undeserved. He was unjustly critical of a composition which still sounds exciting. "That was a novelty record," he insisted. "It's the only one I've done since I left the Beatles to get to number 1. We didn't get a good take on the musicians, but I just quite like the words. It was more commercial than, say, 'Imagine', but in my opinion, 'Imagine' should have been number 1 and 'Whatever Gets You Thru The Night' should have been number 39. It just doesn't make sense. Who knows?"

Lennon's positive comment on the lyrics emphasize a feature of the song not usually appreciated. There is a touch of Yoko Ono imagery in the line about not needing a sword to cut through flowers and, significantly, this is followed by the refrain, 'oh no, oh no' [Ono, Ono]. In common with 'Going Down On Love', the lyrics emphasize a phlegmatic acceptance of the need to survive an ordeal, while acknowledging how easy it is to waste time or blow your mind. Both songs are anthems of Lennon's 'lost weekend', expressing inner turmoil through exuberant music which is as intoxicating as the Brandy Alexanders he regularly consumed.

Old Dirt Road

Jesse Ed Davis' distinctive bottleneck guitar opens this song, perfectly enhancing its down-home, lazy mood. In common with parts of *Imagine*, Lennon and Nicky Hopkins both play acoustic piano, this time abetted by Ken Ascher's electric keyboards. Harry Nilsson also plays a crucial part as backing vocalist and co-writer. Possibly inspired by Charlie Patton's 'Down The Dirt Road Blues', the lyrics feature several blues phrases such as 'lazyboning', 'cool clear water', and the more contemporary soul cliché 'keep on keeping on'. Amid these stock references is some startling imagery, most notably the intriguing allusion to 'shovelling smoke with a pitchfork in the wind'. As with the previous two tracks, the dominant mood is stoical rather than despairing with Lennon's *laissez-faire* lyrics evident. The inclusion of some subtle string work enhances the mood, establishing the song as another strong contender on an album that rivals *Imagine* as Lennon's most consistent and engaging work since the epochal, unbeatable *John Lennon/Plastic Ono Band*.

What You Got

Funky rhythms, scorching vocals and belting brass characterize this track in which Lennon attempts a marriage between Sly Stone, the Isley Brothers, early Tamla Motown and Philadelphia soul. He stressed the latter influence in a contemporary radio interview, admitting that the song was partly inspired by the O'Jays' 'For The Love Of Money'. Lyrically, this could be the theme song of Lennon's lost weekend as he bemoans the absence of Yoko before begging for one last chance. Like 'Whatever Gets You Thru The Night', the song advocates indulgent escapism as the panacea for emotional loss. Although the party atmosphere suggests one long drinking binge, neither the musicianship nor the arrangement is slack. On the contrary, this song sounds much better than most of the material on *Mind Games*, which was recorded at a time when Lennon was supposedly more in control. The need to 'cut the string' still attaching him to Ono transforms his desperation into an exhilarating defiance. Significantly, these songs are neither angry nor moody but strangely cathartic in their celebratory tone.

Bless You

One of the most striking melodies on the album, this love song to Yoko added fuel to the romantic notion that their separation was never intended to be permanent. The break-up is seen as the roaming of 'restless spirits' and, for those critics who insist that it's over, Lennon confides to his estranged partner, 'but we know better, darling', then states with conviction that their love is eternal. In one of his best vocal and lyrical lines of the decade, he describes his current feelings as the 'hollow ring of last year's echo'. In the final verse, he addresses the suitor who may be with her now and, with unprecedented magnanimity, blesses their union, asking only that his replacement be caring and 'kind-hearted'. Emotionally, it's a long way from 'Jealous Guy'. Yet there is an air of defiance accompanying the nobility and a sense of calm control not always evident elsewhere on the album. Ken Ascher's electric piano and mellotron add a supper club glitz to the track, as if they were already convinced that Lennon had composed a standard. The composition remains one of his most prophetic and convincing love songs.

Scared

The ominous sound of a howling wolf prefaces Lennon's confession of his fears, which consist largely of passing time, encroaching age, and lost opportunities. Not since 'Help!' has a single-word song title so nakedly expressed his insecurities. In common with 'I Am The Walrus', which sampled *King Lear*, he returns to Shakespeare, partly quoting the Bastard's lines from *King John*: "Bell, book and candle shall not drive me back/When gold and silver becks me to come on" (Act III, scene iii). Here, the Bastard is himself quoting from the words of excommunication, which end with "Do to the book, quench the candle, ring the bell." Lennon uses the words as an incantation that proves powerless, prompting that familiar plea 'oh no' [Ono]. With Jesse Ed Davis' fluent guitar accompaniment setting the scene, Lennon adds the full weight of the horn section to ram home the third verse in which his darker side emerges. Here, he tears away the familiar Lennon persona of the past few years, ridiculing his 'love and peace' philosophy and confronting the red meat of human emotion that is gnawing at his heart. At one point, he becomes so passionate that he screams in frustration, convinced that hate and jealousy will prove his undoing, in marked contrast to the stoicism previously voiced on 'Bless You'. 'Scared' is another powerful statement and proof positive that the pain of his separation from Yoko Ono could work to his artistic advantage.

"I was terrified when I wrote it, if you can't tell," he recalled. "It was the whole separation from Yoko, thinking I lost the one thing I knew I needed. You know, I think Mick Jagger took the song and turned it into 'Miss You'." In Lennon's imagination, the Rolling Stones' hit sounded like a faster version of 'Scared'. "I like Mick's record better. I have no ill feelings about it. It could have been sub-conscious on Mick's part, or conscious. Music is everybody's possession. It's only music publishers who think that people own it."

9 Dream

One of the highlights of the album, this sumptuous, Spectoresque production displayed Lennon's love of melody to excellent effect. The velvet vocal and whispered backing from May Pang is spine-tingling stuff and it was no surprise when the song was selected as a single. "That's what I call craftsmanship writing," Lennon explained, "meaning I just churned that out. I'm not putting it down, it's just what it is. I just sat down and wrote it with no inspiration, based on a dream I had . . . I wrote it around the string arrangement I'd written for the Harry Nilsson album I produced: [based on] 'Many Rivers To Cross', the Jimmy Cliff number. I'd done this string arrangement for that and it was such a nice melody . . . So I wrote words to the string arrangement, that was '# 9 Dream'. [It was a] psychedelic, dreamy kind of thing." Those elements were evident in the rich imagery, which included references to 'heat whispered trees', allusions more appropriate to a song like 'Lucy In The Sky With Diamonds'. When the album first came out, I assumed that 'ah bowakama' was a Japanese phrase, like 'Aisumasen' on the previous album. Lennon later confirmed it was pure nonsense, a word emerging from a dream, like those invented words you sometimes hear during an intense LSD trip.

Jesse Ed Davis' wah-wah guitar playing on this track has been compared to that of George Harrison and it may be that Lennon was attempting to pay passing tribute to his former colleague. As further evidence, listen closely and you can hear May Pang, her voice apparently reversed, intoning the word 'Krishna' in the background. Lennon was also aware of the significance of the number nine in his life. As he told journalists, he once lived at 9 Newcastle Road in Liverpool and had already featured the number in such songs as 'One Over 909' and 'Revolution 9'. When he married Yoko, he added Ono to his Christian names John Winston, thereby ensuring that the total number of 'O's in both their names came to nine. And, as everyone knew, his son Sean had been delivered by Caesarean section on the same birthday as his father, supposedly completing the nine sequence for a new generation. "I was born on the ninth of October, the ninth month," Lennon noted. Lennon's numerological theories relating to his and Sean's birthdays should be greeted with scepticism, not least because October is the tenth month of the year!

Surprise Surprise (Sweet Bird Of Paradox)

With Elton John on harmony, Lennon offers a love song, clearly directed at May Pang. The sentiments are hardly romantic, however. There are even strong hints that the relationship is merely functional and probably temporary. Evidently her main task is ensuring that he gets through this 'God-awful loneliness'. There is even a suggestion that May Pang, although a positive influence on his libido, somehow deadens his true feelings: 'She makes me sweat and forget who I am'. Yet, there is also a brief acknowledgement that he loves her and a sense of exuberance at this unexpected discovery. The bracketed sub-title, ostensibly a throwaway pun on 'sweet bird of paradise', nevertheless expresses the paradoxical nature of his feelings for his new love, who seems both needed and used in equal measure. In a more playful mood, Lennon closes the song with phrasing borrowed from the fade-out of the Beatles' 'Drive My Car', significantly one of their most anti-romantic compositions. In 1980 when David Sheff interviewed Lennon for *Playboy* he contemptuously dismissed 'Surprise Surprise' as a "piece of garbage", an excessively harsh assessment no doubt prompted by the fact that Yoko was at his side and the memory of May Pang as any form of creative inspiration a subject conveniently forgotten.

Steel And Glass

The playfulness continues in the opening to this composition as Lennon chuckles, then teases the listener with the clue: "Hee hee

hee! This here's a story about your friend and mine?" as offstage whispers hiss, "Who is it?" The question remains unanswered in the song, although most critics credit Allen Klein as the unlucky recipient of Lennon's wrath. Certainly, many of the unflattering descriptions could be applied to the pugnacious American, as various journalists gleefully pointed out. Of course, as ever with Lennon's accusative songs, the sentiments can all too easily be turned inwards. The line about losing your mother during childhood, for instance, applied to both Klein and Lennon. With the use of strings recalling the equally vituperative 'How Do You Sleep?' Lennon spits out a series of cheap insults, which are just vague enough to preclude litigation. Later, Lennon attempted to obfuscate its meaning by pointing out that although Klein may have had a New York 'walk', he was not known for displaying an 'LA tan' and therefore the song was an amalgam of various people or resentments. Although the song stands as one of the best on this album, the bile sounds a little contrived in comparison to the genuine hurt evident on the more convincing 'How Do You Sleep?' Nevertheless, the intensity of Lennon's vocal carries the song with conviction and it remains one of his best compositions of the period. A starker version of 'Steel And Glass' would later be unearthed for the posthumous Lennon album, *Menlove Avenue*.

Beef Jerky
This funky instrumental workout, based around a blues progression during the session for '# 9 Dream', features some fine guitar interplay between Lennon and Jesse Ed Davis. The Little Big Horns, featuring Bobby Keyes, provide a neat approximation of Stax soul, while part of the song brings to mind the sassy 'Tight A$' from *Mind Games*. It came as a complete surprise to hear an instrumental on a Lennon album. Unexpected and high-spirited, the track was perfectly placed serving as a party romp before the hangover that was about to follow.

Nobody Loves You When You're Down And Out
After the excitement of 'Beef Jerky', Lennon provides the ultimate example of his world-weariness with this bluesy lament. A chilling

commentary on the hollowness of his sabbatical 'lost weekend', it betrays Lennon's cynicism and despair in equal measure. Midway through, he testifies to the extent of his disillusionment by telling his listeners that the whole rock star circus is simply 'showbiz'. Lennon had been here before, of course, most notably at the conclusion of 'God' when he pronounced 'the dream is over'. But whereas that composition was sung with the clear-eyed passion and commitment of a convert, the sentiments expressed here are of a defeated spirit, whose last refuge is the self-protective detachment of a cynic.

An instrumental break, which includes some exquisite wah-wah guitar from Jesse Ed Davis, sustains the downbeat ambience of quiet reflection. Then, suddenly, there is an unexpected shift of tempo and mood as Lennon wrestles himself from the apathy of his situation to cry out in a sudden burst of emotion. The description of his early morning routine recalls the equally unexpected interjection of Paul McCartney's vignette midway through 'A Day In The Life', but without the breezy detail. Lennon never gets beyond describing seeing himself in the mirror before we're swiftly taken to late evening when he's lying in darkness, unable to sleep. A sarcastic 'oo wee' concludes this cry from the wilderness, after which he slips back into his former ennui. The sentiments, at once desperate, sardonic and full of self-loathing, lead to the cynical consideration, familiar to all rock gods, that everyone will love you when you're dead.

"Well, that says the whole story," Lennon summed up. "That exactly expressed the whole period I was apart from Yoko. I always imagined Sinatra singing that one. I don't know why. It's kind of Sinatraesque. He could do a perfect job with it. Are you listening, Frank? You need a song that isn't a piece of nothing. Here's one for you. The horn arrangements, everything's made for you. But don't ask me to produce it!" Lennon even provided some lounge singer whistling at the close, recalling 'Jealous Guy'.

Sinatra never did record the song but its lyrics obviously impressed the appeal judge in the subsequent Morris Levy case. Quoting the lines, 'Everybody's hustling for a buck and a dime', he pointed out: "The words of John Lennon are an appropriate introduction to this case, which involves alleged broken promises and acrimony between supposed friends in the record industry."

Ya Ya

In a vain attempt to pacify the litigious wrath of Morris Levy, Lennon included this throwaway version of Lee Dorsey's hit at the end of the album. With 11-year-old Julian Lennon on drums, the track was a brief, hilarious coda, which sounded like it had been recorded in a bathroom. It starts off with the father about to offer some toilet humour before stopping himself with the quip, "We won't get into that!" Although it works as a playful coda to a great album, Lennon was evidently embarrassed about the recording. "It was a contractual obligation to Morris Levy," he admitted. "It was a humiliation, and I regret having to be in that position, but I did it. That's the way it turned out. Julian was playing the drums and I just leapt on the piano and sang, 'Ya Ya'."

Levy failed to appreciate Lennon's humour and was not content with the share of publishing royalties received from the song's inclusion at the end of the album. As a result, the track would reappear in more sophisticated form on Lennon's next release.

In October 2005, *Walls And Bridges* was reissued on CD in a remixed/remastered format with three bonus tracks:

Whatever Gets You Thru The Night (Live)

Previously available on the Mark Lewisohn compiled 1990 box set *Lennon*, this recording captures Lennon's return to live performance after a two-year absence. Elton John can take responsibility for goading Lennon into joining him onstage. As Lennon recalled: "Jokingly, he was telling me he was going to do this Madison Square Garden concert and said, 'Will you do it with me if the record's number 1?'" When 'Whatever Gets You Thru The Night' unexpectedly topped the US charts, Elton called in that promise and the former Beatle appeared before an audience of 20,000 at Madison Square Garden on 28 November 1974.

After a fulsome introduction, Lennon wandered onstage, accompanied by the familiar riff from 'I Feel Fine'. Their tentative but pleasing reading of the chart-topping hit was saxophone heavy, with Elton John singing lead alongside Lennon, rather than merely providing backing vocals. "It was an occasion where grown men, even Scottish road managers who'd seen it all, cried," Elton recalled. "I've never seen anybody get an ovation like that. When he walked onstage, it shook him. He was physically sick when he came onstage that night, he was so scared. But he kept his bargain."

Nobody Loves You When You're Down And Out [alternate version]

As the engineer announces that this is the ninth take, Lennon suddenly brightens. "Nine? That's a lucky number!" This quiet, acoustic reading of the composition, sounds even more desolate than the more familiar album version. It also has a pensive quality, with Lennon intoning the 'what you say?' line four times. He reaches a froth of emotion during the 'get up in the morning' section which threatens to leave him hoarse. Immediately after, you can hear him counting in the song again, as if settling himself after a cathartic outburst. A whistling coda concludes the song on a more restrained and stoical note.

This recording was probably attempted towards the end of 1973, well in advance of *Walls And Bridges*. "I had been sitting on the song because I knew I would ruin it if I tried to record it at the time I wrote it," Lennon explained. "My head wasn't together to deal with it so I just kept it in my pocket."

John Lennon Interview

This late 1974 promotional interview for the forthcoming release of *Walls And Bridges* was effectively a call to arms for the sales staff at EMI Parlophone. Lennon urges them to "Do your best" in selling the record into the shops. Asked whether he misses England, he counters: "Well, I call it Britain. I miss Britain but I try not to miss it too much because then I'd get that homesick bit, which I went through for a period." Stressing his stubbornness in staying in

America to fight for his much prized green card, he reveals that a final legal decision will be forthcoming within 18 months. He sounds philosophical about the outcome. "'Que Sera, Sera' as Doris Day used to say . . . I'll take whatever comes." The interviewer then encourages him to list every musician on the new album and offer his record company a final message. "Come on EMI!" Lennon cheers. "Show me what you can do!"

ROCK 'N' ROLL

Released: February 1975

Original UK issue: Apple PCS 7169. US issue: Apple SK 3419. CD reissue with
bonus tracks: EMI 8 74329 2 (UK)/Capitol 8 74329 2 (US)

The litigious Morris Levy was never likely to be satisfied with a couple
of minutes of 'Ya Ya' from *Walls And Bridges* and soon made it clear
that he would be suing Lennon for reneging on his promise to record
three songs owned by his publishing company. Aware of Levy's
legendary Mafia connections and hard man reputation, Lennon soon
realized that he would not be easily fobbed off. On 8 October 1974, a
meeting was arranged at Levy's Club Cavallero in Manhattan during
which Lennon poured out a persuasive list of excuses for his failure to
meet the recording deadline. He blamed Spector for running off with
the tapes, related salty tales of drunken antics in the studio, and insisted
that the final product was incomplete and so appalling that it could not
possibly be released. "There was a psychodrama happening called Phil
Spector!" he told Levy. "He apparently had an auto accident. I don't
know for sure whether he did or didn't – but that was what I heard. I
tried everything to get the tapes back. Then I had to do *Walls And
Bridges*. I've now listened to the tapes and there's only about four of
the rock 'n' roll songs worth using."

Levy listened patiently, then pressed Lennon for a solution. The
singer was evasive and later admitted in court: "All I was interested in
saying was what I had to say about the tapes. I was very nervous
because I did not know the man and I heard he was annoyed at me.
So I told him, as best I could, all about the Phil Spector tapes and
what had happened: 'I am sorry you didn't get what you were supposed to get, but this is why.' I explained that for about three-
quarters of an hour, or an hour. And he said something like, 'Well
that is all very well and good, but I am out of pocket.' And he started
writing some figures down on a bit of paper. I don't know what they
were, maybe $250,000 or something. I could not follow the

reasoning, but if he thought he was out of pocket, he was out of pocket as far as I could see."

In the end it was Levy who came up with an ingenious compromise. He suggested that Lennon should complete the rock 'n' roll album and license the work to his television mail order company, Adam VIII. The legality of any such agreement would prove highly questionable, as both parties must have known, but Lennon 'the television addict' was intrigued by the possibilities. "I was thinking perhaps I could put it straight on TV and avoid the critics and avoid going through the usual channels." Bamboozled by Levy's optimistic figures and promises of making a financial killing, Lennon was intoxicated with the idea of creating history as the first major artiste to offer new product exclusively through television mail order. At that moment, Levy convinced himself that he had secured a verbal agreement from Lennon, although nothing was ever committed to paper and the whole mail order concept seemed little more than a fanciful idea that still needed careful negotiation, not least with EMI and Capitol Records.

Urged on by Levy, Lennon rushed the project through. Rehearsals took place at the entrepreneur's dairy farm in upstate New York. Levy was the perfect host and a charming raconteur, regaling the assembled musicians with tall tales of his times in the music business. After selecting material and salvaging the best of the Spector sessions, Lennon completed the re-recordings at the Record Plant in New York with assistance from the musicians used on *Walls And Bridges*. Lennon later admitted that he was initially unsure how the *Rock 'n' Roll* album might be reconfigured. "I didn't know whether to forget it or carry on, but I hate leaving stuff in the can. I thought of putting out an EP, but they don't have them in America, and I thought about a maxi-single. In the end I decided to finish it off and produce the rest myself. I did 10 tracks in three days in October, all the numbers that I hadn't got around to with Phil. I had a lot of fun and mixed it all down in about four or five days. My one problem was whether it sounded weird going from the Spector sound to my sound, from 28 guys down to eight. But they matched pretty well . . ."

This was Lennon's positive spin on the album's reconfiguration. At other times, he claimed to have few fond memories of the project. Ploughing through endless hours of drunken takes from the Spector sessions in search of a decent performance had proven immensely frustrating. "It cost a fortune in time and energy and it was the most expensive record I ever made. All I thought I wanted to do was just sing a bit of rock 'n' roll . . . It was the worst time of my life, that record!"

In early November 1974, Levy asked for a copy of the completed tapes and Lennon despatched two reels, comprising early rough mixes of all the material. Soon after, under pressure from Lennon's lawyer, Levy provided a breakdown of estimated costs, confirming that the album would be marketed at a bargain price of $4.98. After all the deductions had been calculated, it was evident that neither Lennon nor Capitol would make much money from the release, which seemed patently unworkable. Capitol also received word from their sales representatives that retailers were unhappy about the idea of a mail order deal which they believed would prove detrimental in the marketplace. An impasse was reached but Levy was in no mood to back down and recklessly went ahead with the project.

On 8 February 1975, advertisements appeared on American television for an album titled *Roots*. The package featured an out of date, out of focus photo of Lennon set against a garish yellow cover bearing the slogan: *John Lennon Sings The Great Rock & Roll Hits*. On the back cover there were even a couple of ads for two Adam VIII soul compilations: *Soul Train Super Tracks* and *20 Solid Gold Hits*. The artwork looked shoddy, the pressing lacked even writers' credits for the individual songs, and the sound resembled that of a glorified bootleg.

Capitol wasted no time in issuing their own official album of the sessions titled *Rock 'n' Roll*. In order to scupper Levy's promotion, they wired radio stations, television companies and pressing plants threatening legal action. The tactic worked and it was later estimated that Levy sold a mere 1,270 albums, although that figure may have been deliberately downgraded in view of the court proceedings that followed.

Following legal advice, Lennon promptly sent a telegram to Adam

VIII which read: "The use of my recorded performances and my name and likeness in the album entitled *Roots* and/or *John Lennon's Rock 'n' Roll Hits* and advertising in connection therewith is unauthorized." Predictably, Levy responded by attempting to sue Lennon and Capitol for $42 million for breach of contract and damages. Eventually that fanciful figure was beaten down, but it was not until April 1977 that the argument was finally resolved by the courts in Lennon's favour. Levy's Big Seven Music publishing company was granted a derisory $6,795, while the counter suit from Lennon netted $144,700 damages. Outside the court, Lennon announced: "The reason I fought this was to discourage ridiculous suits like this. They didn't think I'd show up or that I'd fight it. They thought I'd just settle, but I won't." Unsurprisingly, the much maligned *Roots* became a valuable collectors' item, not least because it featured two songs that were not included on the Capitol/EMI release: a cover of Rosie & The Originals' 'Angel Baby' and a histrionic reading of the Ronettes' 'Be My Baby'.

The official *Rock 'n' Roll* was superior in every respect, boasting a wonderful cover photograph from Jürgen Vollmer featuring a sneering leather-clad Lennon standing in a Hamburg doorway back in 1961. Lennon was struck by the iconic power of the image. "I thought, is this some kind of karmic thing? Here I am with this old picture of me in Hamburg . . . I'm ending as I started, singing this straight rock 'n' roll stuff." Musically, the album proved a welcome diversion, enabling Lennon to return to the pre-Beatles days and perform the songs that had inspired him to greatness. His determination to imitate, as closely as possible, the vocal styles and instrumentation of the originals was endearing, but also limiting. On the better known songs, he merely inclined the listener to return to the originals in order to hear a superior performance. But as Lennon remarked in his press release: "Rock 'n' roll will never die. Why should it? Too many people love it, including me. Many of the songs on this album I've been singing since I was 15. They have a special place in my soul."

The work proved a modest success, climbing to number 6 in both the US and UK charts. Media reaction was almost universally positive. *NME*'s scholarly critic Ian MacDonald reckoned it was the singer's most sustained work since *John Lennon/Plastic One Band*: "'Re-lived by J.L.' it says on the sleeve – and that's where *Rock 'n' Roll* scores over last year's spate of retrospective enterprises. Possessing no equivalent of Lennon's crazily alienated youth to obsess them, Bowie, the Band, Ferry *et al* could only look back in warm nostalgia and attempt, with artistry, to *re-create*. By comparison, Lennon is fixated. His focus on his early teen years has the gleam of genuine obsession. He *re-lives* – and that's what prevents *Rock 'n' Roll* from being charged with the archness, the indulgence, the ambiguity, and the general decadence that surrounded the attempts of Ferry and Bowie. Lennon isn't into perspectives: *Rock 'n' Roll* is what it claims to be and no more . . . One comes away from this album with the hope that these old forms are still viable; their simple strengths are very much what's needed today." For many listeners, the work was no doubt appreciated as an aperitif to Lennon's next album of new material. Who would have guessed that his return to rock 'n' roll roots was actually the prelude to a career retirement that would remain unbroken for the remainder of the decade?

Be-Bop-A-Lula

Lennon starts the album with a faithful copy of Gene Vincent's classic, including a decent imitation of the Virginian's distinctive vocal phrasing. Inevitably, it lacks the period charm of the original which seems far too familiar to warrant a xeroxed cover version. For Lennon, of course, the Vincent tune had deep significance. "There's a picture onstage with the group before Paul had joined and I'm in a white jacket," he recalled. "That was the day, the first day I sang 'Be-Bop-A-Lula' at a church fête with the Quarry Men. It was the day I met Paul and he was in the audience, a mutual friend had brought him." McCartney was eager to impress and subsequently played Lennon his own cover of the song, along with Eddie Cochran's 'Twenty Flight Rock'. He had even seen Vincent and Cochran perform at the Liverpool Empire in March 1960 on the ill-fated tour that cost Eddie his life. In a press release, Lennon wrote of 'Be-Bop-A-Lula': "One of my all-time favourite records [by] Capitol's answer to Elvis. Gene was the first great rock 'n' roller the

Beatles met in person (at the Cavern Club, Liverpool). As soon as we could afford it, we dressed in leather suits. We looked like four Gene Vincents."

Stand By Me

One of the undisputed highlights of the album, this version of Ben E. King's 1961 hit was subsequently chosen as a single and graced the US Top 20. Lennon's acoustic strumming leads into a powerhouse production, featuring his most confident and expressive vocal on the album, plus some impressive slide guitar work. As he explained to Chris Charlesworth: "Every time I make an album I jam on oldies to warm up. There must be tons of tapes around with me doing songs like this just to get the feel of being in the studio. We'd do these numbers to break the ice in case we were getting too uptight about a song. If it wasn't a 12-bar, it'd be something like 'Stand By Me'. With the Beatles, we covered a lot of rock 'n' roll on the early albums, but we were really loath to do it on record because we always thought the originals were so great we couldn't touch them."

Medley: Ready Teddy/Rip It Up

The inclusion of a Little Richard medley was not particularly surprising since he had once headlined over the Beatles back in 1962. "We met Little Richard in Liverpool," Lennon confirmed. "Later meeting both Gene and Richard in Hamburg, Germany. We played onstage and off, Hamburg still hasn't recovered. Billy Preston was Richard's organist in Hamburg." Preston, of course, later appeared on the Beatles' 'Get Back', even receiving a separate billing on the single. It was during this period that Lennon first mentioned the possibility of a covers album that would include 'Rip It Up', the second song on this medley. "I think we'll make an album of the straight stuff," he said, "and maybe later release a collection of daft things like 'Rip It Up' and 'Blue Suede Shoes'." The ubiquitous Little Richard was still on his mind during the September 1969 Toronto Rock 'n' Roll Revival Festival. Even though Lennon had yet to enrol with therapist Arthur Janov, he anticipated the importance of the primal scream when describing Richard's influence to Barry Miles. "The most exciting thing about early Little Richard was when he just screamed, just before the solo, and that was howling. It used to make your hair stand on end when he did that long, long scream into a solo. I still imitate him – when it comes to a solo on a record I always have to prevent myself going 'arrrgh', which I've been doing ever since I first heard Little Richard. So it's just eliminating the song bit and elongating the howling bit because that definitely got everybody I knew . . ."

You Can't Catch Me

This was the song that prompted Morris Levy's plagiarism suit. With Spector at the controls, the sound is deeply compressed as Lennon provides an atmospheric opening that makes no attempt to disguise the song's similarity to the Beatles' 'Come Together'. In interviews, Lennon was always ready to admit his debt to Chuck Berry as a key influence on his musical career, as evidenced by such Beatles live or studio recordings as 'Roll Over Beethoven', 'Sweet Little Sixteen', 'Carol', 'Memphis, Tennessee', 'Too Much Monkey Business' and 'Rock And Roll Music'. "Chuck Berry's lyrics were intelligent. In the Fifties, when people were singing about virtually nothing, he was writing social comment, songs with incredible metre to the lyrics, which influenced Dylan, me, and many other people."

Despite the lawsuit and Lennon's indisputable admission of his borrowings, there was no doubt that 'You Can't Catch Me' and 'Come Together' were very different songs in other respects. As Lennon later argued: "I left the line in 'Here comes old flat top'. It is nothing like the Chuck Berry song, but they took me to court because I admitted the influence . . . I could have changed it to 'Here comes old iron face' but the song remains independent of Chuck Berry or anybody else on Earth."

Lennon's case was best made during the court hearing by Apple's attorney, who argued: "In order to meet the burden of showing substantial musical similarity, plaintiff cannot merely dissect the two songs and show similarity of a few measures here and there. In short the two songs neither sound similar . . . nor do they convey the same idea to the average listener." It was argued that the songs differed in various aspects, including theme, music and style. Apple noted:

" 'You Can't Catch Me' deals with the exploits of a person who purchased a new automobile, then describes an occasion when he was driving on the New Jersey Turnpike and was passed by another car, a 'flat top', meaning a convertible, and then chased by a policeman. 'Come Together' concerns the characteristics and personality of an individual, 'an old flat top'. The song portrays the change from his 1950s clean-living, conservative existence, as epitomized by his flat top haircut, to his present existence as a person with long hair, unshined shoes, and a free-living existence."

Ain't That A Shame
A Top 10 US hit for Fats Domino in 1955 and a number 1 that same year for Pat Boone, this song held special significance for Lennon. " 'Ain't That A Shame' was the first rock 'n' roll song I ever learned," he told journalist Chet Flippo. "My mother taught it to me on the banjo before I learned the guitar." It's a faithful reading of the song, with saxophone dominant and Lennon hamming up the vocal on the chorus. Lennon and Domino met in Las Vegas during 1973, possibly for the first time since the Beatles' appearance in New Orleans' City Park Stadium in September 1964.

Do You Wanna Dance
Bobby Freeman's 1958 hit 'Do You Wanna Dance' had already spawned several chart successes, from the Beach Boys and Bette Midler in the USA to Cliff Richard and Barry Blue in the UK. It was therefore rather too well covered to warrant yet another version. Lennon's reading sounds weary and over-familiar despite an attempt to add a reggae rhythm. It is probably a truism to say that the more familiar the listener is with the original recording, the less likely he is to be impressed by Lennon's adaptation, and vice versa.

Sweet Little Sixteen
Lennon had already rehearsed Chuck Berry's 'Thirty Days' for the album, but stuck to this familiar classic, which he took at a slightly slower tempo and embellished with horns. This was the second of four songs retrieved from the original Spector tapes and reinvested

with a fresh vocal. Lennon had no hesitation about recording two Berry songs for the album. "When I hear good rock, the calibre of Chuck Berry, I just fall apart," he confessed. "I have no other interest in life. The world could be ending and I wouldn't care." In his press release, he eulogized Berry as "Rock's first poet. His influence is still reverberating now. I could write a book but I'll sing instead. There were so many great artistes and songs I would love to have included. I could go on forever: Elvis Presley, Eddie Cochran, Carl Perkins, Jerry Lee Lewis, Bo Diddley . . ."

Slippin' And Slidin'

Having already recorded Little Richard's 1956–57 hit 'Long Tall Sally' with the Beatles, Lennon decided to tackle its B-side. It's a rousing vocal performance, although Lennon would be the first to admit that, in common with many of the songs on the album, it pales in comparison to the original. "It was a song I knew," he casually observed. "It was easier to do songs that I knew than trying to learn something from scratch." Lennon was equally familiar with the Buddy Holly version, which he also loved, but selected the original on merit. Interestingly, 'Slippin' And Slidin'', along with 'Stand By Me' and 'Imagine', were the songs chosen for what became Lennon's final television performance in June 1975. As a final conciliatory gesture, following the lingering dispute over Ono's involvement as a co-writer on Lennon songs in the early Seventies, he agreed to appear on *Salute To Sir Lew – The Master Showman*, a tribute to the head of ATV Music, who had purchased the Lennon/McCartney songwriting catalogue from Dick James. The same month as the Grade television screening, 'Slippin' And Slidin'' was scheduled for release as the second single from the album. Despite being allocated a serial number (Apple 1883), the release was cancelled at the last minute.

Peggy Sue

One of the first songs Lennon learned to play on guitar was the Crickets' 'That'll Be The Day'. It was also the first known recording of the Quarry Men, surviving as a private demo and featuring regularly in their live performances. The Beatles loved Buddy Holly songs, enlivening their early repertoire with such classics as 'It's So Easy', 'Maybe Baby' and 'Think It Over'. During their famous Decca audition on New Year's Day 1962, they recorded 'Crying, Waiting, Hoping' and dutifully included 'Words Of Love' on 1964's *Beatles For Sale*. Here, Lennon tackles 'Peggy Sue' in as faithful a version as modern technology allows. As well as the familiar lead guitar breaks and primitive percussion, there's a chance to hear him attempting Holly's hiccupping vocal style, which is quite amusing. Lennon described 'Peggy Sue' as "one of Buddy's great records; his influence on Lennon/McCartney's early songs was immense; he also made it OK to have four eyes!" Perhaps the only case against the song is its over-familiarity, leaving the listener wondering what Lennon might have made of a less well-known Holly number such as the rocking 'I'm Looking For Someone To Love'.

One irony, in view of his previous falling out with Paul McCartney, was that the ex-Beatle received the publishing royalties for 'Peggy Sue', having purchased the Buddy Holly catalogue. "What a clever move that was," Lennon said at the time. "I hope he gives me a good deal. Klein owns the Sam Cooke back catalogue too, which includes 'Bring It On Home To Me'. I don't care who gets the money. With Paul it's cool because we're pals, and even Klein's all right really. I'm not going to get much money from this album anyway."

Medley: Bring It On Home To Me/Send Me Some Lovin'
Contributing to Klein's publishing income, Lennon offers a short medley of Sam Cooke hits. 'Send Me Some Lovin'' (co-written by Lloyd Price) was familiar to Lennon from earlier versions recorded by Little Richard and Buddy Holly, while 'Bring It On Home To Me' was one of John's "all-time favourite songs". Bassist Klaus Voormann was surprised to be asked to add backing vocals and even more amazed when Lennon captured his contribution after a single take.

Bony Moronie
This was the third song on the album retrieved from the Phil Spector sessions and probably the weakest of the batch. Lennon

provides a dull, mid-tempo reading that is largely unmemorable. He always liked Larry Williams whom he found easier to imitate than Little Richard. The Beatles had recorded Williams' 'Slow Down', 'Dizzy Miss Lizzy' and 'Bad Boy', so it was always a good bet that one of his songs would feature on *Rock 'n' Roll*. 'Bony Moronie' also had a strong sentimental significance in Lennon's life. "This was one of the few rock songs my mother saw me perform. This was before George and Paul joined the group. She only saw me once before she died."

Ya Ya

Having angered Morris Levy with a deliberately throwaway version of this song at the end of *Walls And Bridges*, Lennon made amends with a straighter rendition which nevertheless retained the childish fun of the Lee Dorsey original. Although light in tone, the song fitted reasonably well on the album and was less well known than some of the other rock 'n' roll classics having never reached the UK charts.

Just Because

The final song was probably the best on the album. Lennon sets the scene, asking his listeners: "Remember this? I must have been 13 when this came out? Or was it 14? Or was it 22? I could have been 12, actually." In fact, he was 16 when Lloyd Price enjoyed his début hit with this in April 1957. Lennon later admitted that he was not that familiar with the track, which Phil Spector had strongly recommended. It works extraordinarily well as a song of emotional defiance from a former 'lost weekender'. Lennon instructs us to note the use of two basses on the track and towards the end of the record offers the following signing-off message: "This is Dr Winston O'Boogie saying goodnight from the Record Plant East, New York. We hope you had a swell time. Everybody here says, 'Hi.' Goodbye."

Looking back, Lennon realized that his hammy disc jockey style signing-off message might have held deeper significance: "Something flashed through my mind as I said it. 'Am I really saying farewell to the business?' It wasn't conscious and it was a long, long time before I did take time out."

In September 2004, *Rock 'n' Roll* was reissued in remixed, remastered format. Some of the tracks were slightly elongated. "[Yoko Ono] wanted to have little extras, like the dialogue on the ends, instead of the fade-outs which appeared on the original release," her spokesperson said. In addition, there were four bonus tracks, as follows:

Angel Baby
Previously available on *Menlove Avenue* (see Posthumous Releases section) and Morris Levy's *Roots*, this homage to teenage apotheosis was a welcome addition to the CD. Coincidentally, it even fitted in with John and Yoko's belief in angels, as famously expressed in their newspaper advertisements, published in 1979. This version of 'Angel Baby' was not remastered or remixed.

To Know Her Is To Love Her
A second borrowing from *Menlove Avenue* (where it is discussed at greater length), this Spector classic had previously been attempted in concert by the Beatles, who also recorded the song for the BBC during 1963. The composition deserved to be included on the original *Rock 'n' Roll*, but failed to make the final list, a fate that also befell a cover of the Ronettes' 'Be My Baby', which was belatedly premièred on *Anthology*. Like 'Angel Baby', this was not subject to the remixed/ remastering process.

Since My Baby Left Me
This Arthur Crudup composition, which became a hit for Elvis Presley, is an alternate take of the track that appears on *Menlove Avenue*. The choral singers are still there in abundance, but the tune is taken at a slightly bouncier pace.

Just Because (reprise)
For those who wondered what happened after the original fade on 'Just Because', here is the answer. Lennon mentions 'Goodnight Vienna', then passes on Christmas greetings to Ringo, George and Paul and the people of Britain.

In January 1975, one month before the original album's UK/US release, Morris Levy's label Adam VIII issued an alternative version of the work titled *Roots* (Adam VIII A 8018) with the following:

Full track listing: *Be-Bop-A-Lula; Ain't That A Shame; Stand By Me; Sweet Little Sixteen; Rip It Up; Ready Teddy; Angel Baby; Do You Wanna Dance; You Can't Catch Me; Bony Moronie; Peggy Sue; Bring It On Home To Me/Send Me Some Lovin'; Slippin' And Slidin'; Be My Baby; Ya Ya; Just Because.*

SHAVED FISH

Released: October 1975

Original UK issue: Apple PCS 7173. US issue: Apple SW 3421. CD reissue: EMI
CDP 7 46641 2 (UK)/ Capitol EMI CDP 7 46641 2 (US)

The mid-Seventies saw the withdrawal of John Lennon from the record business. But, on a personal and professional level, 1975 was to prove one of the most rewarding years of his life. He anticipated as much, telling writer Pete Hamill: "This last year has been extraordinary for me personally. I got such a shock that the impact hasn't come through. It has to do with age and God knows what else. But I'm through it. It's 1975 and I feel better and I'm sitting here and not lying in some weird place with a hangover. I feel like I've been on Sinbad's voyage and I've battled all those monsters and I've got back." The year began with Lennon appearing at a David Bowie session during which he played on a cover of the Beatles' 'Across The Universe' and collaborated on a new song 'Fame', which would later climb to number 1 in the US charts. In March, Lennon was back in the news following speculation that he and Yoko Ono were reunited. A press statement followed confirming: "The separation didn't work out."

Recalling a meeting at their Dakota apartment in New York, Lennon revealed: "I was just going over for a visit and it fell into place again. It was just like I'd never left. I realized that this was where I belonged. I think we both knew we'd get back together again sooner or later, even if it was five years, and that's why we never bothered with divorce. I'm just glad she let me back in again. It was like going out for a drink, but it took me a year to get it." Soon after, it was learned that Ono was pregnant with his child.

Meanwhile, Lennon's long battle against the US immigration authorities reached a critical stage in October when an appeal court overruled a deportation order against him and instructed the Immigration Service to reconsider his request for resident status. As they concluded: "Lennon's four-year battle to remain in our country is a testimony to his faith in that American dream."

A week after that momentous announcement, Yoko Ono gave birth to Sean Taro Ono Lennon on 9 October 1975 (John's 35th birthday). Two weeks later, this album was issued. It was the only Lennon compilation sanctioned by the singer during his lifetime and served as an excellent opportunity to collate the A-side singles that had been issued by himself and the Plastic Ono Band since 1969. Although extremely popular, the package did not break sales records, peaking at number 8 (UK) and number 12 (US). Nevertheless, the fact that it was the only Lennon 'Greatest Hits' selection of the decade ensured its continued appeal.

Detailed below are the tracks featured on the compilation that had not previously appeared on Lennon's albums.

Give Peace A Chance
The sole crime perpetrated by this compilation was the decision to feature an agonizingly truncated version of this wonderful track, which was faded after a mere 58 seconds. Still, it partly works as a tease, reminding us of the glorious origins of the Plastic Ono Band. This remains one of the freshest and most exuberant songs ever captured on vinyl. Originally recorded on an 8-track portable during their 1969 Montreal bed-in, the song featured a unique line-up of backing singers and amateur percussionists, including Yoko, Timothy Leary, Abbie Hoffman, Tommy Smothers, Murray The K, Derek Taylor, Roger Scott, several members of the clergy, a chapter of the Radha Krishna Temple and, most surprisingly, Petula Clark.

Lennon's amusing lyrics sound like a spontaneous overflow of instant rhymes, but there is a certain sardonic glee in his litany, which embraces bagism, shagism, evolution, revolution, masturbation and much more, before leading up to the central chant, 'give peace a chance'. Intriguingly, Paul McCartney still receives a writing credit, although he had nothing to do with the song. "I wasn't ready to take his name off yet," Lennon admitted.

The composition was rapidly adopted as an anthem by the peace movement and over the years took on a far greater significance. As

Lennon acknowledged: "I was pleased when the movement in America took up 'Give Peace A Chance' because I had written it with that in mind really. I hoped that instead of singing 'We Shall Overcome' from 1800 or something, they would have something contemporary. I felt an obligation, even then, to write a song that people would sing in a pub or on a demonstration." Today, this all–purpose chant is still used by all sorts of pressure groups and is not only sung on marches, but in pubs and on football terraces, where the familiar refrain "All we are saying is give us a goal" echoes through television and radio commentaries. No doubt, Lennon would have been amused.

Cold Turkey

Unquestionably one of the most harrowing and forceful songs ever written about drug addiction, this enabled Lennon to use the primal scream to express something more than personal salvation. Set against a searing guitar backing from Eric Clapton and the emphatic percussion of Ringo Starr, Lennon dramatizes the disorientating effects of heroin withdrawal with feverish pleading. His moans and screams culminate in an intense coda during which he re-enacts the horrors of cold turkey, almost writhing in agony as he pleads, 'Oh, no . . .', words that also translate as a plea to his soul mate. The song is probably the best advertisement against taking heroin ever issued, but the controversial subject matter discomfited many radio programmers in America. "It was banned because it referred to drugs," Lennon lamented. "To me, it was a rock 'n' roll version of *The Man With The Golden Arm*. It's like banning *The Man With The Golden Arm* because it showed Frank Sinatra suffering from drug withdrawal. To ban a record is the same thing. It's like banning the movie because it shows reality."

The combination of a then unusual title and some of Lennon's most incessant wailing intrigued reporters. Speaking about the song in 1969, Lennon patiently explained: "The screaming effect is only a progression from the end of 'Strawberry Fields Forever' or the end of 'I Am The Walrus' or 'A Day In The Life'. The expression 'cold turkey' isn't only known around drug addicts, but is also known to ordinary people, and not just [as] the meat. It's not exclusive to drug addiction. I like words or expressions and 'Cold Turkey' just happens to be one of them. I wrote the song 'I'm A Loser' after I'd picked up the expression. 'Kick Out The Jams!' is a nice expression. I'd write that if there already weren't so many of them. 'Day Tripper' I made out of hearing about trips before I had anything to do with tripping. Cold turkey means suffering. It can mean a three-day flu or dying in Biafra. It means many things that have nothing to do at all with drugs."

Originally released in October 1969 as the follow-up to 'Give Peace A Chance', 'Cold Turkey' reached number 14 in the UK charts and number 30 in the US. Its modest chart achievements were transformed into a hubristic joke by Lennon who, when returning his MBE, informed Prime Minister Harold Wilson and Her Majesty: "I am returning this MBE in protest against Britain's involvement in the Nigeria-Biafra thing, against our support of America in Vietnam and against 'Cold Turkey' slipping down the charts." Lennon's flippancy brought criticism from some quarters, which left him both amused and bemused. "It was a gag. I'm not too serious a person. People get bored with seriousness. Had I done it like some silly colonel it wouldn't have had that effect . . . I'd been seriously considering returning it privately. People say I should have done it that way, but what they don't understand is that there is no way to return an MBE privately. Therefore, rather than wait for the story to break, I made use of the stories that were going to be in the paper anyway. Look, if I have an accident and I have to go to hospital, it's going to be in the press. So, on the way to the hospital, if I can change it into a peace event, I will. I'm getting press anyway whether I like it or not. I found that out a long time ago, so I might as well get used to it."

It would have been fascinating to hear the song played by the Beatles who were the intended recipients of the composition in 1969. Historians, critics and fans can only wonder and savour the idea of how this would have sounded and fitted in the context of *Abbey Road*.

Instant Karma!

This was the ultimate example of Lennon's dream of using the medium of the 45rpm single as an aural newspaper to despatch his latest message to the world. He wrote the song on the morning of 27 January 1970 and it was in the shops 10 days later. The recording, which featured a hastily assembled Plastic Ono Band line-up of George Harrison, Klaus Voormann and Alan White, was produced by Phil Spector. The tycoon of teen provided many of his sonic tricks from the early Sixties, using lots of echo, heavy percussion, tambourine, handclaps and multi-dubbed pianos. Lennon's passionate but controlled vocal almost bristles with static on the recording, while the thunderous drums are played in a different metre for maximum dramatic effect. White's crisp drum beats also serve as a playful counterpoint to the singer's relentless questioning. Vocally, Lennon sounds both frantic and restrained, the bottled genie in Spector's Wall Of Sound. The record label admonishes the listener to play the record loud, which is good advice for it is the sound that propels the lyric.

After working on the instrumentation and vocals at EMI, backing singers were required to complete the track. Seemingly determined to break down the barrier between performer and audience, Lennon declined the opportunity to employ a professional choir in favour of an untutored proletariat. He duly instructed his roadies to round up some people from a night-club – variously identified as the Speakeasy, the Revolution and Hatchetts by different sources. The unsuspecting patrons were brought to the studio to participate in the grand finale singalong of 'we all shine on'. Spector, no stranger to mass ensembles, captured their contribution with aplomb.

Recalling the genesis of the song from conception to completion, Lennon explained: "I wrote it in the morning on the piano, and I went into the office and I sang it many times, and I said, 'Hell, let's do it.' We booked the studio, and Phil came in and he said: 'How do you want it?' I said, '1950s,' and he said, 'Right,' and boom, I did it, in about three goes. He played it back and there it was. The only argument was [when] I said 'a bit more bass', that's all, and off we went. Phil is great at that, he doesn't fuss about with stereo or all the bullshit, just 'Does it sound all right? Then let's have it!' It doesn't matter whether something's prominent or not prominent; if it sounds good to you as a layman or as a human, take it . . . just take it, and that suits me fine."

On first hearing, the lyrics caused confusion to many listeners as the word 'karma' was not in such general use at the time among the general public. In Lennon's circle, by contrast, 'karma' was slowly on its way to cliché status. "Everybody was going on about karma, especially in the Sixties," he explained, a decade on. "But it occurred to me that karma is instant as well, as it influences your past life or your future life. There really is a reaction to what you do now. That's what people ought to be concerned about. Also, I'm fascinated by commercials and promotion as an art form. I enjoy them. So the idea of 'Instant Karma!' was like the idea of instant coffee, presenting something in a new form."

For those unsure about karma, the song offered various meanings. Some latched on to the concept of receiving enlightenment like instant coffee, while others saw a political or even Christian message in its advice to recognize your brother as everyman. There was even a hint of tart Lennon sarcasm in the line, 'Who do you think you are, a superstar?' And only Lennon could manage to combine empathy and accusation in the reprimand 'yeah you', as if attempting to liberate the passive listener from the role of the apolitically entertained into a full engagement with the song's sentiments of personal revolution.

In a determined attempt to bring his message to the masses, Lennon premièred the song on BBC's *Top Of The Pops* on 11 February 1970, the first time he had appeared on the show since the heyday of the Beatles. The two taped performances from the Plastic Ono Band were visually striking, with rarely seen Beatles' roadie Mal Evans playing tambourine, Irish journalist B.P. Fallon clapping along, John wearing headphones and a white armband saying 'People For Peace', and Yoko sitting, wearing a blindfold, holding up peace cards ('Love', 'Peace' and 'Hope') and, most strikingly, knitting.

Power To The People

Although this was the first occasion on which 'Power To The People' appeared on album, it had since been added as a bonus track to the October 2000 CD reissue of *John Lennon/Plastic Ono Band* where it is discussed at greater length. The sloganeering song was not Lennon's most memorable political statement, but a good performance was transformed by Phil Spector's production in true Wall Of Sound fashion. The composition also allowed Lennon to express his new radicalism in interviews. "They knock me for saying 'Power To The People' and say that no one section should have the power," he complained. "Rubbish! The people aren't a section. The people means everyone. I think that everyone should own everything equally and that the people should own part of the factories and they should have some say in who is the boss and who does what. Students should be able to select teachers. It might be like communism, but I don't really know what real communism is. There is no real communist state in the world . . . Russia isn't. It's a fascist state. The socialism I talk about is a British socialism, not the way some daft Russian might do it, or the Chinese might do it. That might suit them. We'd have a nice socialism here. A British socialism."

Happy Xmas (War Is Over)

Recently added as a bonus track to *Some Time In New York City*, where it is analysed in detail, this song was a festive favourite, whose release in the UK was delayed until December 1972. Thereafter, it was a regular Christmas chart contender. Lennon was proud of its longevity. As he explained to the BBC's Andy Peebles: "What we wanted to do was have something besides 'White Christmas' being played every Christmas. And there's always wars, right; there's always somebody getting shot. So, every year you could play it . . . the lyric stands in that respect . . . I've always wanted to write something that would be a Christmas record, that would last forever."

Give Peace A Chance: Reprise

The compilation ends with 'Happy Xmas (War Is Over)' segueing into this 50-second live version of 'Give Peace A Chance' taken from the August 1972 One To One concert. *Newsweek* magazine neatly summed up the impact of the song: "It will serve as the centrepiece for sing-ins at shopping centres planned in Washington and will join the list of carols to be sung in projected nation-wide Christmas Eve demonstrations . . . The peace movement has found an anthem."

Full Track Listing: *Give Peace A Chance; Cold Turkey; Instant Karma!; Power To The People; Mother; Woman Is The Nigger Of The World; Imagine; Whatever Gets You Thru The Night; Mind Games; # 9 Dream; (a) Happy Xmas (War Is Over) (b) Give Peace A Chance: Reprise.*

DOUBLE FANTASY

Released: November 1980

Original UK issue: Geffen K 99131. US issue: Geffen GHS 2001. CD reissue with
bonus tracks: EMI 5 28739 2 (UK)/Capitol 5 28739 2 (US)

The second half of the Seventies saw Lennon finally settled in
America having successfully obtained a much prized green card in
July 1976. During the hearing, which took place in New York, a
number of witnesses testified on his behalf including sculptor Isamu
Noguchi, television news reporter Geraldo Rivera, actress Gloria
Swanson, and writer Norman Mailer who said: "I think John Lennon
is a great artist who has made an enormous contribution to popular
culture. He is one of the great artists of the Western world. We lost
T.S. Eliot to England and only got Auden back . . . it would be splen-
did to have Mr Lennon as well." Outside the courtroom, Lennon
paid special tribute to Yoko Ono, who had given birth to his son
Sean the previous year. "It's great to be legal again. I'll tell my baby. I
thank Yoko and the Immigration Service who have finally seen the
light of day. It's been a long, slow road, but I am not bitter. I can't get
into that. On the contrary, now I can go and see my relations in Japan
and elsewhere. Again, I thank Yoko. I've always thought there's a
great woman behind every idiot."

Lennon cut down his social and media activities after securing his
green card. In January 1977, he and Yoko attended President Jimmy
Carter's inaugural ball in Washington, but such high profile sightings
became increasingly rare. True to his word, he did visit Japan with
his family, spending four months there in the summer of 1977 and
returning for further lengthy visits in 1978 and 1979, seemingly
beyond the glare of the Anglo-American media. As he correctly
informed one friendly journalist in search of an interview: "I am
invisible."

After the birth of his son Sean, John Lennon elected to become a
house husband, attempting to fulfil the fatherly obligations that had

been so patently lacking in the rearing of his first boy Julian. The decision meant that he could finally break the cycle of abandonment that had begun in his own disrupted childhood, when his parents had given him no time instead of it all. Although Lennon's retreat to domesticity was later seen as a fully fledged retirement, he had always intended to return to his musical career once Sean had reached five years of age. As he said: "We've basically decided, without a great decision, to be with our baby as much as we can until we feel we can take the time off to indulge ourselves creating things outside the family. Maybe when he's three, four or five then we'll think about creating something else other than the child." For the remainder of the Seventies, he kept his word and never once entered a recording studio or appeared on a stage. His only concession to the creative urge was to tinker with some home demos, usually just after his birthday each year. Several of these fragments and works in progress would be revived and completed when he re-emerged to record a new album at the end of the decade.

Lennon's 'Dakota days' have since become the subject of legend with wildly varying accounts of his everyday activities. Tales of eccentric behaviour, fad diets, nicotine and caffeine addiction, drug consumption, temper tantrums, sexual frustrations, erotic fantasies, spiritual unrest, religious conversions, magic rituals, neurotic behaviour, wild mood swings, extreme fasts and vows of silence, spending sprees, excessive indolence, elongated periods in front of a television, horoscope readings, 'secret' vacations and much else have been mentioned by 'insiders', gossip columnists and biographers. Given the four-year period in question and Lennon's mercurial personality, some of the contradictions are not surprising.

His seemingly erratic relationship with Yoko, childlike dependency and interaction with Sean have also prompted provocative comments, especially from those claiming to have read his unpublished diaries. When viewed in strict, chronological form, detailed diaries and letters often provide a penetrating but unbearably banal account of everyday life, full of inconsistencies, petty details, passing preoccupations, exaggerated hopes and fears, pseudo-profound ruminations, digressions, endless self-absorption and seemingly erratic progress. Although Lennon's diaries remain unpublished, their contents have infiltrated the pages of several biographies and memoirs and, given their existence, the unexpurgated complete version will no doubt appear at some future point. Their bleakness will inevitably colour any serious account of his final years, but it is necessary to add that had Lennon documented the Beatle period or any other stage of his life in such detail then the results would probably have seemed equally dark and filled with doubts and moments of self-loathing. As his lyrics revealed, Lennon's introspection was almost always accompanied by brutally honest admissions and sometimes shocking confessions. Iconoclasm was his watchword.

With time on his hands during the late Seventies, Lennon resembled a chameleon, zig-zagging through life in apparently purposeless fashion, a changing character from week to week – a drug user, a health obsessive with a strict regime, a sluggish loafer, a student of Japanese, an airy presence obsessed with numerology, astrology and documenting his dreams, an adventurer who enjoyed learning how to sail and teaching his child to swim, a distant, grumpy person and an engaging, loving, devoted father. The listless Lennon was quite capable of retiring to the sanctum of his Dakota bedroom for a spell, then suddenly rousing himself from his inertia and jetting around the world, visiting various locations ranging from Egypt to the Caribbean and South Africa. Many of these excursions were at the behest of his wife whose interest in tarot cards and fortuitous travel was much commented upon. Inspired by oriental numerology and astrology, she believed in 'directional trips', specific routes that can change a person's fate, which partly explains Lennon's veritable circum-navigation of the globe. For a supposed recluse, he remained a well-travelled man.

There were similar contrasts in his own private comments on his life during this period. In the prose piece 'The Ballad Of John And Yoko', later included in his posthumously published book *Skywriting By Word Of Mouth*, he portrayed himself as a man fully in control of his destiny. "I am blessed with a second chance. Being a Beatle nearly cost me my life, and certainly cost me a great deal of my health . . . I will not make the same mistake twice in one lifetime . . . If I never 'produce' anything more for public consumption than 'silence', so be it. Amen." Of course, at other times, in his audio diaries, he sounded thoroughly disillusioned and embittered, although even then there was a lively reptilian bite to his observations, particularly when discussing fellow rock icons, Paul McCartney and Bob Dylan. His inner thoughts and outward actions were frequently in conflict.

For the general public, Lennon remained a shadowy figure. Our only clues to his whereabouts and well-being were sporadic tabloid reports and occasional asides from former friends and colleagues. In May 1979, as a response to the ongoing rumours, a full-page advertisement was placed in newspapers in New York, London and Tokyo titled 'A Love Letter From John And Yoko To People Who Ask What, When, And Why'. Its message was the familiar litany of love, peace and good vibes, written in Ono's distinctive meandering style, and veering between the metaphorical and the literal. An extensive account of their spring cleaning routine took up a paragraph and there was a strong recommendation that we invest in the 'logic of magic': "Wishing is more effective than waving flags. It works." Drawing halos over pictures of their enemies' heads was another positive action, leading them to conclude that "all people who come to see us are angels in disguise carrying messages and gifts from the universe." After eulogizing Sean, the plants and cats, the letter concluded with the assurance "our silence is a silence of love and not of indifference . . . We are all part of the sky."

Statements such as the above perpetuated the 'John & Yoko' myth, causing cynics to suggest that the entire Dakota period was nothing more than an idyllic fantasy, a view reinforced by the allegedly explicit contents of Lennon's diaries. The truth was surely far more complex and intriguing. Even at his worst moments, Lennon never denied the enduring intensity and sometimes desperate nature of his love for Yoko Ono. For all his private protestations of fear, hopelessness, acrophobia, inertia and unsociability, the public man was the complete opposite. His final interviews were a testament to positive thinking, optimism, humour, good grace and industry. Their conviction can be qualified but never negated by troubled writings seemingly designed to purge his soul of negativity. Both the private and the public persona are subject to excessive pronouncements and Lennon sounded a lot more logical and cogent in his best interviews than in his prose ramblings. To choose one over the other in search of the 'real Lennon' seems at best inadequate and unimaginative.

It was not until 1980 that Lennon felt ready to record a new album and, in complete contrast to the doubts expressed in his private meditations, he again displayed a confident presence, clearly eager to work hard and enjoy the company of his fellow musicians. An important catalyst, according to Lennon, was a trip from Newport, Rhode Island to Bermuda during which he was called upon to navigate a yacht during a sea storm. "No one else could move," he recalled. "They were sick as dogs, so there I was, driving the boat. I was smashed in the face by waves for six solid hours. I was screaming sea shanties and shouting at the gods. I felt like a Viking. Once I got to Bermuda, I was so centred after the experience at sea that I was tuned in to the cosmos." A flurry of songwriting activity followed, convincing Lennon to push ahead with an album project. The work soon developed into a musical dialogue between himself and Yoko, who was keen to showcase her material as a complement to his own. During a visit to the Bermuda Botanical Gardens, Lennon saw a hybrid freesia named Double Fantasy, a title which he felt would be perfect for their new record. Tellingly, he described the work as "an exploration of sexual fantasies" rather than a romantic saga.

In choosing a co-producer, they settled on Jack Douglas, who had previously worked as an engineer on *Imagine*, later establishing himself with such acts as Cheap Trick, Aerosmith and Alice Cooper. A tight team of session musicians was enlisted for the recording sessions at New York's Hit Factory, including guitarists Earl Slick and Hugh McCracken, bassist Tony Levin, drummer Andy Newmark, keyboardist George Small and percussionist Arthur Jenkins.

News that Lennon had entered a recording studio for the first time since April 1976 rapidly reached the executive heads of the world's largest record companies. Telegrams were despatched expressing interest, but most of the requests were directed to John Lennon, an unintended slight on his wife whose role in his business and creative life was paramount. One person who did not make that mistake was the canny David Geffen, who was then in the process of setting up his own company, Geffen Records. Geffen had managed the talented singer-songwriter Laura Nyro in the late Sixties, before finding his niche as a record company man with the founding of Asylum Records, the artiste friendly label that launched the careers of Judee Sill, the Eagles and Jackson Browne. Along with Elliot Roberts (manager of Neil Young and Joni Mitchell), Geffen was a prominent figure in the convoluted career evolution of Crosby, Stills, Nash & Young. At one point, he even resurrected the original Byrds for a reunion album. In perhaps his greatest coup, Geffen had prised Bob Dylan from CBS for a spell, during which the master recorded two albums for Geffen: *Planet Waves* and the double live set *Before The Flood*. If he could win over Dylan, Geffen reasoned, then signing Lennon was worth a try. He succeeded by ingratiating himself with Yoko and finally offering to release their record 'unheard'.

After signing with Geffen Records on 22 September, Lennon concluded the sessions at the Record Plant East and prepared for the media blitz attending his 40th birthday and 'comeback' album. When *Double Fantasy* finally appeared, critical reaction was sharply divided. British reviewers, still caught up in the maelstrom of post punk, felt disappointed by its flaccidity and found it cloying in comparison to his previous work. They were hoping for something in the spirit of 'Cold Turkey' and found only cosy sentimentality. A sneering review in *Melody Maker* concluded, "The whole thing positively reeks of an indulgent sterility – it's a god-awful yawn." *NME*'s Charles Shaar Murray was equally damning: "For people imprinted with the passions and preoccupations of the Beatles years, the release of *Double Fantasy* is, of necessity, an Event, though maybe not a happy one. Everybody else – straight to the next review please . . . let's waste no more time on John Lennon. On this showing he can get back to the kitchen and mind the kid and the cows, because all the most interesting material on *Double Fantasy* is Yoko's . . . Still Yoko's vision is by no means unflawed . . . *Double Fantasy* is right: a fantasy made for two (with a little cot at the foot of the bed). It sounds like a great life. But, unfortunately, it makes a lousy record . . . That's why I look forward to a Yoko Ono solo album, why I wish that Lennon had kept his big, happy trap shut until he had something to say that was even vaguely relevant to those of us not married to Yoko Ono, and why I'm pissed off because I haven't heard the new Jam album yet. Now bliss off."

Lennon was probably unsurprised by the negative reaction in the UK rock weeklies. He was happy enough to have escaped the more serious backlash against the rock aristocracy that had occurred during the first flowering of punk. "God help Bruce Springsteen when they decide he's no longer God," he had said. "When he gets down to facing his own success and growing older and having to produce it again and again, they'll turn on him and I hope he survives it."

American critics were generally more generous and less judgemental than their UK counterparts, although a number of negative reviews were pulled at the eleventh hour following the news of Lennon's death. Unlike the UK writers who saw their work printed on 24 November, the Americans had no weekly national music papers. So there was still time to 'kill' a review. Nonetheless, there was certainly some strong criticism in the US news media. The *Boston Phoenix*'s Kit Rachlis was evidently not alone in expressing annoyance at the assumption "that lots of people care deeply about John Lennon and Yoko Ono." In the influential New York paper *Village Voice*, Geoffrey Stokes' review was pointedly titled 'The Infantilization Of John Lennon'. One month later, the *Village Voice*'s self-styled 'dean of American rock criticism' Robert Christgau wrote an eloquent appraisal, testifying to Lennon's new maturity in what was effectively a re-review of the album.

"The simplistic words and less adventurous music were off-putting at first," he admitted. But, it seemed in the wake of Lennon's assassination everything was changed utterly and a terrible beauty was born. "*Double Fantasy* is now a pop event, its slightest moments here gained pathos, impact and significance . . . The elementary device of alternating cuts between the two spouses (no duets) makes their union come alive more than any of the often one-dimensional lyrics. But I ought to admit that, for the most part, I like the lyrics, especially John's. I liked the lyrics on his *Plastic One Band* too, not so much for what they said or how they said it, but for what they said *about* how they said it – that John's commitment to the outspoken and straightforward knew no bounds. Nine years later, though he's more mature, more amiable, happier, that commitment is unchanged. I use the present tense, of course, to refer to art . . . A great album? No, but memorable and gratifying in its slight, self-limiting way – connubial rock 'n' roll is hard to find."

While Christgau reacted positively to the dialogue of alternating perspectives, others were more critical of the device. Author and critic Francine Prose countered: "*Double Fantasy* is a conceptual piece, but the concept doesn't work. John's song, then Yoko's . . . we can't keep making the necessary transitions and adjustments, it doesn't function as dialogue or harmony or counterpoint, so what we're left with is the jumpy unease one gets around a couple who keep interrupting each other."

Structural arguments aside, *Double Fantasy* was more important as possibly the first album by a major Sixties figure to address the issues of middle age in a culture obsessed by youth and faux rebellion. "I cannot be a punk in Hamburg and Liverpool any more," Lennon said. "I'm older now. I see the world through different eyes." In his last ever interview, conducted with RKO Radio on 8 December 1980, Lennon eloquently expressed his own feelings about the album's significance: "When I was writing this, I was visualizing all the people of my age group . . . being in their thirties and forties now, just like me, and having wives and children and having gone through everything together. I'm singing for them . . . I'm saying, 'Here I am now. How are you? How's your relationship going? Did you get through it all? Wasn't the Seventies a drag, you know? Here we are. Well, let's try to make the Eighties good, you know, because it's still up to us to make what we can of it' . . . We were the hip ones in the Sixties, but the world is not like the Sixties. The whole world's changed and we're going into an unknown future, but we're still all here."

Albums released by major artistes after long absences always prompt high expectations and *Double Fantasy* was no exception. Despite certain critics' reservations, it clearly contained some of Lennon's best work, and some pretty average material too. Perhaps the most surprising aspect of the album was the emergence of Yoko Ono as a convincingly commercial writer, with a couple of harder-

edged songs that had a punch missing from her husband's more contented meditations. While the overall feel of the album suggested
middle-aged satisfaction, a closer listen to several of the tracks indi-
cated some conflict amid the Edenic bliss. The production gloss
sometimes disguised the starker moments on the record, but they
were there, dramatized within the 'answer song' format. As Lennon
said: "The work we did on this is really a play, but we used ourselves
as characters."

The role-playing was extremely effective in fashioning the concept
of the 'heart play'. Lennon included some of the most poignant love
songs of his career on this record, leaving Ono to offer the occasional
rebuttal. The structure recalled the totally contrasting *Some Time In
New York City*, albeit from a different viewpoint. There, in such
songs as 'Luck Of The Irish', it was Ono who offered the overtly
sentimental perspective, while Lennon provided the lyrical bite, just
as he had frequently done when writing with Paul McCartney. On
Double Fantasy, the roles were audaciously reversed, with Lennon
playing the Ono role of dreamy romantic while she provided the
barbs that cut through the occasional mawkishness. Judging from the
album's outtakes and rehearsals, Lennon might easily have assembled
a very different work in which his idyllic portrayals were qualified by
some characteristically sardonic musings. Some claim that this was his
original intention. That Ono was allowed the privilege was part of
the play. Indeed, had this been a Lennon solo album, it is likely that
he would have taken on both roles as arch sentimentalist and
debunker. Oddly, most critics failed to appreciate the fantasy role-
playing favoured by Lennon and Ono and treated the album too
literally, as if it was a confessional piece rather than a carefully constructed artifice, designed to celebrate an idealized mythology.

For most listeners, uninterested in the critical debate, it was just
good to hear Lennon singing again after such a long hiatus. In interviews, he spoke of taking the record on tour in the New Year and
promised that a follow-up, already apparently under way, would
be completed soon. Given his restless spirit, it is not easy to predict
what Lennon might have done next, especially considering the
contemporaneous work of Yoko Ono, whose intriguing 'Walking

On Thin Ice' he was producing during the final days of his life. He spoke of "a new era of Lennon/Ono music", which presumably embraced the ongoing romantic saga of John and Yoko in the form of a sequel to *Double Fantasy*, plus the more radical experimentation that he had enjoyed since the controversial days of *Two Virgins*. No doubt, Lennon and Ono would have continued to release work, together and apart. Whatever might have been achieved was lost in the madness that prompted a deranged Beatles' fan to murder his tainted idol. The dream was over.

(Just Like) Starting Over

The album opens with the sound of Yoko's wishing bell, its gentle tinkling deliberately intended to remind the listener of the contrasting funereal bells of 'Mother', the first track on Lennon's premier solo work. Whereas 'Mother' had revealed Lennon in the throes of intense pain, 'Starting Over' is an optimistic reiteration of love's vows, and looks optimistically towards a happy middle age. Despite the upbeat, playful arrangement, there are signs of past tension, most notably in the plea about why they can't be making love which takes on a subtextual importance if considered alongside Lennon's alleged diary entries. But it is the revitalization of the relationship that propels the song.

The composition was one of the last completed during Lennon's writing spell in the summer of 1980. "I wrote it when I was in Bermuda with Sean, while Yoko was attending to business. It just came out that way. All the other songs were finished and it and 'Cleanup Time' came out sort of like fun after the work was done. It has the Fifties-ish sound because I have never really written a song that sounded like that period, although that was my period, the music I identified with. So I just thought, 'Why the hell not?' In the Beatle days that would have been taken as a joke. One avoided clichés. But, of course, now those clichés are not clichés any more." At one point, Lennon seriously considered omitting a line from the song which contained the word 'wings' for fear that it might be interpreted as another comment on Paul McCartney.

Musically, the song is quite simple, with Lennon undercutting the schmaltz arrangement and sentimental lyrics with a mock rockabilly vocal. Although not the best song on the album, its theme of renewal could be interpreted as an advert for the Lennons' comeback. According to John, the song's title was slightly amended at the eleventh hour: "It was really called 'Starting Over' but, while we were making it, people kept putting things out with the same title. There was a country & western hit called 'Starting Over', so I added '(Just Like)' at the last minute . . . The musicians got very loose because it was so simple rock 'n' roll . . . 'Starting Over' was the best way to start over. And, to me, it was like going back to 15 and singing *à la* Presley . . . I was referring to 'Elvis Orbison'. It's kind of 'I Want You, I Need You . . . ', 'Only The Lonely' . . . a kind of parody, but not really parody." '(Just Like) Starting Over' was issued as a pilot single at the end of October and climbed into the UK Top 10. In the wake of his death, it topped the charts on both sides of the Atlantic.

Kiss Kiss Kiss

This track showed evidence of Yoko's commercial instincts, employing a contemporary sound, with a bright new wave arrangement, featuring Andy Newmark's drums prominent in the mix and the vocal surprisingly orthodox. In earlier years she might have screamed her lungs out for 10 minutes, but here she offers a brief and erotically charged orgasmic moan to bring the song to a startling conclusion. Her faked climax, culminating in the Japanese 'mote, mote, mote' ('more, more, more') both astounded and amused those present. As she told the BBC: "I started to do it, and then I suddenly looked and all these engineers were all looking and I thought, 'I can't . . .' So I said, 'Turn off all the lights' . . . They put the screen around me and I did it that way."

The composition has a visceral edge with dark images of a shattered mirror, blood, terror, and death. According to Ono, the song expressed her feelings about modern society's denigration of emotional expression and the way a patriarchal culture creates divisions and a lack of communication among people from an early age. "In our childhood we were more capable of touching and kissing each other more freely, but even childhood society has these restrictions."

Cleanup Time

"It's a piano lick, with words added," Lennon explained, when recalling the origin of this satisfied tale of domestic union. "I was talking to [co-producer] Jack Douglas on the phone from Bermuda. We were talking about the Seventies and about people's getting out of drugs and alcohol, and those kind of things. And he said, 'Well, it's clean-up time, right?' And I said, 'It sure is.' That was the end of the conversation. I went straight to the piano and just started boogieing and 'Cleanup Time' came out. Then I had the music and thought, 'What is this about?' I only had the title. So then I wrote the story on top of the music. It's sort of a description of John and Yoko in their palace, the Palace of Versailles, the Dakota: 'The queen is in the counting house, counting up the money; the king is in the kitchen . . .'" The latter quote adapts the nursery rhyme 'Sing A Song Of Sixpence' to humorous effect and there is also a reference to the couple's interest in angels, astrology, numerology and tarot with the allusion to consulting the oracle and casting the perfect magic spell.

Give Me Something

An acid answer to 'Cleanup Time', and far more impressive, this chilling and accusative song features Ono tearing down the John and Yoko myth of domestic bliss. Set against an edgy new wave arrangement, it is dominated by images of frustration as cold eyes result in a 'cold bed'. It sets a pattern for much of the album with Lennon romanticizing their relationship while Ono takes a more cynical view of proceedings. At the end of the song, she even adopts a self-martyred tone, offering 'tear and flesh' before adding contemptuously, 'you can have it'. For those who claimed that *Double Fantasy* was nothing more than an idyllic myth, this song – along with the next two – contradicted that popular notion.

I'm Losing You

Lennon returns to the more familiar lyrical territory of emotional insecurity for this track, one of the best on the album. An earlier, more jagged version had been recorded with Rick Nielsen and Bun E. Carlos of Cheap Trick, but was vetoed and only appeared as late as

1998 on *Anthology*. Producer Jack Douglas was sufficiently impressed with the original to run it through the musicians' headphones for inspiration while they were tackling this. The song's pent-up anger and fear of losing Yoko propels Lennon back to memories of their last estrangement. Indeed, one verse in the song reads like an outtake from the lost weekend. Recalling how he hurt her in the past, he complains that the incident is now ancient history and even accuses her of carrying a cross of bitterness based on old resentments. There is even some of that familiar blood imagery, also heard on 'Kiss Kiss Kiss'. Lennon confirmed that his song spanned two eras of emotional disturbance: "It's about the past, but I actually started writing it when I called from Bermuda and I couldn't get through to Yoko. I was just mad as hell, feeling lost and separate. But it's also a description of the separation period in the early Seventies when I physically couldn't get through."

He later added, "But, getting a bit distant from it, it is expressing the losing you . . . losing one's mother, losing one's everything, losing everything you've ever lost in that song . . ."

I'm Moving On

'I'm Losing You' dramatically segues into Yoko Ono's answer song, which is her best moment on the album. The lyrics actually date back to 1973, when their relationship was clearly in trouble, but the idea of reviving the composition as a spiteful riposte was truly inspired. In a remarkable diatribe, Ono accuses Lennon of fickleness, suspected infidelity and, worst of all perhaps, being a phoney. There's even a cold, erotic allusion to sticking a finger in a pie that echoes a similar line in the Beatles' 'Penny Lane'.

'I'm Moving On' provides a welcome moment of harsh realism, which splendidly undercuts the romantic depiction of John and Yoko's fairy-tale marriage. It also underlines the extent to which they constructed the album as a play, using contrasting songs for dramatic effect. This was a more complex mythology than some writers and biographers give them credit for. Clearly, the Lennons were not afraid to admit that there was trouble in paradise and anyone listening to the album in search of autobiography must have felt caught between the confused belief that they were still love's young dream yet seemingly close to splitting up. That contradiction remains in the 'I'm Losing You'/'I'm Moving On' segment, which provides the backbone to the album. The Cheap Trick duo that graced the original 'I'm Losing You' also appeared on the first attempt at this song, but their contribution has yet to be released on any archival album.

Beautiful Boy (Darling Boy)

Although some felt this song to be over-sentimental, it was still a fine example of Lennon's rejection of traditional macho rock ideals. His description of the father/son relationship is very poignant in places and there is even a touch of homespun philosophy in the line about life being a process that happens while you're vainly pursuing different plans. The bedtime advice closes with Lennon whispering goodnight, followed by the dream-like sounds of children playing in the water.

The ballad was apparently in the back of Lennon's mind for some time, even before he completed a home demo of the song in late 1979. As he explained: "I was with Sean in the kitchen with the bread . . . I kept thinking, 'Well, I ought to be inspired to write about Sean' . . . I was going through a bit of that and when I finally gave up on thinking about writing a song about him, of course, the song came to me." The track retained a tropical, Caribbean feel, complete with Robert Greenidge's steel drum prominent in the mix. In common with several other compositions on the album, the lyrics took on a sadly ironic ring in view of Lennon's impending death. Almost in passing, he sings about his desire to come of age and the need to be patient. These were the words of a man who felt he still had all the time in the world.

Watching The Wheels

Another of Lennon's great tracks, this was his provocative defence of indolence, a theme previously heard to strong effect on the Beatles' 'I'm Only Sleeping' and, to a lesser extent, on 'I'm So Tired'. The inspiration for the song came from reading other people's comments on his extended sabbatical from the music business. Among these was a 1978 issue of *NME* which carried the headline: 'Where The Hell Are You, John Lennon?' In addition, there were some flippant remarks in the media from Paul McCartney and Mick Jagger that Lennon evidently took to heart. "People have been saying I'm lazy, dreaming my life away, all my life," he pointed out. "Pop stars were getting indignant in the press that I wasn't making records. I couldn't believe it. They were acting like mothers-in-law. I don't know whether it was Mick [Jagger] or who. What's it got to do with them if I never do another record in my life?"

His rejection of the music business rat race is almost as radical a statement as 'Give Peace A Chance' or 'Woman Is The Nigger Of The World'. He often recalled the surprise he felt in realizing that life did not stop when his name no longer appeared in the music trade magazine *Billboard*. "I just had to let it go," he could say, with satisfaction. There is only one moment in the song where Lennon's contentment is qualified by a Freudian slip. Towards the end he refers to himself sitting around just 'doing time', as if his self-imposed isolation in the Dakota is akin to a prison sentence.

The image of the wheel in the song's title also allowed Lennon to indulge in some quasi-mystical speculation during interviews. "The whole universe is a wheel, right?" he imparted sagely to *Rolling Stone*. "Wheels go round and round. They're my own wheels, mainly. Watching myself is like watching everybody else. And I watch myself through my child too . . . The hardest part is facing yourself. It's easier to shout about 'Revolution' and 'Power To The People' than it is to look at yourself and try to find out what's real inside you and what isn't . . ." Musically, this was arguably the strongest song on the album with a memorable melody and some delicate touches, like the hammer dulcimer played by Matthew Cunningham.

I'm Your Angel

Between the fade-out of 'Watching The Wheels' and the beginning of this track, there is a brief segue of music and recorded conversation. Journalist Jonathan Cott was sufficiently intrigued by the effect to tease the following lengthy explanation from Lennon: "One of the voices is me going, 'God bless you, man, thank you, you've got a lucky face,' which is what the English guys who beg or want a tip say, so that's what you hear me mumbling. And then we re-created the sounds of what Yoko and I call the Strawberries and Violin room – the Palm Court at the Plaza Hotel. We like to sit there occasionally and listen to the old violin and have a cup of tea and some straw-berries. It's romantic. And so the picture is: there's this kind of street prophet, Hyde Park Corner-type guy who just watches the wheels going around, pronouncing on whatever he's pronouncing on. And people are throwing money in his hat, and he's saying, 'Thank you, thank you.' And then you get in the horse carriage and you go around New York and go into the hotel and the violins are playing and then this woman comes and sings about being an angel."

Alas, the actual song proves terribly anti-climactic, with Yoko reverting to her baby voice, set against a 1920s style arrangement. Essentially a 'happy birthday' song, presumably to celebrate Lennon's 40th, the composition is full of Cinderella imagery, including refer-ences to angels and magic, followed by the ambiguous quip, 'You're my fairy!' The melody so closely resembled the evergreen 'Making Whoopee' that its publishers subsequently sought damages for alleged plagiarism.

Woman

This song features the most beautiful melody on the album and it was no surprise when it climbed to number 1 in the UK charts after Lennon's murder. On one level, the composition can be seen as an obsequious tribute to Yoko Ono, but Lennon felt that it held a more universal message. "That's to Yoko and to all women in a way," he told *Playboy*'s David Sheff. "My history of relationships with women is a very poor one – very macho, very stupid . . . very sensitive and insecure but acting aggressive and macho. You know, trying to cover up the feminine side, which I still have a tendency to do. But I'm learning to acknowledge that it's all right to be soft. I tend to put my cowboy boots on when I'm insecure, whereas now I'm in sneakers and it's comfy."

While some commentators saw the song simply as a mainstream ballad, those familiar with Lennon's *oeuvre* took a wider view of its significance. Tracing a history of Lennon's love songs and comments on women, it is possible to see a gradual development from the macho cool narrator of 'Girl', through the proselytizing new man campaigner in 'Woman Is The Nigger Of The World' to the humble house husband of 'Woman'. Lennon was equally keen to place 'Woman' in some kind of historical context. When interviewed by the BBC, he suggested: "It sounds a bit like 'Girl' and a bit Beatley, but I do like it . . . I'm supposed to be macho, Butch Cassidy or something and tough Lennon with the leather jacket and swearing. And I really am just as romantic as the next guy, and I always was. It's sort of an Eighties version of 'Girl' to me. I call this one the Beatle track . . . It suddenly hit me about what women represent to us, not as the sex object or the mother, but just their contribution. That's why you hear me muttering at the beginning 'For the other half of the sky', which is Chairman Mao's famous statement. That it *is* the other half. All this thing about man, woman . . . is a joke. Without each other, there ain't nothing . . . It was a different viewpoint of what I'd felt about woman and I can't express it better than in the song."

Beautiful Boys

Yoko extends the thematic framework of Lennon's 'Beautiful Boy' to comment on both her son and husband. Addressing each in turn, she includes an interesting observation on John's psychology: that in one sense he has everything he can carry, yet somehow still feels empty. Beginning with an Eastern-style feel, the musical arrangement includes some fleeting flamenco guitar midway through. The song encourages exploration, but concludes with the gentle warning, 'Don't be afraid to be afraid'. While mulling over that line, Lennon added: "I'm not afraid to be afraid, though it's always scary. But it's more painful to try not to be yourself. People spend a lot of time trying to be somebody else."

Dear Yoko

If '(Just Like) Starting Over' was Lennon's vocal tribute to Elvis Presley and Roy Orbison, then this was an even more obvious homage to Buddy Holly. It is also 'Oh Yoko!' revisited, with Lennon again expressing affection for his wife by cataloguing her ever present influence upon the most mundane aspects of his daily life. While other writers might have fictionalized the experience or referred more obliquely to an unnamed muse, Lennon clearly preferred to be as particular and direct as possible. As he noted: "The track's a nice track and it happens to be about my wife instead of 'Dear Sandra' or some other person that a singer would sing about who may or may not exist." The barely audible dialogue at the end of the song presents a caricature of Ono as the busy businesswoman, with Lennon playfully complaining: "When you come over next time, don't sell a cow. Spend some time with me and Sean. You'd like it." The 'cow' allusion referred to Ono's successful sale of a Holstein bovine at the New York State Fair in Syracuse for a supposedly record-breaking $265,000.

Every Man Has A Woman Who Loves Him
With its overtly contemporary arrangement and production, this sounded like one of the lesser tracks on the album, although the melody line is memorable enough. The lyrics feature Ono musing over the contradictory elements of her relationship with Lennon. Rarely for Yoko, there are hints of self-reproach in the lyrics. There is also a strong suggestion of her own fickleness, most notably the admission that she suffers wanderlust and roams, even though she knows her husband is 'the one'.

Ono's new-found melodic accessibility divided critics, some of whom questioned her motives and means of expression. While the *NME*'s Charles Shaar Murray praised her efforts, with some qualification, and later chroniclers like Peter Doggett championed the radicalism of her early work, others were left cold. Cultural commentator Francine Prose, who wrote a challenging essay on Ono in *The Lives Of The Muses*, recognized "the desperate competition for individual attention suffusing *Double Fantasy*" and responded negatively to the artist's apparent pop/disco makeover. "Yoko's contributions to *Double Fantasy* are so awful and disingenuous that they make you long for the howling of her earlier compositions, which at least seemed sincere. It's not merely that they suggest bad disco versions of bad Japanese pop music but that they seem calculated to please, to amuse, and most important, to sell. Yoko's songs appear to have been composed by someone who deconstructed the work of currently popular musicians – Blondie, Talking Heads, Patti Smith – and tried to figure out why they were so successful . . . Everything is airless, programmatic . . . In its own way, *Double Fantasy* is as tough to listen to as *Two Virgins*."

Hard Times Are Over

Yoko is allowed the last word with this anthemic finale, which offers the comforts of middle-aged security after a lifetime of struggle. It also brings to a positive end the ups and downs of a relationship dramatized in the *Heart Play*. According to its composer, it was written in the form of a prayer, inspired by memories of a car trip across America. While travelling from New York to San Francisco, Lennon and Ono stopped off in a city (neither could remember the exact location) to fill up the car with gasoline. For no explicable reason, they both experienced one of those epiphanic moments. All they could recall was looking into each other's eyes and realizing everything was well in their world. The chorus includes a crucial qualification to the main theme: 'hard times are over *for a while.*' Soon, it would be clear how short those good times were to be.

In October 2000, a remixed/remastered version of *Double Fantasy* was released, with three bonus tracks as follows:

Help Me To Help Myself

"What's the matter with this thing? It's sticking on my feet here. That's why we've been interrupted. Very bad." This humorous preamble, in Lennon's familiar Peter Sellers' 'Indian' voice, gives no indication of the bleak composition that is to follow as a funereal piano accompaniment, similar to 'Imagine', sets the scene for a most unexpected journey. Angels appear frequently in the written work of Lennon and Ono and are mentioned in certain songs, always as a force for good. Here, however, he faces the Angel of Death, a destructive entity that threatens to hound him to the grave. As early as the opening line, Lennon laments how he tried so hard to remain alive, as if the struggle has already been lost. Tellingly, the lyric sheet replaces the words 'stay alive' with the innocuous 'settle down' in a flagrant misinterpretation of the songwriter's intent. In common with a similar amendment on the incorrectly spelt 'The Rishi Kesh Song', it reads as if there has been a retrospective attempt to censor or banish such suicidal speculations. In his despair, Lennon turns to the Lord for salvation, but is seemingly undone by memories of that old adage: 'God helps those that help themselves'. Although recorded as a home demo in 1980, this is a song that could have been written at Lennon's lowest ebb during the hangover that accompanied the 'lost weekend'. Indeed, this may be the case. Beneath the encroaching despair and candid acknowledgement that he has never been satisfied with life, is a plea, seemingly directed at Yoko Ono. The line in which he states his conviction that they never really parted, thematically echoes the assurances offered in the otherwise cheerless 'Bless You'. Could 'Help Me To Help Myself' have been a leftover from that same era?

Walking On Thin Ice
It says much for Lennon that his final creative act was working on this Yoko Ono single. He was excited about the composition and production, which he saw as presaging a new era in the evolution of their partnership, a view that found favour with most critics, albeit after his death. As Ono recalls: " 'Walking On Thin Ice' was what we were remixing that night [8 December 1980]. The past weekend we had listened to the song all day and all night. It was as if we were both haunted by the song. I remember I woke up in the morning and found John watching the sunrise and still listening to the song. He said I had to put it out right away as a single."

No Yoko Ono release received such positive reviews or looked more likely to succeed commercially. Unlike the songs on *Double Fantasy*, it sounded voguish and contemporary, its New York disco edge allied to some avant-garde touches and characteristically opaque lyrics. The screams were still there, but now reduced to whelps and used as a backbeat for Tony Levin's upfront bass. The song's title is evoked in the chilling and oddly soulless ambience, complete with desolate lyrics in which hearts turn to ashes and real life events and emotions are reduced to mere stories. In the final verse, Ono switches to a spoken-word account of a girl who tried to walk on thin ice. It has the feel of a modern-day Grimm's fairy-tale, minus the narrative drama.

Released as a single in February 1981, it came as no surprise when 'Walking On Thin Ice' entered the UK charts. Peaking at number 35, its progress was probably halted by the lack of a chorus or easily remembered melody. Geffen may well have pressed too many copies in anticipation of greater things, as the single was subsequently included as a free gift inside Yoko Ono's next solo album, *Season Of Glass*.

Central Park Stroll (dialogue)
Seventeen seconds and 13 words long, this snippet captures Lennon walking with Yoko Ono in Central Park at a time when he genuinely believed it was safe to saunter around the streets of New York. With an air of sarcasm in his voice, he portrays himself and Ono as just 'two average people', knowing that everyone else in the world saw them as extraordinary.

POSTHUMOUS RELEASES

THE JOHN LENNON COLLECTION

Released: November 1982

Original UK issue: EMI EMTV 37. US issue Geffen GHSP 2023.
CD reissue: EMI CD-EMTV 37 (UK)/Capitol 7 91516 2 (US)

With strong television promotion in the UK, this compilation climbed to number 1, in striking contrast to its disappointing performance in the US charts, where it stalled at number 33. Reasonably generous, with 19 tracks on the CD version ('Move Over Ms L' and 'Cold Turkey' are missing from the vinyl release), the collection inevitably concentrated on Lennon's more commercial material. The fact that it featured only one track from *John Lennon/Plastic Ono Band*, placed quietly out of the way near the end of side one, spoke volumes. However, it did offer the first appearance of the original single 'Give Peace A Chance' on album, although the inner sleeve erroneously states "From the EMI album *Shaved Fish*." Those responsible were apparently unaware that the previous compilation had only offered the first 58 seconds of the song and a coda from the One To One concert.

Give Peace A Chance

The album was worth the retail price for the chance to hear the full version of this song on CD for the first time. It remains as fresh and exuberant as ever and the perfect example of Lennon's desire to make the Plastic Ono Band a people's collective. Recalling the recording for the BBC, he explained: "There was Tommy Smothers and Tim Leary and Dick Gregory and all people sort of clapping along and singing on the chorus. And if you hear the record, it's funny actually, because my rhythm sense has always been a bit wild and, half-way through it, I got on the on-beat instead of the backbeat and it was hard because there was non-musicians playing along with us. So I had to put a lot of tape echo to double up the beat to keep a steady beat right through the whole record . . ."

In order to ensure that the record did not receive a radio ban, Lennon subtly altered the lyric sheet to remove a potentially offensive word. "I sort of cheated," he admitted. "I'd had enough of bannings and all . . . I'd been banned so many times all over that I copped out and wrote 'mastication'." In the lyric sheet to this collection, the self-censorship is overridden and the third verse now features the line: "Revolution, evolution, *masturbation* . . ."

Move Over Ms L

The CD release of the album features this surprise bonus track, which had previously been available only on the B-side of the single 'Stand By Me', although Keith Moon included a cover version on his 1975 solo album, *Two Sides Of The Moon*. Written during the famous 'lost weekend' exile, it's a sardonic and irreverent riposte by John to his estranged wife. Musically, it borrows heavily from the Fifties rock 'n' roll lexicon, at once recalling the work of Chuck Berry, Elvis Presley and Jerry Lee Lewis. That it should end up as the flip-side of one of the *Rock 'n' Roll* tracks was therefore appropriate, but it would also have made a wonderfully acerbic complement to the Yoko Ono-inspired songs on *Walls And Bridges*. Ono had good reason to dislike the song. Even its title sounded like an affront, and she always insisted on being called Yoko Ono rather than Mrs Lennon. Although the composition was never annexed to any of Lennon's re-released, remastered albums, it later appeared on 1998's *Anthology*.

Full track listing: *Give Peace A Chance; Instant Karma!; Power To The People; Whatever Gets You Thru The Night; # 9 Dream; Mind Games; Love; Happy Xmas (War Is Over); Imagine; Jealous Guy; Stand By Me; (Just Like) Starting Over; Woman; I'm Losing You; Beautiful Boy (Darling Boy); Watching The Wheels; Dear Yoko; Move Over Ms L; Cold Turkey.* The original UK pressing issued in November 1982 featured: *Happy Christmas (War Is Over); Stand By Me; Power To The People; Whatever Gets You Thru The Night; # 9 Dream; Mind Games; Love; Imagine; Jealous Guy; (Just Like) Starting Over; Woman; I'm Losing You; Beautiful Boy (Darling Boy); Dear Yoko; Watching The Wheels.*

HEART PLAY – AN UNFINISHED DIALOGUE

Released: December 1983

Original UK issue: Polydor 817 238-1. US issue: Polydor 817 238-1 Y1 (US)

This interview disc consists of chunks of conversation with the Lennons during the promotion of *Double Fantasy*. It is dominated by choice extracts from the *Playboy* interview which are spoiled only by the interviewer's acquiescent tone and nervous habit of saying 'a-ha' every few seconds. In fact, it's more of a monologue than a conversation, with Lennon in sparkling form throughout. He reveals that *Double Fantasy* is the first of a two-volume work and hopes that the world is at last ready to accept Yoko as his equal musical partner. At one point he credits her for refusing "to live with a bullshit artist, which I'm pretty good at."

At times, it's poignant and painful listening, as Lennon marvels at the old adage 'life begins at 40' and expresses great excitement for the future. His current album is described as the product of "love and a lot of sweat and life's experiences of two people."

On the second side of the record, he reflects on the Beatles' break-up and cuts through the myths and nostalgia with his usual forthrightness. Denying his guru role for the umpteenth time, he tells his audience, "I can't cure you – you cure you." The album ends on an eerie note, with Lennon discussing the world's great peace campaigners and adding, with prophetic poignancy, "What does it mean when you're a pacifist that you get shot? I can never understand that."

MILK AND HONEY: A HEART PLAY

Released: January 1984

Original UK issue: Polydor POLH 5. US issue: Polydor 817-160-1Y-1 (US).
CD reissue with bonus tracks: EMI 5 35959 2 (UK)/Capitol 5 35959 2 (US)

Released shortly after the third anniversary of Lennon's death and his first album to appear on CD, this was seen by some as tantamount to the follow-up to *Double Fantasy*. The assumption was that the Lennon songs were outtakes intended for an album already named as *Milk And Honey*. Tracing back the origins of the songs, however, it is clear that what we have here are demos that were recorded at the very beginning of the *Double Fantasy* sessions and subsequently discarded. Some of the tracks are so impressive that it is difficult to believe that Lennon wouldn't have unearthed and revamped them at a later date. Then again, he might have gone ahead and recorded a completely new set of songs and left these languishing in a tape vault. At the time of these recordings, Lennon had unwittingly summed up their potential with the quip: "I'm going back to my roots. It's like Dylan doing *Nashville Skyline*."

The second misconception surrounding this album was that the Yoko Ono tracks were also *Double Fantasy* outtakes. It has since emerged that, with the exception of 'Let Me Count The Ways', all this material was recorded after her husband's death.

Despite the piecemeal way it was put together and the different timescale of the recordings, the album works far better than might have been expected. Some of Ono's songs cry out for the quality control that Lennon might have provided, but most of his previously rejected stuff sounds startlingly good. Many of the critics who lampooned *Double Fantasy* openly stated that it would have been a much better and more sprightly album if Lennon had only included a couple of the rough hewed tracks present on this set.

I'm Stepping Out

"1-2-3-4," Lennon begins in classic rock 'n' roll fashion, as he narrates the following autobiography: "This here's the story about a house husband who, you know, just has to get out of the house. He's been looking at the kids for days and days, he's been washing the dishes and screwing around . . . until he's going crazy." What follows is a refreshingly upbeat opener, in striking contrast to much of the more polished material on *Double Fantasy*. The rawness of the rehearsal fits Lennon's bristling statement of independence. What impresses most is his irrepressible excitement at the prospect of simply going out into the street. Like a cured agoraphobic, he can barely suppress his joy at the prospect of stepping out.

Sleepless Night

Yoko's voice is reinforced with lots of echo as she relates this humorous tale of a sleepless night. Her lyrics are characteristically odd. In consecutive verses she addresses her legs and head, then speculates on the monetary value of a bath brush. There's a basic rock 'n' roll beat, with some playful feline phrasing as she quizzically wonders at the end: 'What am I asking for?'

I Don't Wanna Face It

Another ebullient rocker from Lennon with basic lyrics and all the spirit of an early rehearsal. Musically, the song reveals his immemorial debt to Fifties' rock 'n' roll. There is an endearing lack of self-consciousness about the track, with Lennon content to keep things simple. It is worth contrasting the sentiments with those of 'I'm Stepping Out'. Instead of unsuppressed exuberance, he fully expresses his fears. Each verse lists opposing aspects of his personality, detailing his humanitarianism and his misanthropy in equal measure. A reconciliation is provided in the final stanza, when he faces down his fears and confidently tells us: 'I can make it'.

Don't Be Scared

Yoko offers a series of quaint aphorisms set against an insistent reggae beat. Had this been written in the Seventies, it would no doubt have been interpreted as an 'answer song' to Lennon's 'Scared'. By her unorthodox musical standards, the composition is overly simple with no surprises, vocally or melodically. Whether Lennon would have deemed this track worthy of album release without substantial development or revision seems doubtful.

Nobody Told Me

Originally intended for Ringo Starr ("This one's for Mr Richard Starkey, MBE"), this was issued as a Lennon single just before the release of *Milk And Honey*. A revelation to many critics and fans, it provoked several commentators to suggest that *Double Fantasy* would have been considerably better if only Lennon had approached the work in the same spirit as this song. In many respects, it's Lennon at his spontaneous best, using a catchy melody and getting a quick take with piano, guitar and drums. The sound is upfront, in the spirit of the Plastic Ono Band, the lyrics are witty and unselfconscious, and Lennon's vocal is at its biting best. His phrasing is delicious throughout and only he could invest humour in a simple, seemingly throwaway aside like 'most peculiar, mama'. It should have been a number 1 hit.

O' Sanity

The first side of the vinyl album ended with this short, simple melody from Yoko Ono, which proves surprisingly effective. She includes the usual lyrical aphorisms, but also addresses 'sanity' as though it were a recalcitrant child: 'O' sanity, why don't you let me go . . . cut it out!'

Borrowed Time

Another posthumous single, this Caribbean-flavoured track, complete with simulated steel drum, is another of Lennon's testimonies to the virtues of growing old. There's a comic monologue in a thick Scouse accent and some playful singing towards the end, but in the aftermath of his death the lines about living on borrowed time took on a painful poignancy.

Your Hands

Yoko sings in Japanese and translates accordingly. The backing is fairly rudimentary as she once again revisits the theme of John and Yoko's insatiable love. The most notable feature of the composition is her seeming lyrical fixation on individual body parts. In 'Sleepless Night', she addressed what were presumably Lennon's legs and head, while here she tackles hands, skin, arms and eyes.

(Forgive Me) My Little Flower Princess

There's some debate as to whether Lennon was inspired to write this track for May Pang or Yoko Ono, although the lyrical evidence points firmly towards the latter. Some of the sentiments recall the *mea culpa* confessionals on *Mind Games*, combined with subtle suggestions that Ono is still carrying the cross alluded to in 'I'm Losing You'. It's Lennon at his most deferential and submissive, singing an early take that would, most likely, have been changed substantially if released in his lifetime.

Let Me Count The Ways

This would appear to be the one Yoko Ono song on the album that was recorded, however primitively, during Lennon's lifetime. Taken from a standard cassette recording, the basic tune on piano testifies to a composition that might have been impressive, if developed. The lyrics are expansive and completely unlike Ono's usual instant haikus, a discrepancy explained by the source of the song – nineteenth century poet, Elizabeth Barrett Browning. Yoko explained the genesis of the composition: "One early morning in the summer of 1980, I woke up with 'Let Me Count The Ways' ringing in my head. I called John who was then in Bermuda and played it over the phone. 'How do you like it? . . . How about you writing one with a Robert Browning line and we'll have portraits of us as Elizabeth and Robert on the cover?' (This needs a little explaining. John and I always thought, among many other things, that we were maybe the reincarnation of Robert and Liz. So he immediately knew what I was talking about.) We discussed [the] *Double Fantasy* cover, that it should be two portraits, one of Elizabeth and the other of Robert, only the faces would be ours. John thought we should look very prim and proper with just our hands coming out of the paintings and holding in the middle, the funny touch. We both laughed. 'OK then, just tell downstairs (our office) to send me the collection of Robert Browning and let's see what happens.' It wasn't necessary, however, to send the collection to Bermuda. John called me that afternoon. 'Hey, you won't believe this!' He explained that he was watching the TV, a Fifties film of a baseball player. In the film, John saw the girlfriend send a poem which was one by Robert Browning called 'Grow Old Beside Me'. 'Can you believe that? . . . so, anyway, this is my version.' John proudly played his song over the phone. That's how our two songs happened."

The portraits described by Yoko Ono were included in the CD artwork and look surprisingly authentic. Presumably, it was the romantic story of the Brownings' meeting and marriage that prompted the reincarnation fantasy. In 1845, Robert Browning wrote to Elizabeth Barrett expressing his love for her verses. She was eight years his senior and suffered from a lung infection and spinal injury that left her incapacitated. They enjoyed a platonic, epistolary relationship, exchanging hundreds of letters which later inspired the 'How do I love thee? Let me count the ways' sonnet. In 1846, they eloped, married in secret and subsequently moved to Italy. Elizabeth gave birth to a son and lived until 1861. As Browning wrote: "Then, always smiling happily, and with a face like a girl's, in a few minutes, she died in my arms, her head on my cheek." Some of the comparisons between the Brownings and the Lennons are self-evident and the death scene adds a bittersweet ending to the story.

Grow Old With Me
John's answer to Yoko's 'Let Me Count The Ways' was inspired by Browning's *Rabbi Ben Ezra* ('Grow old along with me! The best is yet to come'). The song survives in this rough, home-made cassette version on which he plays piano and rhythm box and sings falsetto. Melodically, it's not unlike 'Woman', with romantic lyrics that again proclaim the joys of love in old age. According to Yoko: "To us, these two songs were the backbone of *Double Fantasy*, and we kept discussing how we would arrange them. For John, 'Grow Old With Me' was one that would be a standard, the kind that they would play

in church every time a couple gets married. It was horns and symphony time. But we were working against [a] deadline for the Christmas release of the album, [so we] kept holding 'Grow Old With Me' to the end, and finally decided it was better to leave the song for *Milk And Honey* . . . 'Grow Old With Me' was a song John made several cassettes of, as we discussed the arrangements for it. Everybody around us knew how important these cassettes were. They were in safekeeping, some in our bedroom, some in our cassette file, and some in a vault. All of them disappeared since then, except the one on this record. It may be that it was meant to be this way, since the version that was left to us was John's last recording. The one John and I recorded together in our bedroom with a piano and a rhythm box."

You're The One
Yoko closes the album with the sound of a thunderstorm as she backs herself with rhythmic yelps and lyrics that are as sparse and elliptical as anything she ever wrote. Her familiar use of nature imagery is once more present in the lyrics. It's a powerful finale which continues the literary analogies evident in the previous two tracks, this time referencing Emily Brontë's *Wuthering Heights* and Cervantes' *Don Quixote*.

In October 2001, *Milk And Honey* was reissued with the following bonus tracks:

Every Man Has A Woman Who Loves Him
At one of the sessions for this song, Lennon brutally teased Ono with the quip: "Start writing ones that you can sing from now on." It was a surprise, therefore, to hear his own version of her song. Although he sounds hesitant while phrasing some of the lines, his reading is impressive, and arguably superior to Ono's.

Stepping Out
This acoustic demo, pointedly titled 'Stepping Out' rather than 'I'm Stepping Out', has identical lyrics to the released band version, but

inevitably sounds more subdued. Lennon has clearly readied the song
for recording, requiring only the animation of a more engaged vocal
to complete the performance.

I'm Moving On
Yoko Ono's best song on *Double Fantasy* is presented here in its original state, an eerie sounding demo, with a more mournful tone than
the released version. Ono's singing is strangely affecting and the stark
piano accompaniment adds to the ambience.

Interview With J&Y December 8th, 1980
Recorded on the afternoon before his death, this uncredited
22-minute interview was taped for RKO Radio. Most credit Dave
Sholin as the sole interviewer but in his post-Beatles diary *After The
Break-Up*, Keith Badman mentions three others: Laurie Kaye, Ron
Hummel and Bert Keane. Despite the 'J&Y' title here, there is not
much of 'Y' in the contents as Lennon is in full flow throughout,
discussing the origins of *Double Fantasy*, songwriting technique, his
relationship with son Sean, his first meetings with Paul McCartney
and Yoko Ono, her artwork, his peer group, the importance of
'Woman', the role of the artist in society, an excited reprise of his old
'Declaration of Nutopia' ideal, his working relationship with the
Beatles, his return to his early rock 'n' roll influences, the importance
of 'conceptual thinking' and 'goal projection', some passing references to Aldous Huxley and George Orwell, his disbelief in an imminent apocalypse, a restatement of the importance of the Sixties as a
time of optimism, the possibilities of touring in the future and, most
poignantly, his concluding observation: "I've come through . . . And
the Eighties is like we've got a new chance."

LIVE IN NEW YORK CITY

Released: January 1986 (US) February 1986 (UK)

Original UK issue: Parlophone PCS 7301. US issue: Capitol 7 46196 1 (US).
CD reissue: EMI 7 46196 2 (UK)/Capitol 7 46196 2 (US)

The famous One To One concert had been issued on bootleg but this was its first official appearance, nearly 14 years after the original performance at Madison Square Garden on 30 August 1972. Yoko Ono remixed the record and receives the production credit on the album. Commenting on the memorable recording, she explained: "The concert was held . . . to help improve the living conditions of the mentally handicapped children. Starting with the Toronto Peace Festival in 1969, John and I did a series of rock concerts as our statement of Peace and Love, and to spotlight various social issues effectively. All proceeds from the concerts were given to the needy. This one in Madison Square Garden turned out to be the last concert John and I did together."

The Lennons topped the bill at the afternoon and evening shows which also featured Sha Na Na, Roberta Flack and Stevie Wonder. It proved an unexpected triumph that left Lennon exultant. After the event, he said: "It was just the same feeling as when the Beatles used to really get into it." But even the Beatles never performed a show so full of cathartic passion and primal release. It was raw, intense and, sadly, never to be repeated. Television rights were sold to ABC TV, which screened an edited version of the afternoon show on 14 December 1972.

As an archive live recording, *Live In New York City* was a pleasing addition to the Lennon canon, enabling us to hear several classic studio songs in a concert setting.

New York City
A chant of 'Power To The People' opens the concert before Lennon launches into a stirring version of 'New York City', with the grandly

named Plastic Ono Elephant's Memory Band providing a suitably rudimentary but vibrant backing. The vocals are mixed surprisingly low in places, which robs the song of some of its power.

It's So Hard
Continuing with a basic blues riff, Lennon tackles one of the harder-edged songs on *Imagine*, while saxophonist Stan Bronstein is given leave to let rip. Lennon slows the pace so that his singing is virtually reduced to a spoken word recitation in places. "Welcome to the rehearsal," he chirps at the end of the number.

Woman Is The Nigger Of The World
With Yoko's 'We're All Water' edited from the original tape, we move straight into the Lennons' most famous feminist statement. Although the vocal is a little flat in places, the performance transcends such minor quibbles, providing us with a welcome opportunity to hear a live version of one of the best Lennon songs of the decade. John was always disappointed that the song never reached a wider audience, and later told Chris Charlesworth: "They banned it and made such a fuss . . . it was never played because they said it insulted blacks, which it didn't at all. I know a lot of black people, and they know what's going on. I know it was political, but that was what I had in my bag at the time and I wasn't just going to throw the song away. I still like 'Woman Is The Nigger Of The World'. I like the sound of it and it gets me off, but it just happened that it didn't please people."

Well Well Well
'Sisters O Sisters' was the next song at the concert, but Yoko edits her version, moving swiftly on to another blues based item. Somebody shouts for Ringo just before the song starts, prompting Lennon to retort, "That was yesterday, or four years ago." Although this track is far from the best song on *John Lennon/Plastic Ono Band*, it works remarkably well in live performance and Lennon even attempts some screaming at the end, albeit in less tortured fashion than on the studio version.

Instant Karma! (We All Shine On)

"I'm only beginning to understand what this record was about," Lennon remarks, as they attempt a relatively sparse version of 'Instant Karma!', complete with a parenthetic addition to the title not featured on the original single. Without Phil Spector's studio magic, the song sounds strangely denuded and even the presence of two drummers, Jim Keltner and Rick Frank, cannot quite produce a sound to equal the percussive power of the original. A better mixed version might have brought up the drums in the appropriate places. By the end, the song is turned into a chant, after which Lennon apologizes: "We'll get it right next time."

Mother

"This is another song from one of those albums I made since I left the Rolling Stones," Lennon jokes. "And a lot of people thought it was *just* about my parents, but it's about 99 per cent of the parents alive, or half-dead." Again, it's most gratifying to hear one of Lennon's finest compositions in live performance and this version is particularly striking. With a strong saxophone backing, Lennon turns the song into a blues, bringing out much of the pain in such paraphrased lines as 'I needed you so bad, you didn't need me, oh no!' Towards the end, he attempts the primal scream, investing as much passion in his voice as possible, albeit with the knowledge that he cannot risk shouting himself hoarse for fear of destroying the rest of the show.

Come Together

"We'll go back in the past just once," Lennon concedes. "You might remember this better than I do, actually. Something about a flat top, that's all I know." The song must have been on his mind at the time, as music publisher Morris Levy was suing him for alleged plagiarism of Chuck Berry's 'You Can't Catch Me'. Lennon provides a potent performance and Elephant's Memory find an impressive R&B groove. Their intense contribution to the Lennon story has been continually undervalued, as this performance demonstrates. As the song ends, Lennon proudly says: "Thank you, I nearly got all the words right too."

Imagine

"This song's more about why we're here, apart from rocking and all that," Lennon notes. Both his vocal and piano playing are tentative here, but he relates the song to the audience, amending the lyrics a little to say 'Imagine no possessions, I wonder if *we* can' and expressing his feminist leanings by suggesting 'a brotherhood and sisterhood of man'.

Cold Turkey

"This is something that happens to us, one way or another," Lennon stresses as he conjures the harrowing memories of heroin withdrawal. The song is taken at a surprisingly fast pace and some of the menace of the original recording is lost due to the chug-along accompaniment. Towards the end, though, Lennon unearths the buried pain with some expressive vocal outpourings.

Hound Dog

Recalling Elvis Presley's version of 'Hound Dog', Lennon noted that it often sounded as though it was being played at a different speed, depending on his mood of the moment. "One day it would sound very slow," he considered, "and one day it would sound very fast. It was just my feeling towards it . . . the way I heard it." Surprisingly, perhaps, he chooses to play the song in exactly the same tempo as the original. It's a great finale, complemented by a thrilling sax break and some excellent boogie-woogie piano.

Give Peace A Chance

"This is what you call an encore," Lennon announces. "You're going to be the encore too!" At this point, the audience really does become the Plastic Ono Band. As Yoko recalled: "The concert was filled with love of brotherhood and sisterhood. We passed out tambourines to the audience, true to our slogan, '*You* are the Plastic Ono Band'. Everybody joined in onstage at the end when we sang 'Give Peace A Chance'. People could not contain themselves and marched down Fifth Avenue after the performance, singing 'Give Peace A Chance'." It is a pity that the album could not include more than a few seconds of this atmospheric conclusion, which went on for nearly a quarter of an hour. Journalist Roy Hollingworth, who attended the event, recalled the grand finale. "David Peel was already onstage with his back-up shouters. Then Lennon started 'Give Peace A Chance' and the stage began to crowd with people, all wearing tin helmets and chanting. There was Phil Spector and poet Allen Ginsberg. Then Stevie Wonder, plus more and more people. There must have been a couple of hundred onstage at the end. The Garden was up, and singing too – for a full 15 minutes, dancing and clapping, and letting it all fall out, and come up, and up, and explode. It was ultra-emotion."

MENLOVE AVENUE

Released: October 1986

Original UK issue: Parlophone PCS 7308. US issue: Capitol 7 46576 1.
CD reissue: EMI 7 46196 2 (UK)/Capitol 7 46196 2 (US)

Shortly after what would have been Lennon's 46th birthday, Yoko Ono sanctioned this archive release, which offered a side of outtakes from *Rock 'n' Roll* and a side of rehearsal sessions from *Walls And Bridges*. The packaging was slight, but the cover featured an illustration of Lennon drawn by Andy Warhol. The album title alluded to Lennon's childhood home in Liverpool at 251 Menlove Avenue. In March 2002, Ono bought the house, which she donated to the National Trust. As she said: "I think Menlove Avenue has an important place in Beatles' history and it saddened me to think that it might be lost."

Overall, *Menlove Avenue* was a welcome release for collectors and hard-core fans, and provided insights into the making of both albums. The *Rock 'n' Roll* outtakes offered the chance to consider several songs that might have improved the album, while the rehearsals for *Walls And Bridges* revealed occasional emotional depths that were later hidden by production gloss.

Here We Go Again

Boasting that rarest of writing credits 'Lennon/Spector', this was an outtake from the late 1973 sessions that were subsequently salvaged for *Rock 'n' Roll*. As this was not a rock 'n' roll classic, it failed to appear on the album and was not considered as a strong enough candidate for *Walls And Bridges*. In many ways, it fits the mood of the latter record. Lennon begins the song in reflective mode, abruptly changing tone midway through as he becomes more anguished. There is a sense of disillusionment and defeat that permeates the song ('Everybody's an also-ran'), as Lennon testifies to an enveloping feeling of directionlessness in the midst of the lost weekend. Spector adds a suitably grandiose production, using an array of instruments, most notably piano, slide guitar and orchestration.

Rock 'n' Roll People

Originally cut during the sessions for *Mind Games* back in 1973, this was an easy-going romp, which might have served as a warm-up for the *Rock 'n' Roll* sessions. Lennon's voice is outstanding throughout this derivative, catch-all rock 'n' roll tribute. Johnny Winter previously premièred the song on his 1974 album *John Dawson Winter III*.

Angel Baby

"This here is one of my favourite songs," Lennon states, while introducing this number. It's ironic then that he failed to include the track on *Rock 'n' Roll*, the more so when you consider that Morris Levy slipped it on to his unofficial release *Roots*. Lennon's production is particularly noteworthy as he attempts to outdo Phil Spector as the master of the mixing board. The vocal is also impressive and John expertly accents the teenage angst at the core of the composition. Overall, it's far better than many of the songs on *Rock 'n' Roll* and an excellent addition to this album.

Since My Baby Left Me

Better known under the title 'My Baby Left Me', this old Elvis Presley hit, composed by Arthur Crudup, was taken from the original Phil Spector sessions with Lennon in late 1973. The song is performed at a much slower tempo than expected, with a gaggle of backing singers providing an overt party atmosphere.

To Know Her Is To Love Her

It was most appropriate that Lennon should cover the song that gave Phil Spector his first experience of pop stardom as a member of the chart-topping Teddy Bears in 1958. Lennon had already name-checked the song on the front sleeve of *Some Time In New York City*, where there is a photo of Phil Spector encased in an apple with the motto 'To Know Him Is To Love Him' written underneath. The phrase 'To Know Him Was To Love Him' was originally inscribed on the gravestone of Spector's father, before Phil altered the tense and wrote a song that became a million seller. On the record he was joined by Marshall Lieb and Annette Kleinbard, and it was the latter's distinctive voice that proved particularly memorable. Covers by male artists obviously prompted a change of gender. Peter And Gordon altered the title to the unspecific 'To Know You Is To Love You', while Lennon preferred 'To Know Her Is To Love Her'. His version, complete with an affected and occasionally histrionic conclusion, would have been a prized addition to *Rock 'n' Roll*.

Steel And Glass
Opening quietly, with a gentle, strumming acoustic guitar, this could almost have been a reflective, introspective ballad rather than one of Lennon's more vicious put-downs. It serves as a pleasing companion piece to the more produced version on *Walls And Bridges*, with Jesse Ed Davis' solo enhancing the subdued mood. In the final verse, Lennon unexpectedly resorts to infantile insults, sneering about a toilet, Mickey Duck and 'your Donald Fuck'. These words were subsequently deleted from the final version on *Walls And Bridges*, in which Lennon contented himself with a snipe at his adversary's animal instincts and backyard odour, even referring to him as an alley cat. In many respects, this track sounded more menacing and direct than the previously released version.

Scared
This is another stripped-down acoustic rehearsal, minus the Little Big Horns. Again, the sense of melancholy underlying the composition is more prevalent, with Lennon's voice painfully cracking up half-way through the song. At times, it's like hearing *Walls And Bridges* reprogrammed in the naked manner of *John Lennon/Plastic Ono Band*.

Old Dirt Road
The strong country influence on this Lennon/Nilsson composition is even more prevalent here, with Jesse Ed Davis' guitar heard in isolation. There is also a more discernible borrowing from chain gang songs in the refrain 'cool, clear water'. It makes you realize how

incongruous this track actually sounded amid the self-analytical material on *Walls And Bridges*.

Nobody Loves You When You're Down And Out

Although it sounds slight in relation to the full-blown version on *Walls And Bridges*, this is another interesting addendum to the Lennon catalogue. While the song seems firmly directed towards Lennon's estranged wife, the sentiments could equally apply to his demanding audience (whom he informs, 'it's all showbiz') and back-stabbing music critics ('I'll scratch your back, if you knife mine'). Lennon's vocal sounds like a blunted razor at times, especially when he launches into the 'mirror-gazing' lament, at which the song peaks. Like several other once exclusive tracks on this album, time has diluted its initial impact and rendered *Menlove Avenue* less import-ant as an archival repository. You can now hear 'Nobody Loves You When You're Down And Out' in acoustic form as a bonus track on *Walls And Bridges*, some of the Spector sessions on the reissue of *Rock 'n' Roll*, and more rarities than you could ever have imagined on the 1998 *Anthology*.

Bless You

Lennon again has trouble staying in tune during this rehearsal as he reflects on his confused relationship with Yoko Ono. It's a tentative and often emotional rendition, but Lennon's voice cracks up rather too much for comfortable listening.

IMAGINE: JOHN LENNON

Released: October 1988

Original UK issue: Parlophone PCSP 722. US issue: Capitol C1-90803.
CD reissue: EMI Parlophone CD PCSP 722 (UK)/Capitol 7 90803 2 (US)

John Lennon was the perfect subject for a film documentary. Since meeting Yoko Ono, the separation between his life and his art had become increasingly blurred. As early as 1969, he was urging: "Why shouldn't I be a poet, a film-maker, a dancer, an actor? Let's do it all while the going's good."

The film soundtrack of this celebrated documentary on Lennon's life pooled together nine Beatles songs, the single version of 'Give Peace A Chance', selections from *John Lennon/Plastic Ono Band*, *Imagine*, *Rock 'n' Roll* and *Double Fantasy*, plus the live version of 'Mother' from *Live In New York City*. There were also two tracks, previously unavailable, as follows:

Real Love

Unlike 'Free As A Bird', which was later released exclusively under the name Beatles, 'Real Love' exists as both a solo and a group recording. The song began life in 1977 under the title 'Real Life' and part of the original melody and some of the words were incorporated into 'Watching The Wheels' and 'I'm Stepping Out'. From the remaining skeleton, Lennon worked on 'Real Love', cutting seven demos of the song in late 1979. This, the sixth take, is very much a work in progress, featuring a strumming acoustic guitar and plaintive vocal. Lyrically, Lennon harks back to 'Isolation' with the line 'I don't expect you to understand', which seems quite appropriate given the song's air of emotional desolation. Yoko Ono subsequently passed this song over to the remaining Beatles and it was later issued as a single (peaking at number 4 in the UK) and lead track of their second anthology album. The song was probably too slight to warrant the hype and lacked the sparkle and poignancy that was present in the Beatles' excellent exhumation of 'Free As A Bird'. Yet, listening to 'Real Love' as it was first presented on this album, an unheralded demo distinct from the Beatles' catalogue, its charm and potential can be better appreciated. Remarkably, this version is arguably of superior sound quality to the take released under the Beatles' name.

Imagine (Rehearsal)

The second unreleased item on the soundtrack is this two-minute rehearsal of 'Imagine', which features a croaky-voiced Lennon preparing the song for the forthcoming studio take. Towards the end of his rendition, he slips into a country & western style reading, which is quite amusing.

Full track listing: *Real Love; Twist And Shout; Help!; In My Life; Strawberry Fields Forever; A Day In The Life; Revolution; The Ballad Of John And Yoko; Julia; Don't Let Me Down; Give Peace A Chance; How?; Imagine (Rehearsal); God; Mother; Stand By Me; Jealous Guy; Woman; Beautiful Boy (Darling Boy); (Just Like) Starting Over; Imagine.*

LENNON

Released: October 1990

Original UK issue: Parlophone CDS 79 5220 2

In the continued absence of Lennon's full catalogue on CD, this box set offered a comprehensive introduction to his work. There had previously been a special issue, limited edition John Lennon box set issued in June 1981, but that merely collected the albums from *Live Peace In Toronto 1969* through to *Shaved Fish* in a gift package. This 1990 4-CD set was something much more, a genuine compilation spanning Lennon's solo work since the demise of the Beatles. Compiler Mark Lewisohn ensured that it was a decent package, with an excellent track selection, in strict chronological order. Basically, it's John Lennon denuded of Yoko Ono, whose own songs are systematically removed, although some would later appear on her own box set, *Ono*. Apart from a couple of questionable omissions from *Some Time In New York City*, Lewisohn carefully trawls through Lennon's complete solo work to produce a representative collection. Full marks for including the groundbreaking *John Lennon/Plastic Ono Band* in its entirety.

The only tracks on this set not previously issued on album at the time were the three songs recorded live with Elton John at Madison Square Garden on 28 November 1974.

Whatever Gets You Thru The Night (Live)

"Seeing as it's Thanksgiving and Thanksgivings are joyous occasions, we thought we'd make tonight a little bit of an occasion by inviting someone up with us onto the stage. And I'm sure he'll be no stranger to anybody in the audience when I say it's our great privilege and your great privilege to see and hear Mr John Lennon." Elton John's effusive introduction was followed by Lennon's first stage appearance since the One To One concerts at Madison Square Garden on 30 August 1972. As the chords of 'I Feel Fine' linger in the background, the pair launch into an entertaining rendition of the song that unexpectedly took Lennon to number 1 in the US charts for the first time since the glory days of the Beatles. The track, once an exclusive here, has since been added as a bonus to the remixed/remastered CD of *Walls And Bridges*.

Lucy In The Sky With Diamonds

"I wanna hear you raise the roof up to the ceiling," Elton John enthuses. "This is one of the best songs ever written." He then takes lead vocal on a reggae-style version of this Lennon/McCartney classic, with John joining in the chorus. "I had fun with Elton," Lennon later told *NME*'s Lisa Robinson, "but that was just because it was Elton. He was really more nervous than I was, because he was nervous for me. I think he felt, 'Poor old bugger, maybe he'll collapse . . .' It was just a weird feeling being up there alone, but I knew Elton, and I knew the band, and it was just a one-off thing."

I Saw Her Standing There

Lennon concludes proceedings, by announcing: "I'd like to thank Elton and the boys for having me on tonight. We were trying to think of a number to finish off with so's I could get off here and be sick. And we thought we'd do a number by an old, estranged fiancé of mine called Paul. This is one I never sang – it's an old Beatle number and we just about know it."

A rousing finale follows with this carefree version, which remains the most impressive of Lennon's three cameo appearances with Elton John. Privately, this historic evening was eclipsed by an even more newsworthy event: the reconciliation of John and Yoko. She had been persuaded to attend by a young art gallery owner, who was evidently keen to see and meet Lennon. "It was Elton's show and John came out at the end as a surprise guest," she recalled. "People were so excited that the whole Garden was shaking. I looked at him and tears rolled down my cheek. He was looking lonely. He was looking scared. He bowed once too often. This was not the John I knew. When he was with me, he wasn't afraid of anything. I couldn't stop crying. Everybody else was ecstatic."

Full track listing: *Give Peace A Chance; Blue Suede Shoes; Money (That's What I Want); Dizzy Miss Lizzy; Yer Blues; Cold Turkey; Instant Karma!; Mother; Hold On; I Found Out; Working Class Hero; Isolation; Remember; Love; Well Well Well; Look At Me; God; My Mummy's Dead; Power To The People; Well (Baby Please Don't Go); Imagine; Crippled Inside; Jealous Guy; It's So Hard; Gimme Some Truth; Oh My Love; How Do You Sleep?; Oh Yoko!; Happy Xmas (War Is Over); Woman Is The Nigger Of The World; New York City; John Sinclair; Come Together; Hound Dog; Mind Games; Aisumasen (I'm Sorry); One Day (At A Time); Intuition; Out The Blue; Whatever Gets You Thru The Night; Going Down On Love; Old Dirt Road; Bless You; Scared; # 9 Dream; Surprise Surprise (Sweet Bird Of Paradox); Steel And Glass; Nobody Loves You (When You're Down And Out); Stand By Me; Ain't That A Shame; Do You Want To Dance; Sweet Little Sixteen; Slippin' And Slidin'; Angel Baby; Just Because; Whatever Gets You Thru The Night (Live Version); Lucy In The Sky With Diamonds; I Saw Her Standing There; (Just Like) Starting Over; Cleanup Time; I'm Losing You; Beautiful Boy (Darling Boy); Watching The Wheels; Woman; Dear Yoko; I'm Stepping Out; I Don't Wanna Face It; Nobody Told Me; Borrowed Time; (Forgive Me) My Little Flower Princess; Every Man Has A Woman Who Loves Him; Grow Old With Me.*

LENNON LEGEND

Released: October 1997

Original UK issue: EMI 8 21954 1. US issue: Capitol 8 21954 1.
CD issue: EMI 8 21954 2 (UK)/Capitol 8 21954 2 (US)

This double album was an attempt to improve and update 1975's *Shaved Fish*. It's a reasonably representative collection of Lennon's most popular songs, with a strong emphasis on singles. Inevitably, 'Imagine' is used as a lead track, while the harrowing 'Cold Turkey' does not appear until after 'Jealous Guy'. Even 'Working Class Hero' is safely held over till near the end, presumably in case it scared off mainstream listeners. These niggles aside, the set was well conceived, although containing nothing new for the collector. It proved very successful in the UK, peaking at number 3, while stalling at number 65 in the US. The DVD edition featured some additional fade-outs for the discerning listener.

Full track listing: *Imagine; Instant Karma!; Mother (single edit); Jealous Guy; Power To The People; Cold Turkey; Love; Mind Games; Whatever Gets You Thru The Night; # 9 Dream; Stand By Me; (Just Like) Starting Over; Woman; Beautiful Boy (Darling Boy); Watching The Wheels; Nobody Told Me; Borrowed Time; Working Class Hero; Happy Xmas (War Is Over); Give Peace A Chance.*

ANTHOLOGY

Released: November 1998

Original UK issue: EMI 8 30614 2. US issue: Capitol 8 30614 2

The origins of this anthology can be traced back 10 years to January 1988 when Yoko Ono sanctioned the Westwood One radio series *The Lost Lennon Tapes*. The series lasted four years, covering 218 broadcasts featuring a wealth of Lennon recordings, demos, rehearsals and studio chat from his seemingly exhaustive tape archive. The *Anthology* packaging boasts "94 previously unreleased tracks including intimate home recordings, live rarities and illuminating alternate takes of his most classic songs". Split into 4 CDs, titled 'Ascot', 'New York City', 'The Lost Weekend' and 'Dakota', this sumptuous set was a veritable treasure trove for collectors. Seldom, if ever, in rock history has an anthology boasted so much previously unheard material. For those fascinated by Lennon's works in progress and means of composition, this was a revelation and a crucially important historical artefact. The packaging was impressive too, beautifully laid out with rare photographs, handwritten and printed lyrics, and illustrated with Lennon's distinctive drawings. Unfortunately, the session details were frustratingly vague with seemingly little attempt to denote the precise date of the recordings, which are usually identified by year only. Given that much of this information was already in the public domain, the lapse seems odd, especially in a lavishly produced box set, complete with an additional 60-page booklet including essays and annotations.

There was a similar lack of clarity in the album's title. On the front of the box, it clearly says *Anthology* in yellow letters and the artiste's name 'John Lennon' in blue, which seems straightforward enough. The individual discs, which would usually repeat and thereby confirm a title, are only identified by their subtitles: 'Ascot' etc. However, in Yoko Ono's essay, she refers to the package as *The Lennon Anthology*. Later, in Anthony De Curtis' notes, it's referred to as both *Anthology* and *John Lennon Anthology* (the latter was used by most reviewers too). Finally, the simultaneously released *Wonsuponatime* calls its parent album, *Lennon Anthology*, again contradicting what is actually on the box's cover: *Anthology*.

Critical reaction to the set was revealing. *Mojo* recognized its significance with a three-page review. The overcritical Jim Irvin, admitting that he was no great fan of archival recordings of this type, concluded: "This sprawling collection of cast-offs, notes and abandoned music is a real mixed blessing . . . the benefits of half-written, stumbled-through versions of Lennon's tautly crafted songs are dubious . . . *Anthology* is not a selection which will, as Yoko Ono hopes, turn on a new generation to the music of John Lennon. Rather it's a long, unfocused (and expensive) documentary concerning Lennon in the studio and at home with his family. The snippets of dialogue and home-recorded skits are often more engrossing than the songs, hardly any of which surpass the already available versions. This is a portrait of the man rather than his music."

Balancing Irvin's appraisal was a fascinating overview by Beatles' expert Mark Lewisohn who was in the unique position of having previously constructed a parallel box set anthology for EMI in the 1990s, during which he was required to trawl through 477 reels of studio tape, listening to countless outtakes and material from the Lennon archives. "It was, from the first minute, a life-altering experience," he wrote. "John Lennon was a true performer and everything he did was done with gusto. Not for him day after day of the same song, backing track after monotonous backing track. When John Lennon was recording, brevity was the key. A few takes, capture the feel, move on. Even as a lifelong Lennon devotee, it was impossible not to be awed by the artistry of this great man. Fortunately, Lennon's performing instinct meant that he always recorded with a vocal, so every take – provided it passed muster – was a candidate for inclusion in this box set. And he seemed never to know the meaning of the term 'guide vocal', where the singer saves his voice for the essential take later in the session: Lennon gave his all, time after time after time."

So how did Yoko Ono's newly sanctioned *Anthology* differ from

Lewisohn's unissued project? According to the writer, among the major omissions were an alternate 'Cold Turkey', the full version of 'Just Because', the Tittenhurst Park demo of 'Gimme Some Truth', an early 'Luck Of The Irish' and some 'astonishingly powerful' selections from Spector's *Rock 'n' Roll* sessions.

When I spoke to Mark Lewisohn about his original involvement in the *Anthology*, before Yoko Ono replaced him as researcher/archivist, his lasting memory was of the excitement he felt hearing the unexpurgated *Rock 'n' Roll* sessions. "My number one love while doing that project was listening to those Spector sessions on 16-track in the studio. I had the volume up and I was listening to them like they were being recorded. Those were sessions where they were all drunk and Spector's going mad in the control room. I heard it all, and it was just the most wonderful thing I've heard in my life. Of course Yoko couldn't use them because John is pissed and swears a lot. It didn't reflect him in a good light. And I can understand that. John probably wouldn't have wanted them out either. But if we love John for being the honest bloke that he was, always revealing his own warts, then there's something quite nice about hearing them. So I had a lot of tracks from there . . . I'd been working on it for three years and then it just went quiet. The phone stopped ringing . . . Once your relationship with Yoko is damaged you're never healed."

Much of the material mentioned by Lewisohn remains unheard by the public. In the wake of the Westwood One US radio series *The Lost Lennon Tapes* that seems just the tip of the creative iceberg. Remaining on tape are a number of unreleased song fragments and blueprints in various stages of development, including such titles as 'When A Boy Meets A Girl', 'She Is A Friend Of Dorothy's', 'Mirror Mirror On The Wall' (not the Pinkerton's Assorted Colours' classic), 'One Of The Boys', 'Whatever Happened To . . .', 'I'm Crazy', 'The Worst Is Over' and 'You Saved My Soul'. Two other songs, 'India, India' and 'I Don't Want To Lose You', were included in the Ono sanctioned musical on the lives of John and Yoko, but have yet to appear on album. Given the hours of extant taped material still in the vaults, there may even be an *Anthology II* at some future point.

Working Class Hero

CD 1 opens with this 8-track recording from the *John Lennon/Plastic Ono Band* sessions. "OK, I'll try," Lennon announces, as if he is unsure about something, but this version is largely faithful to the classic recording. Apart from a slightly different stress in his voice when he sings 'to be' and a change of lyric from 'smile *as* you kill' to 'smile *when* you kill', the song is clearly ready. Like several of the 8-track recordings herein, the acoustic guitar is more prominent in places. Towards the end, Lennon's voice threatens to waver slightly but otherwise it's a strong rendition. For no apparent reason, the tape then segues into the chorus of 'Well Well Well'.

God

This not quite realized version of 'God' shows how well Lennon worked with the rhythm section of Ringo Starr and Klaus Voormann during the recordings. The playing is confident with Lennon suddenly upping the emotion by shouting 'I'll say it again', then unexpectedly ad-libbing with a 'Yes we do'. Overall though it's a less dramatic or expressive rendition than the final version with a more monotone vocal. Conspicuously absent is that wonderful pregnant pause after 'I don't believe in Beatles', which is arguably the highlight of the finished arrangement, along with the hymnal keyboard work of Billy Preston later added to provide a spiritual aspect to Lennon's atheism.

I Found Out

This home recording features Lennon playing an electric rather than an acoustic guitar with a vocal in a different key. Rough, but intriguing, it sounds as though the lyrics haven't yet been fully determined. The reference to Old Hare Krishna is missing, replaced by a line about not wishing to see Mary Jane, a name familiar from the Beatles' outtake 'What's The New Mary Jane?' Interestingly, despite the song's title, Lennon slightly distances himself from the lyrics preferring to sing 'your ma and pa' rather than 'my ma and pa'. Most noticeable of all, the familiar reference to sitting with 'your cock' in your hand is at this point expressed as the less controversial 'your axe' – which could either refer to an instrument of violence or a guitar, depending upon your preferred interpretation.

Hold On
Recorded in a totally different rhythm, more in keeping with an early Sixties tune, this would have been fascinating to hear in its entirety as an alternate take but alas it fades after 43 seconds and fails to extend beyond the opening verse.

Isolation
Beginning *in medias res* with a lacerating vocal, the song abruptly stops, much to Lennon's chagrin. "That was a gooner," he says. "That was very good, wasn't it? Remember those bits, we'll keep them. What went wrong?" Before a full explanation is forthcoming, the song restarts with that familiar piano introduction. Lennon's vocal is exceptional and reaches a passionate peak in the climactic third verse. Clearly satisfied with the performance, he announces: "You see, I concentrated less on the voice and more on *both* . . ."

Love
Here, Lennon's voice falters almost from the start. "I was thinking about my bum note," he confesses, in mitigation. After restarting, he produces an accomplished version spoilt only by an over-active acoustic guitar and a shrill word or two towards the end. His problems are solved later when the guitar accompaniment is replaced by some striking piano work from Phil Spector.

Mother
Klaus Voormann's bass meanders across the speakers as Lennon offers another strong vocal showing. His primal screams towards the conclusion are as remarkable as the completed album version, but the crucial difference is the inclusion of a growling electric guitar break, which adds a real edge to the composition. Eventually, they decide that the song would work better in starker form which was probably the correct decision, although the electric arrangement is still

welcome. Lennon evidently felt the same. "Well that was *more* like it," he enthuses with obvious satisfaction.

Remember
Beginning at a disconcertingly frantic pace, this leaves Lennon lagging behind the rhythm section before the end of the first line. "It's getting a bit fast," he exclaims, with amused amazement. At the restart he sings in a stately, affected voice and by the fourth line he is collapsing with laughter. While singing 'if you ever change your mind', he adds 'or the rhythm!' prompting further merriment. The song continues, accompanied by jokes about the shifting rhythm until they call a halt at the close of the first verse.

Imagine (take 1)
"Will you be quiet in the kitchen please?" is the instruction that precedes the first take of Lennon's most famous song. This version is distinguished by the presence of a harmonium played by John Barham. It's almost as though Lennon was considering adding his old friend Ivor Cutler to the line-up, which would have been even weirder. The interaction between Barham and session pianist Nicky Hopkins proves productive and it is salutary to consider that even on the more polished *Imagine*, Lennon ultimately elected to feature an austere arrangement of the title track with solitary piano.

"Fortunately"
The inverted commas indicate that this is not a song but a slice of dialogue. Taken from the BBC's *24 Hours* documentary taped in December 1969, this famous exchange features John and Yoko doing their 'Fortunately'/'Unfortunately' routine, which closes with them wondering what will happen next and Lennon concluding, "Fortunately, we don't know." It lasts a tantalizing 18 seconds.

Baby Please Don't Go
Previously titled 'Well (Baby Please Don't Go)' when it appeared in live form on *Some Time In New York City*, this was not of course the song made famous by John Lee Hooker and Them, but a cover of

the B-side to the Olympics' 1958 US Top 10 hit 'Western Movies', written by the group's founder Walter Ward. Lennon is at his most exuberant on this *Imagine* outtake which includes some rasping sax playing by Bobby Keyes and solid drumming by Jim Keltner. Lennon's anguished vocal and intense, improvisational electric guitar playing add an edge to a recording which, at the very least, should have been featured on the B-side to the US edition of 'Imagine' instead of 'It's So Hard'.

Oh My Love
Written by John and Yoko, this is another 8-track from the *Imagine* sessions. A simple and graceful expression of love, it's a faithful precursor of the album version, marked out only by the twin piano accompaniment of Lennon and Nicky Hopkins. The song was first attempted in substantially different form as early as 1968.

Jealous Guy
Recorded by the Lennon, Keltner, Hopkins, Voormann line-up, accompanied by John Barham on harmonium, this is a less busy version of the famous song and, for my money, a more affective rendition which better suits the singer's expressions of insecurity. Lennon adds some humming to the track, later replaced by whistling, which is set against Hopkins' impressive piano work. Phil Spector would later embellish the song with strings, creating a lusher production in the process.

Maggie Mae
Also titled 'Maggie May', this 50-second romp about a Liverpool prostitute was a traditional tune previously recorded by the Beatles on *Let It Be*. According to the notes, this excerpt was taken from a tape in 1979, one year before Lennon's death. It was an easy run-through for the singer who had first performed the song onstage during his days in the Quarry Men.

How Do You Sleep?
"No, we're going right in this time," Lennon warns as they try out

arguably the most accomplished song on *Imagine*. This version is subtly different, with Lennon frequently exhorting 'tell me' and sarcastically asking 'how do you sleep, brother?' There's an odd moment in the fourth line that other Lennon commentators have never mentioned where, instead of singing 'those freaks', he seems to intone 'so deeks(?!)', or something similar. Whatever else, this is a fascinating take, primarily because it's denuded of orchestration, and every nuance of Harrison's slide playing can be heard loudly in the mix.

God Save Oz

This was Lennon's guide vocal for the single that he composed with Yoko Ono and credited to Bill Elliott And The Elastic Oz Band for release by Apple in July 1971. On the single it was always titled 'God Save Us', but the compilers have elected to change the spelling as they do several times on this package. The song was issued as part of a fund-raising appeal for the infamous *Oz* obscenity trial. Full page advertisements, funded by the Lennons, appeared in the under-ground press, proclaiming: "Every country has a screw in its side, in England, it's *Oz*. *Oz* is on trial for its life. John and Yoko have written and helped produce this record – the proceeds of which are going to *Oz* to help pay their legal fees. The entire British under-ground is in trouble, it needs our help. Please listen – 'God Save Oz'." Lennon's song is simple sloganeering with a touch of humour amid the polemic as he intends fighting for Mickey Mouse. The last line asks to be saved from the Queen to whom he'd already sent back his MBE in part protest at the chart failure of 'Cold Turkey'. Although Lennon added his vocal to the song's B-side 'Do The Oz', the public were not interested enough in either Bill Elliott nor, presumably, the fate of the imprisoned *Oz* editors to buy enough copies to register a chart entry.

Do The Oz

This was the 2-track master of the B-side which featured John and Yoko on vocals backed by the Elastic Oz Band. This was the first time it had appeared on an actual Lennon album, although it has since been added to the 2000 CD reissue of *John Lennon/Plastic Ono*

Band. It still sounds impressive as a spontaneous political broadcast from a newly radicalized performer. The basic riff is the backdrop for the infectious slogan and there is sufficient humour in Lennon's lyrical asides to win over the unconverted.

I Don't Want To Be A Soldier
After 12 seconds of this, Lennon interrupts: "That was a bit odd that one, wasn't it?" He then turns to his bass player and enquires, "Klaus, if you're getting fed up of playing the same bit . . ." Following discussions with Voormann, Lennon restarts the track playing jagged electric guitar against the double percussion of Jim Gordon and Jim Keltner. Understandably, it's rougher than the finished *Imagine* version. The jamming is echoed in the impromptu lyrics where churchmen fly instead of cry and the thief, rightly no doubt, dies rather than flies. It's unlikely Lennon cared either way. Spector would improve this early attempt by using lashings of echo on the final version.

Give Peace A Chance
Yet another version of Lennon's enduring anthem, this 52-second rendition was taken from the 4-track rehearsal tapes recorded at the Queen Elizabeth Hotel, Montreal on 1 June 1969. Lennon name-checks the evangelist Billy Graham during the warm-up, and Yoko's voice soars above the congregation. Lennon tries to add some intensity with the ad-lib "I'm warning you", then stops the song to offer some advice. "Now, any of you know an offbeat?" he enquires. "An offbeat what?" is the response. Seeking a solution, Lennon suggests, "The ones that know what an offbeat is, do it so that we get it solid and leave the others if they want to join in." Further instructions follow. Then, we're off again for a few seconds more, but the tape cuts just as it starts to sound interesting.

Look At Me
By contrast to the hordes on 'Give Peace A Chance', this 8-track song from the *John Lennon/Plastic Ono Band* sessions is Lennon backed only by his acoustic guitar. The song was previously attempted

as a home demo in 1968 during sessions for *The Beatles* but failed to appear on that double album. Here, the playing is slightly less precise than that featured on the completed album version, but the differences are marginal and the lyrics identical. It sounds as though it is more than ready to be recorded as a complete and final take.

Long Lost John

"I think the piano maybe is better. I just realized to stop struggling." Presumably, these opening words are in reference to the mistitled traditional folk song that follows. This was Lennon's affectionate cover of the 1956 Lonnie Donegan hit 'Lost John', which reached number 2 in the UK charts. With minimal backing from Voormann and Starr, Lennon returns to his skiffle roots, reviving memories of his time with the Quarry Men. Part of the song's appeal for Lennon was no doubt the self-referential title, which he turned into a self-fulfilling prophecy three years later during his 'lost weekend'. Two minutes into the track, he calls a halt with the perplexing words, "Hello? Richard, Mao, Mao, I'm defunct. That's one of my problems of it!"

New York City

The second CD opens with a home recording approximately dated 1972, although it may well have been December 1971, depending on your source. Later fully realized on *Some Time In New York City*, this work-in-progress does not get beyond the first verse and is no more than 55 seconds in length.

Attica State

This song documents Lennon's famous appearance at Harlem's Apollo Theatre on 17 December 1971, where he played a benefit for the families and dependants of the prisoners killed in the riot at the Attica State Correctional Facility. The show opens with a stately tribute to the Lennons: "It is my pleasure and privilege at this very, very solemn moment to introduce a young man and his wife who saw fit to put down in music and lyrics – so that it will never be forgotten in our country by anyone – the tragedy of Attica State."

Lennon sounds genuinely humbled by this tribute and responds, "It's an honour and a pleasure to be here at the Apollo and for the reasons we're all here." What follows is an extraordinary rendition of 'Attica State' dominated by a prominent slide guitar that reverberates through the auditorium. When he points the finger at Nelson Rockefeller, who had refused to negotiate with the prisoners during the siege, the audience erupts. Lennon namechecks previous Beatle songs by singing of 'revolution' and reiterates his old slogan for Timothy Leary in the paraphrase 'Come Together – Join The Movement'. The atmosphere is electrifying and the playing and recording far sharper than expected, especially in view of a lesser performance of the song in Ann Arbor a week before. Inevitably, there is an explosion of applause as the song ends.

Imagine
Continuing his three-song set at the Apollo, the compilers skip Yoko's 'Sisters O Sisters' in favour of a rather more famous composition. Moving to the microphone, Lennon explains: "Some of you might wonder what I'm doing here with no drummers or nothing like that. Well, you might know I lost my old band, or I left it. I'm putting an electric band together – it's not ready yet – and things like this keep coming up, so I have to just busk it. So I'm going to sing a song now you might know." The lead track of his recent album follows, prompting a round of applause in recognition. It's salutary to consider that at this point the composition had yet to become an international hymn of peace. Lennon offers a subtle acoustic guitar reading, rather than the familiar piano accompaniment, and the result is surprisingly impressive and affective. When singing the line about imagining no possessions, he throws in the cheeky rejoinder, 'Try it!'

Bring On The Lucie (Freda Peeple)
This 16-track recording of one of the better songs on *Mind Games* opens with Lennon attempting some call-to-arms scat singing. It's a solid version, most notable for its playful moments. At the beginning of the third verse, Lennon starts to sing in a deliberately Dylanesque drawl while a slide guitar veers back and forth through the speakers.

"Let's say it's picking up some," Lennon concludes, with evident gratification. But he is not yet entirely satisfied. "Hold on! Let's hear more bass in the earphones and more of the slide guitar and a touch less of the piano, it seems loud."

Woman Is The Nigger Of The World
This quietly recorded acoustic home demo serves as a reflective interlude, taking up a mere 38 seconds. Given the quality and importance of the composition, it is regrettable that there was not more to savour. It sounds slightly more restrained than the released version, but any further comparisons are redundant due to the brevity of the recording.

Geraldo Rivera – One To One Concert
This is not a song, but a testimony to the philanthropy of John and Yoko. Introducing the pair at Madison Square Garden, television reporter and campaigner Geraldo Rivera recalls, "They looked at me and said, 'Not only will we perform for free but we're giving you $60,000 in cash for the mentally retarded.'" Huge applause follows. It seems terribly self-aggrandizing to reproduce this tribute as a separate fully fledged track on the box set without music or even any words from John and Yoko. Presumably, the fact that it was filmed was part of the reason but, if so, its worthiness as a recorded artefact is largely lost without the visual accompaniment.

Woman Is The Nigger Of The World
Rivera's idea for a benefit concert in support of mentally handicapped children in New York's Willowbrook Hospital, with support from John and Yoko, proved so successful that a second show was added on 30 August 1972. The seven-piece backing group Elephant's Memory add a gritty edge to the Lennons' material and this was particularly evident on this rendition of one of the best tracks on *Some Time In New York City*, with Stan Bronstein's saxophone in dominant mode. Lennon provides an intense vocal, but as he reaches the lines about people castigating women for being dumb, his memory deserts him. In a superb ad-lib, he sings "this is the one I can never

remember, but you get the message anyway." As we head towards the final verse, he hollers "Connolly was right – scream it!" after which he provides a hoarse but intense vocal finale.

It's So Hard

Another selection from the second show at Madison Square Garden, this begins with Lennon accidentally reversing the opening two verses. The oompah backing sounds like a musical free-for-all at times but obviously works well in a live setting. Typically, Lennon throws in some sexual innuendo, telling the audience that sometimes 'it's hard to get hard' which presumably explains why the singer feels like orally 'going down'.

Come Together

The final selection from the second One To One concert is the only Beatles released composition to appear on this *Anthology* – discounting a brief parody of 'Yesterday'. 'Come Together' was originally conceived as a political campaign song for LSD guru Timothy Leary, but Lennon liked the work so much that he fobbed off the counter-culture king with a banal slogan, 'Come Together – Join The Party'.

As Lennon explained: " 'Come Together' was an expression that Tim Leary had come up with for his attempt at being president or whatever he wanted to be, and he asked me to write a campaign song. I tried and I tried, but I couldn't come up with one . . . Leary attacked me years later saying I ripped him off. I didn't rip him off, it's just that it turned into 'Come Together'."

By the time the song reached the Beatles, Lennon had completed a bayou blues, full of neologisms, like a cross between Lewis Carroll and a New Orleans witch doctor. Lennon's stream-of-consciousness lyrics, part autobiographical, part sexual innuendo, were the song's highlight. Some of the phrasing and allusions appear to have baffled critics and commentators. Are the chilling opening words of each verse, 'shoot me', as Peter Doggett claims, or 'shook' as Tim Riley hears? The ever reliable researcher, archivist and Beatles' expert Andy Neill confirms: "Peter's right – it's 'shoot me'. In a 1969 Radio Luxembourg interview with Tony Macarthur to promote *Abbey*

Road, Lennon said, 'The word shoot is hidden by tape echo.'" Some of Lennon's phrases like 'spinal cracker' have prompted wildly varying interpretations. Riley reckons it's a description of Lennon's 'notoriously abrasive humour', Ian MacDonald says it's a Japanese technique to relieve back tension and Chris Ingham thinks it's a likely reference to the couple's car accident in Scotland. Lennon would probably have been amused by the confusion. As he said: "The thing was created in the studio. It's gobbledegook . . ."

On the One To One concert version, the sexual innuendo is still present, not just in the obvious 'come together over me' (which prompts the Lennon quip, 'some hope!'), but the suggestion to come 'over you' and the reference to a 'hairy arsehole'. Lest we think it's purely sexual, Lennon adds his revolutionary credentials with the coda, 'Stop The War!'

Happy Xmas

Apart from the loss of the parenthetical 'War Is Over' in the title, this rough mix of Lennon/Ono's festive favourite was similar to the single that reached number 2 in the UK charts. At the end, when the assembled cast ignite in a spontaneous cheer, there's some additional laughter after the clapping subsides.

Luck Of The Irish

This track was taken from the benefit concert for John Sinclair at the Chrysler Arena, Ann Arbor, Michigan on 10 December 1971. With a line-up featuring Lennon and Ono, street-singer David Peel, guitarist Leslie Bacon and political activist Jerry Rubin, the group performed four songs, two of which – 'Attica State' and 'Sisters O Sisters' – are not included here. The rousing 'Luck Of The Irish' worked well in concert, largely thanks to its singalong, anthemic chorus. Ono sings in a characteristically high register and evidently finds some difficulty keeping harmony and enunciating the words clearly. As a result her sentimental lyrics are far less noticeable than on the later *Some Time In New York City*, while Lennon's acerbic polemic comes through more forcibly than ever.

John Sinclair

In one of his more memorable introductions, Lennon tells the Ann Arbor audience: "We came here not only to help John and to spotlight what's going on, but also to show and say to all of you that apathy isn't it and that we can do something. OK, so flower power didn't work. So what? We start again. This song I wrote for John Sinclair." As the musicians warm up, he advises, "nice and easy now, sneaky". What sounds like an array of acoustic guitars and tambourine suddenly meld into an animated protest. The specific reference to Judge Columba sounds and scans better than the more generalized 'judges' mentioned on the later album version. There's a not easily decipherable line in this rendition where Lennon appears to sing something like 'and they got punk in London too'. I'd love to think he predicted the next UK cultural youth movement five to six years in advance, but surely even Lennon was not that fatidical. At the end of the song, the announcer attempts to pacify the audience, some of whom seem not entirely satisfied with a mere four songs. "Thank you all for coming. We're way over time. Sorry we couldn't hear more music. John, if you're listening still in jail – man, I hope this helps. I hope to see you here soon." What happened afterwards is revealed in the next track.

The David Frost Show

Five days after the John Sinclair Benefit, Lennon and Ono appeared on *The David Frost Show*, which was broadcast a month later on 13 January 1972. They performed six songs that evening, but none of them are featured in this extract. Nor is there any evidence of the ill-tempered exchanges between Lennon and the audience. Instead, there is an explanation of the plight of John Sinclair and what happened after the Ann Arbor Benefit. As Lennon recounted: "He spent two years in prison, virtually in isolation, in solitary, in case he infiltrated the other prisoners or something. He didn't want any help for two years because he thought, 'Why bother? Justice will let me out. My appeals will let me out . . .' After two years he began to worry and he asked for some help. We went down and had a rally with 15,000 people . . . By a stroke of good luck, he was released on

Monday." During his explanation, Lennon mentioned that they were joined by Phil Ochs and 'Little' Stevie Wonder at the show. David Frost was sufficiently conversant with pop culture to point out to Lennon that Stevie Wonder was no longer referred to as 'Little', an appellation that he had grown out of before the mid-Sixties.

Mind Games (I Promise)

The evolution of 'Mind Games' began with this piano-led *mea culpa* for Yoko, in which Lennon promises never to hurt her again. The home recording closes after one minute with the 'love is the answer' refrain which would be retained for the completed song.

Mind Games (Make Love, Not War)

The second stage of the 'Mind Games' saga was this one-minute home recording from 1973 which is highlighted by the mantra 'make love, not war'. When Lennon sings 'I know you've heard it before' he is already distancing himself from using the pacific words as the song's title. As he later said: " 'Make love, not war' was such a cliché you couldn't say it any more." By this stage, the song was already formed and required only those spacey 'mind game' lyrics and a Spector-like production to take it to the next level.

One Day At A Time

This early version of 'One Day (At A Time)' (parentheses removed) was arguably more effective than the rendition on *Mind Games*, which featured a legion of backing singers whose presence forced Lennon into an excruciating falsetto. Here he sounds more relaxed and the starker production focuses greater attention on the beautiful melody which was borrowed from 'Love', one of the more affecting moments on *John Lennon/Plastic Ono Band*. Unfortunately, Lennon's lazy lyrics fail to complement the melody. Using the Alcoholics Anonymous mantra 'One Day At A Time', already employed by Lena Martell as the title of her Jesus referenced 1979 hit, Lennon slips into trite rhymes which sound like a poor parody of Cole Porter, minus the songwriter's ingenuity and wit.

I Know

Later titled 'I Know (I Know)' on *Mind Games*, this home recording is a pleasant sketch of a reasonable song with a decent melody. If 'One Day (At A Time)' could charitably be interpreted as some kind of satirical comment on McCartney's 'moon and June' songwriting, then this was even more explicit with its references to 'Yesterday' and an entire line borrowed from 'It's Getting Better' on *Sgt Pepper's Lonely Hearts Club Band*. Lennon once claimed that he'd improved that song by adding the sarcastic rejoinder, 'it can't get no worse', but here he is content to parrot his former partner's simple 'it's getting better all the time'.

I'm The Greatest

Lennon first demoed this track at the end of 1970 when its self-boosting lyrics fitted in well with his post-primal 'genius is pain' persona, as evidenced during the famous *Rolling Stone* interview with Jann Wenner. In February 1971, the song was revived during preliminary recording sessions for *Imagine*, then lay unused until Ringo Starr contacted Lennon two years later in search of material for his third album, *Ringo*. According to Lennon, he had consigned this composition to the vaults fearing that its Muhammad Ali-style boasting would only invite a negative media reaction. The opportunity to rewrite the song with Ringo as the central character was something to be savoured. During the sessions, there was a veritable Beatles reunion with a line-up featuring Lennon, Starr, Harrison and Klaus Voormann. Producer Richard Perry was amazed to be working with three former Beatles instead of one. Judging from the atmosphere on this tape, the session was easy-going and exuberant. Lennon clearly enjoys providing his guide vocal for a song that was both thoughtful and funny. "OK boys, this is it," he cries, after which they reprise his autobiographical account of the three ages of greatness, from childhood through to pop star fame and adult independence. The choppy rhythm enhances the tale with suitably dramatic bombast. In his rewrite, Lennon references Ringo's 'Back Off Boogaloo' and brings back the drummer's alter ego Billy Shears from the prologue of 'With A Little Help From My Friends' on *Sgt Pepper's*. In Lennon's version,

Shears has been transformed into a woman somewhere along the way. The song proved one of the highlights of *Ringo* and Lennon's uproarious version is also a joy to hear.

Goodnight Vienna

Lennon was requested to offer another contribution to Ringo's next album and ended up writing the title track. His guide vocal, premièred here, is another impressive addition to *Anthology*. Before he reaches the end of the first line, he moans, "Oh Jesus, I'm worn out . . . let me try another." What follows is an exuberant rocker, full of what Lennon called his 'gobbledegook' lyrics. The playful stop/start rhythm adds a further note of humour and the song ends with a jocose parody of the applause heard at the end of Ringo's signature tune, 'With A Little Help From My Friends'.

Jerry Lewis Telethon

On 6 September 1972, Lennon and Ono appeared on the annual Jerry Lewis charity telethon performing 'Imagine', 'Give Peace A Chance' and 'Now Or Never'. Rather than including any of these selections from what was the last ever public performance by the duo, Yoko Ono features this overwrought tribute from the comedian. He can be heard cheerleading the audience in a chant of "John – Yoko". Worse follows with the words: "I'll tell you what – cool it! I would suspect that John Lennon is probably one of the wisest showmen I've ever met. He knows what he's doing. He did two things tonight: he came here to help, one, I think that was the primary purpose of his visit; and, two, he meant to say something. I think he did both those things. He has split. Let's thank him very much." Why this testimony from the comedian was considered important enough to warrant inclusion as a fully fledged track on the *Anthology* is a mystery. In common with the Geraldo Rivera tribute mentioned earlier, it sounds at best immodest and at worst self-aggrandizing which, presumably, was not the intention.

'A Kiss Is Just A Kiss'

This 10-second snippet features John and Yoko cooing a line from the standard 'As Time Goes By'. Ever playful, Lennon adds 'A fly is just a fly', no doubt in deference to Yoko's 1971 double album *Fly*.

Real Love

After the preceding whimsical tracks, the listener is suddenly thrust forward in time to 1980 for this haunting home recording which was later passed over to the remaining Beatles and revamped as a single. Several demos of the song were attempted including this poignant piano piece which would have fitted well alongside the contents of either *Double Fantasy* or *Milk And Honey*.

You Are Here

Sounding like a Hawaiian wedding song, this easily identifiable blueprint for the eleventh track on *Mind Games* displays the composition without the lively choral accompaniment. Unlike 'One Day (At A Time)', on which the backing singers sounded intrusive, this tune was actually enhanced by their overdubbed presence. Lyrically, there are some subtle differences here with Lennon singing about love opening his 'mind', rather than his 'eyes', which fits better alongside the word 'blown' in the succeeding line. He also seems to take on the mantle of the Kinks' Ray Davies as the only British songwriter concerned with 'village greens', although that allusion was mysteriously deleted from the version later included on *Mind Games*.

What You Got

This 75-second home recording from 1974 reveals Lennon grappling with a new composition. Quietly sung, with acoustic guitar accompaniment, he has the chorus down, but little else. 'You gave me the world and I threw it away,' he sings, revealing a line that failed to appear on the final version.

Nobody Loves You When You're Down And Out

After singing the 'I'll scratch your back' line, Lennon sarcastically observes, "Oh, wonderful! Wonderful!" before telling the engineer and musicians, "Do it the other way." Meanwhile, the studio intercom tells us that this is "Take 19". Ken Ascher's electric piano is evident early on, sounding suspiciously like a celeste. Although this version of the song is more subdued, which certainly fits the lyrical theme, Lennon rouses himself for the impassioned lines about getting up in the morning, familiar from *Walls And Bridges*.

Whatever Gets You Thru The Night

Recorded at home, this 38-second snatch of acoustic strumming sees Lennon running through the lyrics. Suddenly, he incorporates the opening line of 'Jealous Guy' into the song, as if he really is dreaming of the past. Just as it starts to sound interesting, it cuts out.

Whatever Gets You Thru The Night

"1-2-3-4" Lennon counts in, only to suffer a momentary delay. Using his falsetto, he leads the musicians in a strong rendition of a song that would soon provide a surprise US number 1 hit. It's interesting to hear this less frantic version, minus Elton John's distinctive backing vocal. As the song closes, Lennon expresses his evident satisfaction: "It sounded pretty active."

Yesterday (parody)

As 'Whatever Gets You Thru The Night' closes, Lennon launches into a parody of the Beatles' most recorded song, bringing to mind his comments about McCartney on 'How Do You Sleep?' A silent movie-style piano from Nicky Hopkins accompanies Lennon as he croons about not being half the man he used to be 'because I'm an amputee'.

Be-Bop-A-Lula

Taken from the 16-track *Rock 'n' Roll* sessions, produced by Lennon, this features a wonderfully expressive vocal and strong rock 'n' roll playing from the band. Lennon's singing grows more impassioned as the song progresses. He closes this exuberant performance with the words: "Phew! It's hot in here."

Rip It Up/Ready Teddy

Another strong vocal performance from Lennon characterizes this performance. His handling of these rock 'n' roll standards shows no sense of tiredness or overfamiliarity, but a deep involvement in every aspect of the lyrics and music.

Scared

Taken from the 16-track *Walls And Bridges* sessions, this version underlines how well rehearsed the band were while running through the number. It's a remarkably faithful rendition, sung with verve and featuring Lennon and Ken Ascher trading trills on the piano.

Steel And Glass

"My wall collapsed," Lennon says, as the musicians prepare for a fresh take. "OK – are you ready, Klaus, you old boogie, you!" The familiar spoken preamble to the released version is not included here, but it's a strong work in progress, clearly ready for a final take. Jesse Ed Davis offers some striking wah-wah guitar, Voormann's bass is prominent, as requested by Lennon, and the singing is passionate with some impromptu 'nah nah nahs' towards the end. Lennon assumes it's simply another average run-through, but is soon corrected. "OK, OK, OK – well that was the same as the last one. Better? Oh my God, it's better is it?"

Surprise, Surprise (Sweet Bird Of Paradox)

Lennon begins by instructing the musicians about a break in the song, then advises drummer Jim Keltner of what he has in mind. A very strong performance follows, with Lennon's diction crystal clear and the band sounding impressively tight. Just over two minutes in, he urges them to hold the rhythm, cautioning: "Stay in your 'D' – stay there." He then scat sings the words 'sweet sweet smell' before ordering everybody to "Stop!" There is a sense of anticipation as he asks to hear the playback: "Let me just check it!"

Bless You

The *Walls And Bridges* sessions continue with one of the album's most memorable songs. The band have clearly mastered the instrumental section and Lennon's vocal is exceptionally strong. If this version had been included on the album, nobody would have complained. An excellent take.

Going Down On Love

This 54-second excerpt is included to remind us that the recordings for *Walls And Bridges* weren't just a series of seamless takes without comment. After four exemplary songs, we find Lennon mildly reprimanding his players in order to ensure that he achieves the desired musical effect. "OK, hold it!," he instructs as the song commences. "Don't go 'do-do-dum'. We're having enough trouble keeping the rhythm. I don't want anything other than strict four in the bar unless it's written – the jumps on the letter 'A's and the breaks . . . I just don't want any fills from the guitars or anybody. Just play what you were playing and no 'do-do-dum' or 'chick-a-da-dum' or 'sic-a-dee-dee'. Just hold it at four. Take six! This is it!" We then hear six tantalizing seconds of the actual song.

Move Over Ms L

Lennon opens the song with an Elvis growl, similar to that used at the beginning of the later '(Just Like) Starting Over'. Meanwhile, the musicians provide a backing strongly reminiscent of Elvis Presley's hit 'Don't Be Cruel'. The rock 'n' roll arrangement perfectly fits the song, which serves as Lennon's irreverent riposte to his estranged wife. While songs like 'Aisumasen (I'm Sorry)' and 'I Know (I Know)' were heartfelt pleas for forgiveness, this expresses those same sentiments in a couched, tongue-in-cheek style, more in keeping with 'What You Got'. The emotional maturity evident on 'Bless You', in which Lennon acknowledges his loss with stoical acceptance, is repeated here, but the nobility is replaced by an irrepressible irreverence. Stream-of-consciousness catchphrases and fractured adages pour out of his brain as he deflects his emotions by seeking refuge in the wry witticisms of rock 'n' roll lyrics. There's even a reference to starving in China which he would revive and paraphrase in the lyrics to 'Nobody Told Me'. The ironic humour and playful defiance he displays throughout 'Move Over Ms L' is in striking contrast to the subservient role he usually takes in songs about Yoko

Ono. It's regrettable that this track was omitted from *Walls And Bridges* as it would have complemented some of the more subdued songs therein and provided a rollicking finale. On the CD remastered edition of the album it is again conspicuous by its absence from the bonus tracks. Whether this was a political decision based on the composition's subject matter seems unlikely given Ono's willingness to issue any track uncensored. But that question remains unanswered.

Ain't She Sweet
Lennon adopts a pseudo-Cockney accent for this 29-second pub rendition of the song he once recorded in Hamburg. Always useful for breaking the tension between takes, the singalong can also be heard during the *Abbey Road* sessions where it serves a similar function. Originally part of Al Jolson's repertoire during the Twenties, Lennon's probable inspiration was Gene Vincent's version, although his reading and arrangement were considerably different from those of the Virginian wildcat.

Slippin' And Slidin'
Another previously unissued Lennon production from the *Rock 'n' Roll* sessions, this vibrant take fully displays how well he lent his voice to authentic rock 'n' roll. The song is taken at a furious pace, with clanking piano driving the rhythm. As the performance ends, Lennon cries out 'Oh!' in almost orgasmic relief.

Peggy Sue
"OK, ready?" Lennon enquires at the start. "OK – dynamics with tension, fun and laughter for all. Honky rock!" The instantly recognizable opening of 'Peggy Sue' follows, but with a piano dominant in the mix. Lennon does his best Buddy Holly imitation, complete with hiccups and other unorthodox tonsorial inflexions. During rehearsals, Lennon also attempted Holly's 'That'll Be The Day' but it didn't work out to his satisfaction.

Bring It On Home To Me/Send Me Some Lovin'
"Hold on! Hold on! My cowboy shirt jumped off!" Lennon tells his

musicians as they meander into a bluesy reading of these Sam Cooke familiars. Although the word 'medley' has been dropped from the title, this is the same arrangement that was captured on *Rock 'n' Roll*. Lennon was seemingly determined to complete a decent version of 'Sent Me Some Lovin'' having previously attempted the song with Elephant's Memory during the sessions for *Some Time In New York City*.

Phil And John 1

The 'Phil And John' interludes provide some insight into the chaos attending the original Spector *Rock 'n' Roll* sessions. Daybreak madness is the theme here as the recordings are interrupted by the simulated sound of a tweeting bird, presumably provided by one of the musicians. Spector gets increasingly animated as the bird's singing eclipses the playing. "What is that tweeting bird out there, for godsake?!" Suddenly, it sounds like Spector is conducting a nature field recording as the 'bird' refuses his requests for silence.

"Remember the solo," Lennon intervenes. "That's the bit where I come in."

"Keltner, stand up so we know you're there," Spector says to the drummer, which seems rather presumptuous given his own diminutive stature.

Lennon then screams a swear word at Spector, expertly accompanied by the chirping bird. Settling down, John asks one of his players, "Give me a clue," as he attempts to tune his guitar.

"You haven't been in tune all night," Spector chides. Newly determined to push them forward, the producer then announces: "All right, one of the greatest sessions of all-time history is in the making. John Lennon is here with his brother Jack and, here we go, 1-2-3."

Lennon repeats the count in, but adds a 'four', causing Spector to explode: "No! You yelled four. You can't yell over the players."

"Phil, please accept my 'fours' – it's the only way I can come in," Lennon apologizes.

"You don't have to come in," Spector responds.

"No wonder Ronnie left!" Lennon tentatively teases, which wins

a laugh from Spector, who obviously doesn't mind the cheeky reference to his former wife.

Spector then gets disturbed by some horn playing and rants about
"horns, birds and seagulls".

"It's our big chance with A&M, let's not fuck it," says Lennon,
momentarily considering a change of record company, or perhaps
referring to the A&M studios where some of the work was cut.

"Well, Herbie did!" Spector retorts, obliquely alluding to the
label's founder, Herb Alpert.

Finally, everybody is ready for a take but the tape cuts out before
we are allowed to hear any music.

Phil And John 2

An impressive opening of 'Just Because' is abruptly interrupted by
Spector, who notices that everybody reaches for their headphones
whenever he speaks. Is he shouting too loud? Reassured that everything's fine, he allows the musicians to restart. More repartee follows,
culminating in Lennon's tart, "I'm gonna get an all-girl band."

"You need one," Spector adds. "Let's go!"

"You won't let me do 'Be-Bop-A-Lula'?" asks Lennon.

"I won't let you do anything . . . until you get this."

"And 'Send Me Some Lovin'?"

"You can do anything you want, Johnny . . . after this."

"Take the bandages off!"

"You can even do 'take the bandages off'. You can even do
'Johnny B. Goode'. I wish you would."

Another take is attempted but there's further interruptions and
delays as Spector notices somebody in the band waving their hand.
Tape fades.

Phil And John 3

More banter between the comedy pair, although on this occasion it's
not clear whether they're referring to their own musicians or some
other band.

"What are they gonna do, play jazz with Jethro Tull?" asks
Lennon.

"No, Elton John, probably, at the Roxy," Spector replies.

"Elton John's a friend of mine."

"Well, good, he's got the same name as you, only you spell it at the front and he spells it at the back – and you both go in the same place!"

"No, no I refuse. Elton is gonna die young . . . I'm gonna be a 90-year-old guru."

"All right. Good. I make history. You make gurus."

"Phil, I'm gonna write your history, so be careful."

Having explored sexual innuendo and gurus, the duo finally return to the task of completing 'Just Because'.

"When In Doubt Fuck It"

This 10-second snippet is most memorable for Lennon's stark warning to his drummer: "Keltner, control your prick!"

Be My Baby

After the humorous interludes, it's a relief to hear some music again. Cher's recording of the Ronettes' 'Baby, I Love You' may have convinced Lennon and Spector to tackle the equally famous 'Be My Baby'. Given the previous joke about Ronnie in their dialogue segments, it seems apt. The song builds gradually from acoustic to full band and Lennon waits for over a minute before uttering a growl, then joining in. His voice sounds strained at times, but affecting, vulnerable and sensuous; he savours every nuance in each line. In the same way that he imitated rock 'n' roll singers, Lennon attempts to inhabit the spirit of Ronnie Spector as if he's leading a girl group. Towards the end, the effort almost proves his undoing. He grows increasingly shrill, then loses himself in some primal paroxysms. Regrettably, this performance failed to make the final listing on *Rock 'n' Roll*, although Morris Levy was happy enough to include the rendition on *Roots*.

Stranger's Room

Listed as a 1980 home recording in the CD's booklet (although others suspect it may have had an earlier vintage), this was the prototype of

'I'm Losing You'. A mournful ballad, accompanied by a piano's descending chords, it sent a message of intense loneliness, even bleaker than Graham Nash's song of the same title. What's clear, even at this early stage, is the existence of a powerful song. Lennon includes some of his most visceral imagery, agonizingly describing blood oozing from his veins. Tellingly, these lines were excised from 'I'm Losing You'. In common with 'Jealous Guy', 'Stranger's Room' ends with a whistle, but this is no attempt at forced jollity. Stoical at best, the song retains its oppressive mood till the end.

Old Dirt Road

Identified as "Take 11" in the introduction, this begins with Lennon encouraging the engineer or musicians: "Just keep on the road, you're the white line." The performance that follows rivals the slightly more polished rendition on *Walls And Bridges* in terms of musicianship and emotional intensity. In common with the other outtakes from the album included here, it gives the lie to Lennon's proposition that *Walls And Bridges* was merely the work of "a semi-sick craftsman".

I'm Losing You

The final CD of *Anthology* opens with a lacerating version of 'I'm Losing You' featuring Cheap Trick's guitarist Rick Nielsen and drummer Bun E. Carlos, supported by bassist Tom Petersson and pianist George Small. Lennon's sinewy vocal adds spice to a harder-edged recording that veers close to heavy rock. Nielsen provides a jagged guitar solo that makes for invigorating listening, and certainly better suits the aggressive lyrics. Presumably, Lennon concluded that the sound was too severe to fit unobtrusively in the context of the 'Heart Play', so this was axed along with the Cheap Trick duo's take on Ono's 'I'm Moving On'.

Sean's "Little Help"

This home recording, dated 1979, features four-year-old Sean attempting to sing 'With A Little Help From My Friends', which he names as his favourite tune. His father has to tell him that it was

Ringo rather than himself who sang it on *Sgt Pepper's*, but adds, "Paul and I were singing with him." Amusingly, Lennon struggles to remember the title of the song, even though it was a UK number 1 for Joe Cocker and a Lennon/McCartney standard. Such hesitation speaks volumes about his attitude to Beatles history.

Serve Yourself

Recorded in 1980, this comic diatribe was allegedly inspired by Dylan's conversion to Christianity and his Grammy award-winning song 'Gotta Serve Somebody'. The latter offered a series of propositions followed by a single catchphrase, similar in construction to Lennon's 'Crippled Inside'. But 'Serve Yourself' bore little similarity to either song. It was the title that proved arresting for critics keen to report a Lennon v. Dylan feud. The expectation was that Lennon would roast Dylan with the same relish that he trounced McCartney on 'How Do You Sleep?' While the fast and furious opening strumming and acerbic lyrics promised much, 'Serve Yourself' turned out to be little more than a directionless rant, a novelty song performed in the type of exaggerated Scouse accent that would have mortified John's Aunt Mimi. Given his love of mimicry, Lennon was perfectly capable of delivering the song in a Dylan voice, but even this chance was squandered and the sentiments deliberately deflated. Far from attacking Dylan, it does not even allude to him in the lyrics. Unlike 'How Do You Sleep?' which mentioned 'Yesterday', 'Another Day' and the freaks who claimed that McCartney was dead, nothing in 'Serve Yourself' seems to be directed at Dylan, beyond the title's vague riposte to 'Gotta Serve Somebody'. Neither is Christianity condemned as much as dismissed, along with every other religion and belief system. Beneath the barbed ranting, Lennon finds familiar salvation in eulogizing motherhood, albeit in graphic terms, describing a backroom birth replete with 'piss, shit and midwives'. The song becomes more crude as it progresses, meandering into a complaint about spoilt kids and their materialistic demands, and a cutting, racial reference to 'nig nogs'. By this point, any tentative connection with Dylan has been long lost. The song's title alone is its punchline, the remainder a blue-humoured harangue that sounds like a drunken northern music hall entertainer. Judging from his laugh at the end and its failure to appear on record, Lennon did not take the song seriously and evidently bore no malice towards Dylan. "I was very surprised when Bobby boy went that way," he said, referring to the master's conversion. "But I'm not distressed by the fact that Dylan is doing what Dylan wants to do." An important footnote to this song is the extraordinary revelation, mentioned by those who claim to have read Lennon's diaries, that he also went through a 'born again' phase and was briefly entranced by the tele-evangelists Billy Graham, Pat Robertson, and others.

My Life

"We like to have these things to record – let's not get so hysterical this time," Lennon warns for no apparent reason at the start of this song. A blueprint for '(Just Like) Starting Over', this paean to the union of John and Yoko was a slight tune with fawning lyrics. Yet, it survived in various incarnations within his song catalogue. The accompanying booklet wrongly transcribes the words 'I've only myself to *lose*' as '*loose*'.

Nobody Told Me

The best song from *Milk And Honey* is executed here in almost identical fashion. There are some amusing and revealing moments such as Lennon phrasing 'most peculiar, *mummy*' and directing the band "into the middle" in the break before the final chorus. The playing is full of verve with three electric guitars and great interaction between keyboardist George Small and drummer Andy Newmark among the highlights.

Life Begins At 40

Lennon welcomes us to the 'Dakota Country & Western Club' for a sardonic celebration of his 40th birthday, which was still a few months away. The song was earmarked for Ringo Starr whose 40th had occurred in July 1980. Recorded on acoustic guitar with a rhythm box accompaniment, its mock country vocal would have suited Starr's more nasal whine. The spoken intro tells of Yoko Ono offering us a "wonderful gift of a strange . . ." followed by a frustrat-ingly indecipherable word, which even the booklet's compilers fail to translate.

I Don't Wanna Face It

With its longer instrumental opening, this fierce version is a keen rival to the track that appeared posthumously on *Milk And Honey*. Lennon encourages guitarist Earl Slick to play a solo, which he does with aplomb. Some playful sound effects are included at the end of the track.

Woman

This home recording confirms that 'Woman' was a fully realized composition long before Lennon entered a recording studio. There's no 'Mao' preamble here, but the lyrics are intact, set against an acous-tic guitar and rhythm box backing. It's captivating to hear the com-position in such stark form.

Dear Yoko

Lennon employs his 'Buddy Holly' voice to great effect here. The alternate take is not dissimilar to the version on *Double Fantasy*, although there is a stronger Caribbean/reggae influence in the rhyth-mic interaction between drummer Andy Newmark and bassist Tony Levin. Lennon throws in a few puppy yelps towards the end.

Watching The Wheels

Arguably, the best song on *Double Fantasy*, this composition, premièred here as a home demo, would have survived as a fine folk song in its primitive state. Its defence of indolence as an artistic right serves as the perfect response to his careerist colleagues and critics. There is only one lyrical difference, with Lennon assuming a more active stance by suggesting he's '*making* the wheels go round', although that was probably a Freudian slip.

I'm Stepping Out

"OK, who's got the rhythm?" Lennon asks. "Let's just hear the cassette, then we'll get it." The excited introduction that preceded the version on *Milk And Honey* is absent here but, amazingly, there's an entire new verse, beginning, 'Called up the doctor . . .' The physician apparently went dancing to sweeten his breath and ended up 'sick to death' and unable to make house calls. Thereafter, we're back to those equally eccentric lyrics in which Lennon dons a space suit and bestows blessings on cats. Evidently, Lennon had a peculiar sentimentality towards felines. "I got ants in my pants," he cries as the song closes.

Borrowed Time
"A little reggae, I think," says Lennon in an Indian accent, after which he attempts this home recording with the aid of a rhythm box. He achieves a surprisingly full sound on the limited equipment available. The seeming infatuation with reggae resulted from Lennon purchasing some Bob Marley & The Wailers material while on holiday. On this evidence though, Lennon sounds more like an exponent of Caribbean calypso than a fan of roots reggae.

The Rishi Kesh Song
Another home recording during which Lennon introduces the composition as 'The Happy Rishikesh Song'. Since Rishikesh was where the Beatles went on retreat to witness the teachings of the guru Maharishi Mahesh Yogi, it must be assumed that the song title 'Rishi Kesh' is a mistake on the part of the compilers, unless it was written as such in Lennon's hand. Although this composition was taped in 1980, it sounds like a belated follow-up to 'Sexy Sadie', though why he was thinking about the Maharishi Mahesh Yogi at this late date remains a mystery. The song actually opens with a lilt and a paraphrased line from George Harrison's 1979 hit 'Blow Away'. Clearly the connection between Indian music and Harrison was present in Lennon's mind, subliminally or otherwise. Lennon's affected vocal sounds close to a George Formby imitation, while the lyrics merely repeat two verses. This repetition is echoed in the recurring guitar chords, with Lennon parodying the cyclic chanting favoured by the Maharishi, complete with words that pinprick the pseudo-

profundities of 'Within You, Without You' ('everything that's not here is not there'). Towards the end, there's a brief cessation and a dramatic shift in theme and tone, as if Lennon is singing a completely different song. 'Feel so suicidal . . .' he moans, although the reference to 'suicide' is conspicuously absent from the accompanying lyric sheet. Unlike the remainder of 'The Rishi Kesh Song', this segment, which sounds a completely different entity, is a powerful, despairing lamentation, even by Lennon's most mournful standards.

Sean's "Loud"
On this 35-second snatch of dialogue, Sean discovers 'loudness' by playing around with an electric guitar. His father assures him, "I can't make it any louder – it's on full."

Beautiful Boy
The 'Sean' segment warrants its inclusion as a moving introduction to Lennon's affectionate lullaby to his son. Considered saccharine by some at the time of its release on *Double Fantasy*, the composition achieved instant poignancy after the singer's assassination. This full band version is surprisingly strong with Lennon already including his 'Goodnight, Sean' coda.

Mr Hyde's Gone (Don't Be Afraid)
This home demo is another unusual entry in the Lennon canon. With its emphasis on irrational, childlike fears and the allusion to scary sounds that turn out to be cats playing, it was most likely another soothing song for Sean at bedtime. The bare, piano accompaniment and vocal have a vaguely Nöel Coward quality, with a touch of pre-war vaudeville, not heard on a Lennon disc since McCartney's 'Honey Pie' from *The Beatles*.

Only You
Mysteriously undated in the CD booklet, this was Lennon's guide vocal for Ringo Starr's version of 'Only You', which was included on his 1974 album, *Goodnight Vienna*. Its inclusion among a host of tracks from 1980 seems odd, to say the least. The recording boasts a

formidable list of players, including Starr on drums, guitarist Jesse Ed Davis, keyboardist Billy Preston, drummer Jim Keltner and backing vocalist Harry Nilsson. Despite the stellar line-up, Lennon's vocal is perfunctory – a passionless rendition of the 1955 Platters' hit. Of course, Lennon was only offering a 'guide' for Ringo whose own version, on which John played and sang, was far superior and climbed to number 6 in the US charts.

Grow Old With Me

In the liner notes of *Milk And Honey*, Yoko Ono told us that only one copy of this song survived. Here, the original home demo, featuring Lennon and Ono on acoustic piano and rhythm box, has undergone 'audio restoration' by EMI's studio boffins. Beatles' producer George Martin was then employed to add a full-scale orchestra and woodwind backing. The strings are tastefully incorporated and add a stately gentility to the track. Presumably, Ono felt such enhancement was allowable on the grounds that this was Lennon's last ever recording and an alternate 'improved' version might add some majesty to the composition. Coincidentally, one of Lennon's heroes, Buddy Holly, also had his work embellished with strings after his death.

The theme of 'Grow Old With Me' was long familiar to Lennon, who was always wise beyond his years. Even before the youth-obsessed Sixties had ended, he was looking forward to the prospect of ageing. "I really can't wait to be old. You do your best and then there is a time when you do slow down and it seems nice. I always look forward to being an old couple of about 60, just remembering everything. I suppose we'll still be cursing because we're in a wheelchair."

Dear John

Essentially a quieter companion piece to 'Dear Yoko', this undated home demo was recorded shortly before his death around the same time as 'Grow Old With Me'. In common with 'Watching The Wheels', 'Dear John' celebrates taking life at an easy pace and pictures Lennon watching television, content in the belief that the race has been won. The attractive vocal sounds like a cross between mid-period Beatles and a bossa nova beach tune.

The Great Wok

The final seven tracks on *Anthology* are subtitled 'Something More', as if they are bonus tracks. Lennon's prose and spoken-word recordings offer another facet of his personality: the humorist. Here, the style is not that different from his earlier prose works like *In His Own Write* and *A Spaniard In The Works*. His love for *The Goons* is evident in the mock Indian voice, redolent of Peter Sellers. There's passing puns – "the great wok must be done" – and parodies of Eastern wisdom that recall the aforementioned 'The Rishi Kesh Song': "One way to look at it is simply not to look at it at all."

Mucho Mungo

Recorded in 1976 – you can hear baby Sean crying in the background – this was originally co-written with Nilsson for his album *Pussy Cats*. Lennon had already recorded two home demos in 1974 before returning to the song. Short and lyrically sweet, it was never likely to be considered as album material, post Nilsson.

Satire 1

If proof were needed that Lennon could have sung 'Serve Yourself' in the voice of Bob Dylan, then these 'satires' make the case. Here Lennon parodies 'Knocking On Heaven's Door' ('mama take this make-off off of me') and references 'Ballad Of A Thin Man' and the 'never-ending tour' using the exaggerated pronunciation more in keeping with the Dylan of 1965.

Satire 2

An improvement on 'Satire 1', this features Lennon stretching syllables to record lengths as he immerses himself in the Dylan vernacular. There's some occasionally cutting asides ("This should get me in the *Village Voice*"), complete with what sounds like newspaper reports filtered through Lennon's imagination. Dylan once explained how his early protest songs were often inspired by real life events that he read about in the press, so Lennon takes this notion to its logical extreme by singing 'newspaper prose'. "I'm so cynical I could be doing this forever," he remarks. There's a brief pun on 'Stuck Inside Of Mobile With The Memphis Blues Again' before the song ends with Lennon turning on another favourite target: "Sometimes I wish I was just George Harrison, you know, with *all* the answers. Oh God!"

Satire 3
In this last brief parody of Dylan, Lennon adapts a line from Berry Gordy's 'Money' (made famous by the Beatles): "I'd just like to leave you with this message – they say the best things in life are free, except for MTV."

Sean's "In The Sky"
Recorded in 1979, this brief segment sees Sean asking: "When did we get our house?" His mother tells him it was in 1973, and John adds that this was before he was born, and still in the sky. Lennon goes on to tell the child that he was delivered in a cardboard box.

It's Real
There's no vocal on this 1979 home recording, simply Lennon playing acoustic guitar and whistling the melody. It's a low-key ending to an extraordinary audio documentary.

WONSUPONATIME

Released: November 1998

Original UK issue: EMI 4 97639 1. CD issue: EMI 4 97639 2 (UK)/
Capitol 4 97639 2 0 (US)

Subtitled 'Selections from *Lennon Anthology*', this was a pyrrhic attempt to précis the 4–CD *Anthology* on a single CD. Although it captures many of the highlights, its appeal is questionable. Neither fish nor fowl, it seems too esoteric for the casual purchaser and inadequate for hard-core collectors. Presumably, it was aimed at those fans who wanted an archive release, but not one as extensive or expensive as the definitive *Anthology*. In passing, for those who bought the work for reasons of thrift, it was salutary to see *Anthology* on sale at the Fopp chain of record shops in 2006 for £13, which was around the same price that *Wonsuponatime* cost at the time of its release.

Full track listing: *I'm Losing You; Working Class Hero; God; How Do You Sleep?; Imagine (Take 1); Baby Please Don't Go; Oh My Love; God Save Oz; I Found Out; Woman Is The Nigger Of The World; 'A Kiss Is Just A Kiss'; Be-Bop-A-Lula; Rip It Up/Ready Teddy; What You Got; Nobody Loves You When You're Down And Out; I Don't Wanna Face It; Real Love: Only You; Grow Old With Me; Sean's "In The Sky"; Serve Yourself.*

ACOUSTIC

Released: November 2004

Original UK issue: EMI 8 74428 2. US issue: Capitol 7243 8 74428 2 5

Oddly marketed, this was not a best of Lennon's acoustic work from his standard catalogue, but an album seemingly aimed at budding guitar players. In her brief notes, Yoko Ono dedicates the work to 'future guitarists' and includes a full lyric sheet, complete with musical annotation and chord charts. Disconcertingly, there are no details of the recording dates for any of the songs, even though this information was clearly available. Nor is there any indication in the packaging that most of this stuff consists of outtakes and home recordings. Eight of the tracks were taken from the Lennon *Anthology*, while 'Real Love' was previously heard on the *Imagine* film sound-track. The duplication bothered some critics, who complained, quite reasonably, that fans were being encouraged to purchase a work, half of which they already owned.

For my money, *Acoustic* is still a better buy than *Wonsuponatime*, but for different reasons. What we have here is actually a minor extension of *Anthology* for collectors, rather than guitarists, boasting seven previously unreleased songs (none of them identified in the notes) as follows:

Well Well Well

This home demo, recorded in the summer of 1970, is a rough acoustic run-through, with Lennon playing Delta blues style and including a line subsequently deleted from the released version: 'she looked so beautiful, I could wee'.

Look At Me

Except for the more prominent, strumming guitar work and a slightly different coda, this is virtually a dead ringer for the version that appeared on *John Lennon/Plastic Ono Band*.

248

God

From the same vintage as 'Well Well Well', this rendition of 'God' was preceded by Lennon's hammy American preacher-style voice, intoning: "I had a message from above . . ." The full rap is even included in the accompanying lyric sheet, as if it was part of the song. Instead of the familiar piano version, Lennon plays acoustic guitar, using E7/G# chords to emphasize the names mentioned in the mantra. At this point, he still refers to 'Dylan' rather than the amended 'Zimmerman' and in the concluding section he just believes in himself, with no reference to Yoko Ono. During the fade-out, he cries, "Eureka, brother, I had a concept, vanilla was her name."

My Mummy's Dead

Reputedly the first of only two takes recorded for the *John Lennon/Plastic Ono Band*, this version is slightly longer, with Lennon playing in flat tuning and struggling with some notes towards the end.

Cold Turkey

A most welcome addition to *Acoustic*, this was recorded in September 1969, just before it was premièred at the Toronto Rock 'n' Roll Revival Festival on 13 September 1969. Despite the lack of electricity, the song still pulsates with passion and desperation. Its most distinctive feature is Lennon's bleating, which sounds like a cross between Larry The Lamb, Marc Bolan and Yoko Ono. Towards the end, the bleat is transformed into a feral yowl, part feline, part inhuman. Another take, which we may well hear on album at some later date, features Ono adding her own vocal outpourings.

What You Got

Arguably the most radically different recording available here, this home demo is almost unrecognizable on first hearing. During the introduction, Lennon sounds as if he's about to launch into 'Mystery Train' or some rockabilly standard, then he settles into a country blues style. The first verse features impromptu lyrics, including a reference to a 'shaggy dog'. Lennon seems intent on turning the song into a 'shaggy dog' story, seemingly making up nonsense lyrics for his own amusement. The only certainty is the chorus.

Dear Yoko
One of several songs Lennon wrote during his holiday in Bermuda, this is another playfully affectionate tribute to his wife, in the same spirit as *Imagine*'s 'Oh Yoko!' The sprightly opening chords instantly impress and the performance is strong, spoiled only by some sonic interference towards the end of the song. Overall, it demonstrates how well *Double Fantasy* might have sounded in a revamped acoustic format.

Full Track Listing: *Working Class Hero; Love; Well Well Well; Look At Me; God; My Mummy's Dead; Cold Turkey; The Luck Of The Irish; John Sinclair; Woman Is The Nigger Of The World; What You Got; Watching The Wheels; Dear Yoko; Real Love; Imagine; It's Real.*

WORKING CLASS HERO – THE DEFINITIVE LENNON

Released: October 2005

Original UK issue: EMI 3 40391 1. US issue: Capitol 3 40391 1.

In order to celebrate what would have been Lennon's 65th birthday, Yoko Ono sanctioned another Lennon compilation, this time comprising 38 songs over two CDs. Although it still lacked the definitive stamp of the previously issued *Lennon* box set, it was a more than reasonable introduction for the casual purchaser. Nestled within were five tracks from *John Lennon/Plastic Ono Band*, five from *Imagine*, two from *Some Time In New York City*, four from *Mind Games*, five from *Walls And Bridges*, four from *Double Fantasy*, and three from *Milk And Honey*. There were also all Lennon's major singles, plus three tracks taken from *Anthology*: the alternate 'Cheap Trick' take of 'I'm Losing You'; plus the alternate versions of 'Real Love' and 'Grow Old With Me'. Chronologically, the set is all over the shop as the compilers have vouched for a 'thematic' approach in sequencing the tracks. The compilation proved far more successful in the UK, peaking at number 11 in contrast to a lowly number 135 in the US.

Full Track Listing: *(Just Like) Starting Over; Imagine; Watching The Wheels; Jealous Guy; Instant Karma!; Stand By Me; Working Class Hero; Power To The People; Oh My Love; Oh Yoko!; Nobody Loves You When You're Down And Out; Nobody Told Me; Bless You; Come Together (Live); New York City; I'm Stepping Out; You Are Here; Borrowed Time; Happy Xmas (War Is Over); Woman; Mind Games; Out The Blue; Whatever Gets You Thru The Night; Love; Mother; Beautiful Boy (Darling Boy); Woman Is The Nigger Of The World; God; Scared; # 9 Dream; I'm Losing You; Isolation; Cold Turkey; Intuition; Gimme Some Truth; Give Peace A Chance; Real Love; Grow Old With Me.*

SINGLES

The following singles are UK issues, unless otherwise stated. American releases offering different track selections are featured in chronological order. Chart placings are included.

Give Peace A Chance/Remember Love
Apple 13. Released: July 1969.
Credited to The Plastic Ono Band, this single reached number 2 in the UK charts and number 14 in the US. The B-side, a quietly sung Yoko Ono ballad, was also first recorded in Room 1742 of Hotel La Reine Elizabeth, Montreal, with John on acoustic guitar.

Cold Turkey/Don't Worry Kyoko (Mummy's Only Looking For A Hand In The Snow)
Apple 1001. Released: October 1969.
Credited to The Plastic Ono Band, this single reached number 14 in the UK charts and number 30 in the US. The B-side is arguably Yoko Ono's greatest recorded moment, with Lennon, Clapton, Voormann and Starr providing a riveting backing. On the single it was subtitled 'Mummy's Only Looking For *A* Hand In The Snow', whereas on album it became '. . . *Her* Hand . . .'

Instant Karma!/Who Has Seen The Wind?
Apple 1003. Released: February 1970.
Credited to Lennon/Ono with The Plastic Ono Band, this reached number 5 in the UK charts and number 3 in the US. The B-side, sung like a nursery rhyme in Yoko's slight voice, was augmented by tambourine and woodwind.

Mother/Why
Apple 1827. US Release: December 1970.
Credited to Lennon/Ono with The Plastic Ono Band, this single reached number 43 in the US. The B-side features Yoko Ono at her most intense, screaming against a solid rock backing.

Power To The People/Open Your Box
Apple R 5892. Released: March 1971.
Co-credited to The Plastic Ono Band, this reached number 7 in the UK charts. The B-side features Yoko warbling wildly, her feral squeals aided by some of John's experimental guitar work. As the cries grow more intense, Lennon scrapes the strings of his guitar, creating an undulating sound which threatens to reach a thrilling climax, then suddenly stops.

Power To The People/Touch Me
Apple 1830. US Release: March 1971.
Co-credited to The Plastic Ono Band, this reached number 11 in the US charts. The B-side (originally released on *Yoko Ono/Plastic Ono Band* in December 1970) features another agitated performance by Yoko, reinforced by instrumental contributions from Lennon, Voormann and Starr.

Imagine/It's So Hard
Apple 1840. US Release: October 1971.
This double selection from the album *Imagine* reached number 3 in the US charts. It would be four years later before the A-side was issued as a single in the UK.

Woman Is The Nigger Of The World/Sisters O Sisters
Apple 1848. US Release: April 1972.
Regrettably, this single failed to reach the US Top 40, peaking at a lowly number 57. It was unissued in the UK due to the publishing dispute concerning Yoko Ono's writing collaboration.

Happy Xmas (War Is Over)/Listen, The Snow Is Falling
Apple R 5970. Released: November 1972.
Credited to John & Yoko/The Plastic Ono Band With The Harlem Community Choir, this single was first released in the US, where it failed to chart, in December 1971. Due to a publishing dispute its British release was postponed for almost a year. It reached number 4 in the UK charts in 1972 and number 2 in 1980. The B-side features Yoko Ono's hymn to Christmas, complete with references to the Empire State Building and Trafalgar Square. Lennon provides the reverb guitar.

Mind Games/Meat City
Apple R 5994. Released: November 1973.
This reached number 26 in the UK charts and number 18 in the US.

Whatever Gets You Thru The Night/Beef Jerky
Apple R 5998. Released: October 1974.
This reached number 26 in the UK charts and number 1 in the US.

9 Dream/What You Got
Apple R 6003. Released: January 1975.
This reached number 23 in the UK charts and number 9 in the US.

Stand By Me/Move Over Ms L
Apple R 6005. Released: April 1975.
This reached number 30 in the UK charts and number 20 in the US. The
irreverent B-side is a rare example of a John Lennon track unavailable on
album, although it was subsequently included on the CD version of *The
John Lennon Collection* and *Anthology*.

Imagine/Working Class Hero
Apple 6009. Released: October 1975.
This reached number 6 in the UK charts after its belated release in 1975,
and number 1 in 1980.

(Just Like) Starting Over/Kiss Kiss Kiss
Geffen K 79186. Released: October 1980.
This reached number 1 in both the UK and US charts.

Woman/Beautiful Boys
Geffen K 79195. Released: January 1981.
This reached number 1 in the UK charts and number 2 in the US.

Watching The Wheels/I'm Your Angel
Geffen K 79207. Released: March 1981.
This reached number 30 in the UK charts and number 10 in the US.

Love/Give Me Some Truth
Parlophone R 6059. Released: November 1982.
This stalled just outside the UK Top 40 at number 41. The B-side
amended the song title 'Gimme Some Truth' to 'Give Me Some Truth'.

Nobody Told Me/O' Sanity
Polydor POSP 700. Released: January 1984.
This reached number 6 in the UK charts and number 5 in the US.

Borrowed Time/Your Hands
Polydor POSP 701. Released: March 1984.
This reached number 32 in the UK charts.

Borrowed Time/Your Hands/Never Say Goodbye
Polydor POSPX 701. Released: March 1984.

Give Peace A Chance/Cold Turkey
EMI G45 2. Released: March 1984.
EMI countered Polydor's release by combining two of Lennon's most
famous songs.

I'm Stepping Out/Sleepless Night
Polydor POSP 702. Released: July 1984.
This single reached number 55 in the US charts.

I'm Stepping Out/Sleepless Night/Loneliness
Polydor POSPX 702. Released: July 1984.

Every Man Has A Woman Who Loves Him/It's Alright
Polydor POSP 712. Released: November 1984.

Jealous Guy/Going Down On Love
Parlophone R 6117. Released: November 1985.
This single reached number 65 in the UK charts.

Jealous Guy/Going Down On Love/Oh Yoko!
Parlophone 12R 6117. Released: November 1985.

Jealous Guy/Give Peace A Chance
Capitol B 442230. US Release: September 1988.
This single reached number 80 in the US charts.

Imagine/Jealous Guy
Parlophone R 6199. Released: December 1988.
This single reached number 45 in the UK.

Imagine/Jealous Guy/Happy Xmas (War Is Over)
Parlophone 12 6199. Released: December 1988.
This 12-inch single reached number 45 in the UK charts.

Imagine/Jealous Guy/Happy Xmas (War Is Over)/Give Peace A Chance
Parlophone CDR 6199. Released: December 1988.

Imagine/Happy Xmas (War Is Over)/Give Peace A Chance/Imagine
(video)
Parlophone CDR 6534. Released: December 1999.

Happy Xmas (War Is Over)/Listen, The Snow Is Falling
Parlophone R 6627. Released: December 2003.

Happy Xmas (War Is Over)/Listen, The Snow Is Falling
Parlophone CDR 6627. Released: December 2003.

GUEST APPEARANCES

During his Beatles' years, Lennon contributed songs to several acts in the Brian Epstein stable, including Billy J. Kramer & The Dakotas, the Fourmost and Silkie. However, apart from a backing vocal on the Rolling Stones' 'We Love You', his guest appearances during the Sixties appear to have been minimal. Once he met Yoko Ono and left the Beatles though, he was a lot freer to tackle different projects. This section documents his extra-curricular songwriting, production credits and guest appearances on other artistes' records.

Yoko Ono Album Releases:

Yoko Ono/Plastic Ono Band
Apple SAPCOR 17. Released: December 1970.
Lennon produced and contributed guitar to this album.

Fly
Apple SAPTU 101/2. Released: December 1971.
Lennon co-produced and contributed guitar to this album.

Approximately Infinite Universe
Apple SAPDO 1001. Released: February 1973.
Lennon co-produced and appeared on part of this album, most noticeably 'Move On Fast'. The album is dedicated to John: "my best friend of the second sex".

Feeling The Space
Apple SAPCOR 26. Released: November 1973.
Lennon appears on three tracks: 'She Hits Back', 'Woman Power' and 'Men Men Men'.

Season Of Glass
Geffen K 99164. Released: June 1981.
This album included a free copy of the single 'Walking On Thin Ice'/'It Happened' [Geffen K 79202; originally released February 1981], both sides of which were co-produced by Lennon.

Every Man Has A Woman
Polydor POLH 13. Released: September 1984.
This various artistes' compilation of Ono material included a previously
unissued performance of 'Every Man Has A Woman Who Loves Him',
retitled 'Every Man Has A Woman', featuring John Lennon on vocals.

Ono
Rykodisc RCD 10224/9. Released: March 1992.
This retrospective 6-CD box set features many tracks that Yoko had
recorded or co-produced with Lennon from *Life With The Lions* onwards.

Other Lennon Related Releases:

Aspen
Published: March 1969.
The spring/summer edition of the arts magazine *Aspen* included a flexi-disc
featuring tracks from the soon-to-be-released *Unfinished Music No 2: Life
With The Lions*. As well as 'No Bed For Beatle John' and 'Radio Play', the
magazine premièred a recording that failed to make the final album listing:
'Song For John'. This was effectively an ad-libbed medley of three of
Yoko's songs: 'Let's Go On Flying', 'Snow Is Falling All The Time' and
'Don't Worry Kyoko (Mummy's Only Looking For Her Hand In The
Snow)'.

God Save Us/Do The Oz
[Bill Elliott And The Elastic Oz Band]
Apple 36. Released: July 1971.
Lennon produced and composed both sides of this single and sang on the
B-side. It was issued as part of a fund-raising appeal for the infamous *Oz*
obscenity trial. The record failed to sell enough copies to register a chart
entry.

The Pope Smokes Dope
[David Peel And The Lower East Side]
Apple 1839. US Release: April 1972.
Lennon produced and guested on this album, which did not receive a UK
release.

Elephant's Memory
[Elephant's Memory]
Apple SAPCOR 22. Released: November 1972.
Lennon produced this album from his backing group and also appeared on
several tracks.

Ringo
[Ringo Starr]
Apple PCTC 252. Released: November 1973.
Lennon wrote, played and sang on the track 'I'm The Greatest'.

Pussy Cats
[Nilsson]
RCA APL 1-0570. Released: August 1974.
Lennon produced this album and wrote the track 'Mucho Mungo', which Nilsson placed in a medley with his own 'Mt Elba'.

Goodnight Vienna
[Ringo Starr]
Apple PCS 7168. Released: November 1974.
Lennon co-wrote and appeared on the title track and also played on 'Only You' and 'All By Myself'.

Lucy In The Sky With Diamonds/One Day (At A Time)
[Elton John]
DJM DJS 340. Released: November 1974.
Lennon co-wrote the A-side, wrote the B-side and guested on both sides of this single.

Save The Last Dance For Me/All My Life
[Nilsson]
RCA 2504. Released: January 1975.
Lennon produced both sides of this single.

Philadelphia Freedom/I Saw Her Standing There
[Elton John]
DJM DJS 354. Released: February 1975.
Lennon appears on the B-side of this single, which was credited to the Elton John Band featuring John Lennon & The Muscle Shoals Horns. After Lennon's death, the song reappeared as an A-side in March 1981 and also featured on the posthumous compilation album *Lennon*.

Young Americans
[David Bowie]
RCA RS 1006. Released: March 1975.
Lennon co-wrote the tracks 'Across The Universe' and 'Fame' and sang and played on both versions on this album. 'Fame' was issued as a single by Bowie and reached number 1 in the US charts.

Ringo's Rotogravure
[Ringo Starr]
Polydor 2382 040. Released: September 1976.
Lennon wrote and played on the song 'Cookin'', a composition he never
released under his own name.

I Saw Her Standing There/Whatever Gets You Thru The Night/Lucy In
The Sky With Diamonds
[Elton John Band Featuring John Lennon & The Muscle Shoals Horns]
DJM DJS 10965. Released: March 1981.
This single features the three songs that Lennon performed with Elton John
at Madison Square Garden on 28 November 1974. All three were
subsequently included on the 4-CD compilation box set *Lennon*.

Playground Psychotics
[Frank Zappa/The Mothers Of Invention]
Zapple CDDZAP 55. Released: October 1992.
As Frank Zappa's liner notes explain: "Some of you might have heard
another version of this material on the John & Yoko album, *Some Time In
New York City*. When they sat in with us that night, we were in the process
of recording the *Live At The Fillmore East, June 1971* album, and all of this
insanity was captured on tape. After the show, John and I agreed we would
each put out our own version of the performance, and I gave him a copy of
the 16-track master tape. Here is our version – a substantially different mix
from what they released."

Zappa's mix sounds a lot clearer than the Lennons' version. He retitles
part of the jam, with a new track listing that reads: 'Well', 'Say Please',
'Aaawk', 'Scum Bag' and 'A Small Eternity With Yoko Ono'. He also edits
both the encore screams and closing music played over the PA.

INDEX

Singles releases are in inverted commas and roman type. Albums are in italics.